Film in Australia
An Introduction

Film in Australia: An Introduction is a groundbreaking book that systematically addresses the wide-ranging output of Australian feature films. Adopting a genre approach, it gives a different take on Australian films made since 1970, bypassing the standard run of historical texts and actor- or character-driven studies of Australian film. Comedy, adventure, horror, science fiction, crime, art films and other types are analyzed with clarity and insight so the reader can recognize and understand all kinds of Australian films, whether they are contemporary or older features, obscure gems or classic blockbusters.

Film in Australia explains how particular types of films work, identifies sub-types, and surveys the work of local film makers in the different genres. Authoritatively argued for film studies courses, and based on the authors' deep and extensive knowledge of Australian film, it is also enjoyable and accessible for the general reader. A must-read for all students of Australian film.

Albert Moran is a professor in the School of Arts, Media and Culture at Griffith University.

Errol Vieth is a senior lecturer in the Faculty of Informatics and Communication at Central Queensland University.

Film in Australia

An Introduction

ALBERT MORAN AND ERROL VIETH

CAMBRIDGE
UNIVERSITY PRESS

CAMBRIDGE UNIVERSITY PRESS
Cambridge, New York, Melbourne, Madrid, Cape Town, Singapore, São Paulo

Cambridge University Press
477 Williamstown Road, Port Melbourne, VIC 3207, Australia

Published in the United States of America by Cambridge University Press, New York

www.cambridge.org
Information on this title: www.cambridge.org/9780521613279

© Albert Moran, Errol Vieth 2006

First published 2006

Cover designed by David Thomas
Typeset in India by Techbooks
Printed in Australia by BPA

A catalogue record for this publication is available from the British Library

National Library of Australia Cataloguing in Publication data
Moran, Albert, 1942–.
Film in Australia: An introduction
Bibliography.
Includes index.
ISBN-13 978-0-521-61327-9 paperback
ISBN-10 0-521-61327-2 paperback
1. Motion pictures, Australian.   2. Motion pictures, Australian – History and criticism.
I. Vieth, Errol, 1950–. Title.
791.430994

ISBN-13 978-0-521-61327-9 paperback
ISBN-10 0-521-61327-2 paperback

Contents

Illustrations

Preface

The genesis of this book lies in a dissatisfaction with the accounts of Australian cinema offered elsewhere, which seemed to postpone or retard an engagement with film in favour of other matters. At least three different types of these deflectionary approaches can be noted. First, there is the general history that tells the 'story' of Australian cinema in terms of recognizable patterns including rise and fall, boom and bust, with a series of familiar character types including film directors, actors, subjects and companies. A second kind of account is pitched at a more general level and concerns even larger entities derived from government policy, state agencies, film distributors, exhibitors and, especially, Hollywood. Both of these approaches are valuable in terms of the contextual understanding of the film industry that they provide, yet in both these accounts film, including the analysis of particular films, tends to be incidental, a reminder to the reader that the business in question is that of cinema and not, for instance, manufacturing or mining.

Meanwhile, another kind of inquiry is beholden to Cultural Studies and Australian Studies. Here, too, the investigation of specific films again tends to be elided in favour of more synoptic interpretations of Australian culture and society. Typically, this last kind of account seeks to interpret a supposed *zeitgeist*, the spirit of the times, adducing a conceptual grid, usually a couplet or triad, which becomes the grand framework for understanding the films. In other words, film seems only to be a point on a journey whose real goal is broadly sociological, historical or even philosophical. Seeking another way forward, it seemed worthwhile to write an account that stressed the prevailing presence of film in Australia not as a prelude to something else but as a fact in itself. In turn, an emphasis on genre seemed to be the best way of approaching this goal. Recognizing and understanding film in terms of particular film classes or types is a necessary first step in their analysis and interpretation. It helps the viewer to grasp not only what a film means but how it means. Comparing and contrasting, recognizing similarity and difference, relating one film to another offers a more comprehensive and valuable way to proceed in the understanding of film in Australia. It is surely the case that comprehending what is filmic about these films is a necessary first step towards understanding what is Australian about them.

Various people helped in the research, writing and preparation of this book. Thanks are especially due to Sharon Klein at Griffith University library, who facilitated access to written material and films that were not otherwise available. In turn, Andrew Leavold, owner of Brisbane's Trash Video, was a mine of information and another great source of films on both video and DVD. Andrew is one of the great institutions and embodiments of Australian cinephilia – long may he reign over the Planet of the Tapes! In the early stages of the work, Albert Moran was also most fortunate in being able to tap into some of the encyclopedic film knowledge of Bruce Hodsdon at the Special Collection section at the State Library of Queensland. Various colleagues at Griffith University also deserve thanks for their input. Pat Laughren first suggested the idea of the book although he might not recognize the offspring. Tony May continues to be sceptical of the value of genre criticism while always being prepared to help with particular films. Cory Messenger assisted in the late stages of the work, tracking down specific films and their synopses and suggesting various other titles. Danni Zuvela has been wonderful in sharing her voluminous knowledge of Australian avant-garde and experimental cinema. Elizabeth Davies has been extremely helpful in so many ways. Finally, special thanks to Kate Moran for help in the late stages of the work.

Although the intention concerning authorship was that both writers would each contribute approximately half the text, this did not eventuate. Instead, Albert Moran wrote Chapters 1 to 7, 9 and 11 to 14 as well as providing the Afterword and Bibliography, while Errol Vieth contributed the chapters on horror and science fiction. Jill Henry has been a wonderful publisher while Susan Hanley has helped guide the manuscript during its production. Greg Alford is to be thanked for editing the manuscript and Sally Chick for arranging the cover.

1

Genre and Australian Film

The purpose of criticism by genres is not so much to classify as to clarify such traditions and affinities, thereby bringing out a large number of literary relationships that would not be noticed as long as there was no context established for them.   Frye 1957: 154

When we examine literature from the point of view of literary genre, we engage in a very particular enterprise: we discover a principle operative in a number of texts, rather than what is unique about each of them.   Todorov 1975: 19

Why Genre?

The aim of this book is to promote the study of Australian feature films in terms of genre. As Todorov suggests, genre is synonymous with the idea of kind, a subspecies of the totality of a particular cultural output. While his and Frye's remarks are developed in relation to poetry, drama and prose rather than to cinema, nevertheless many elements to do with these genres are also, broadly, applicable to film genre. Indeed, one significant linguistic development in the past thirty years has been the everyday adaptation of the French term 'genre'. In times past, film genres had been popularly recognized only in their specificity: this film is a comedy and that one is science fiction. Now, there is a common term that identifies film types such as comedy and horror as belonging to a larger class or kind. The French term genre has become an ordinary, taken-for-granted word in the English language used as an immediate way to designate a film kind or type. That said, one might still ask just what are the advantages of investigating Australian films in terms of genre? Several significant advantages come to mind.

First, such a method provides an overview of the system or corpus that is Australian feature film output while also facilitating insight into a particular film within that oeuvre. Hence, one might ask about favourite genres within Australian cinema, not only among authors but also on the part of film makers, financing bodies, audiences, critics, teachers and students, not to mention the public at large. Why, for instance, is social realism so promoted while the genre of the epic seems entirely absent? What is preventing more musicals being produced here? In addition, this emphasis enables one to deal with new films as they appear, noting how these fit into, cross or even call into question the different subtypes of Australian film.

Yet another benefit to this way of understanding is the fact that it connects with the fashion by which feature film is understood in the community at large. Video and DVD hire, retail outlets, popular film reviewing and so on are all organized according to generic schema so that the approach of this book has something in common with these practices. That said, it is immediately worth adding that this book hopes to enrich and increase generic insights beyond some of their present-day, commonplace understandings and applications, not least by examining how particular films consolidate and extend the range of generic possibilities.

A third benefit is the fact that genre criticism helps steer the reader towards those Australian films that are among the pivotal and richest examples of particular genres. Not surprisingly many films are mentioned once whereas others turn up frequently and in different chapters, thus highlighting their range and variety. The ambition of the book has been to be comprehensive and exhaustive, not so much in terms of accounting for all Australian feature films since the Revival but rather in terms of developing an explanatory system that is reasonably thorough and complete.

Fourth, this emphasis also steers one towards some of the more marginal instances of particular genres. Put another way, this kind of study can direct attention to some of the specific filmic elements that have been either impossible to sustain in a specific genre, or else more occasionally and less frequently grasped.

Yet another useful outcome provided by this focus is the fact that it enables the researcher to remain alive to evolution and transformation both within and beyond the Australian feature film. This approach sharpens the sense of how particular genres are developing and changing. Hence, for example, grappling with a generic understanding of *Lantana* (2001) highlights the ways in which the Australian art film has remained the same and the extent to which it is different to what it was in the period cycle in the 1970s and early 1980s. Furthermore, although it is not a path that is embarked on here, a generic inquiry into film might also stress possible broader cultural and social shifts in the society at large in terms of marriage, relationships, sexuality, family, class and policing.

A sixth gain from the genre approach is the fact that it cuts through the Gordian knot of whether specific films have sufficient Australian credentials to be considered worthy of inclusion in a local canon. In the early years of the Revival, there was little doubt of what was the new Australian feature cinema. Now the matter is far more perplexing. Should Movie of the Week co-productions made over the past ten years at the Warner film studios on the Gold Coast be included in discussion? Do Hollywood films that use Australian film artists count? Are Australian telemovies relevant? While the answer to all of these is a provisional 'yes', the more important point is that focussing on genre bypasses these dilemmas. It also supersedes fixated emphasis on the Great (New) Australian Film.

Finally, genre criticism in the case of Australian feature films is by no means restricted to only the more obvious and commercially sanctioned types of film such as adventure, crime and comedy. A glance at the titles of succeeding chapters reveals the presence of several genres not usually found in discussion of more aggressively market-oriented cinema. Of course, the introduction of some of these types – such as the social realist film – is not new to the discussion of Australian feature film. Nonetheless, including them here again emphasizes the extent to which many different generic types and models are at work across the landscape that is Australian feature cinema.

Generic Difference

To put all this another way, one can suggest that approaching Australian cinema through the notion of genre is significant for an understanding of particular films and for a grasp on that cinema as a whole. However, before examining certain genres that offer more specific constructions within the totality of Australian feature film, it is necessary to look in more detail at the notion of film genre. Several conceptual distinctions are in order before we examine the generic system in more detail.

First, the fact is that specific theoretical boundaries apply to the concept of genre. Todorov has differentiated between complex and elementary genres (1975: 12). The latter is that type constituted by one structural feature, an invariable element. When a particular ingredient is not present then a text (including the filmic one) does not belong to the elementary kind of genre. Later in this chapter, for example, it is noted that the World War II combat film has been designated as a Hollywood genre. Obviously, this class or type would seem to constitute an elementary genre along the lines outlined by Todorov. If a particular war film happens to concern a war other than that of World War II or does not involve combat, then the film does not belong to this genre. By extension, complex genres are those composed of multiple elements and register in terms of numerous combinations of elements. Again, the book notes several instances of these, kinds that have also been called major genres. One that includes several subtypes – for instance, the action-adventure film – leans towards this second class of genre. The important point about a complex genre is that no particular text can possibly display all the genre's elements. Only an Ur-text, an abstraction from all specific instances, both historical and imagined, can encompass such a range.

Several writers on film have suggested that certain universal divisions operate between different films. Hence, Bordwell and Thompson distinguish between narrative and non-narrative formal systems of film (1979, 1996: 41–141). More accessibly, Nichols has differentiated between narrative, documentary and avant-garde films as three broad types of cinema (1981: 3–9). In other words, whatever labels are applied, there are important modes of film that lie outside the domain of story telling. In this book, the discussion is restricted to genres within the range of Australian narrative cinema. To do otherwise is to invite problems having to do with the incommensurability of classes. This is illustrated in an early book concerning the New Australian cinema (Murray and Beilby 1980). The editors include avant-garde alongside other narrative genres such as action and comedy. While, as will be seen, some narrative genres of Australian cinema do share borders with components of non-narrative, nevertheless there is more than enough generic variety within Australian narrative cinema to make recourse to these other types unnecessary.

In fact, complex and elementary genres constitute a continuum rather than two polar types. Genres exist at several different levels. As Todorov, quoting Tomashevsky, puts it:

> Works are divided into large classes which are subdivided into types and species. In this way, moving down the ladder of genres, we move from abstract classes to concrete historical distinctions. (Todorov 1975: 5)

Todorov also distinguishes between what he calls evanescent genres and autonomous genres. The former type is at the frontier of other genres, usually at least two, and may merge into another. He provides the example – taken up again in this book in the chapters on horror and science fiction – of the fantastic, a literary genre that 'hesitates' between the uncanny and the marvellous and can dissolve into one or the other (1975: 14–19). Similarly, following Derry (1988: 55–69) and Neale (2000: 71–85), three closely related types of Australian feature cinema are discussed – the detective film, the crime film and the suspense thriller. These are sibling genres, types that are closely related, sharing adjacent borders. What is common to all three is the subject of crime but each concentrates on a different moment and setting. By contrast, the autonomous genre – perhaps the action-adventure film or the musical film – displays much more stability and fixity. Standing apparently alone, the autonomous genre exhibits no particular tendency towards becoming another genre.

Another way of making much the same point involves the notion of the subtractive genre (Anderson 1988: 331). This is a class or type whose designation is, in part, arrived at negatively by a process of designating what it is not. Todorov adopts this procedure in defining the fantastic story as one located between the magical and the strange or bizarre. Similarly, in picking out the suspense thriller in Chapter 12, it is located generally within a broader category called the crime film, although neither the figure of the gangster nor that of the detective is as central in this variant of the general type. This way of arriving at definition is methodological and, of course, usually not exhaustive. Todorov does not leave his designation at the point of saying what it is not and neither is one content to halt the investigation of the suspense thriller at the point of noting that it is different to both the detective film and the crime/gangster film.

One other general distinction – that between historical and theoretical genres – is worth mentioning. Historical genres are the result of an observation of filmic phenomena such as the ocker comedy cycle of the 1970s and 1980s. This type of the historical genre rises and falls, appears and disappears. In other words, such a type or class has strong material roots in particular economic, political, social, cultural and other circumstances. On the other hand, theoretical genres are deduced from a theory of cinema. Hence, Bordwell and Thompson in discussing the area of non-narrative cinema arrive at four logical types: namely, Categorical, Rhetorical, Abstract and Associational (Bordwell and Thompson 1979, 1996). And although these authors find specific films to illustrate each of these types, the point is that these types only exist as conceptual even ideal genres and have no necessary connection with the history of film genre. Meanwhile, to resume another distinction, everything suggests that historical genres are a subgroup of complex theoretical genres (Todorov 1975: 155–9; Bordwell 1989: 249–54).

Finally, given that this study occurs within the class of Australian narrative cinema, it is necessary to specify those elements that serve as components of film genre. Hence, among the ingredients variously emphasized in this book are structural, stylistic and ideological. In particular, narrative, character, imagery, setting, soundtrack, themes and thematic discourse are emphasized. Of course, not all these elements will be commensurate with particular film genres. Different historical genres may be strong or weak in terms of certain of these elements. Soundtrack is usually more significant and more complex in a musical than in a western. Nonetheless, these elements are sufficiently limited in number to allow the tracing of their combination and transformation in the different Australian film genres. This, of course, begs the obvious question of what are the local film classes or types and this problem frames the last part of this chapter.

Identifying Australian Film Types

In seeking to identify a larger system of local narrative screen types, an Australian film genre taxonomy, one is – for the most part – on barren ground. As Turner has noted, genre has frequently been seen as antithetical to the project of an Australian feature film culture (1993: 102–11). In the cultural politics that lies behind a volume such as the *Oxford Companion to Australian Film* (McFarlane, Mayer and Bertrand 1999), this kind of denial leaves its mark. Specific Australian film genres such as the action-adventure film, the war film, social realism, the musical and other types are all denied specific entry in the volume. And while another genre such as comedy is given space in its own right, the editors' main way of dealing with this absence is through single essays on genre both before and after World War II.

Nonetheless, there are a handful of inquiries that are worth outlining here as part of a process of deciding on the generic framework for this study. Three local attempts at taxonomies of Australian feature film should be mentioned. The first book to analyse the new Australian feature cinema proposed no fewer than nine genres as follows:

- Social Realism
- Horror & Suspense
- Fantasy
- Loneliness & Alienation
- Personal Relationships & Sexuality
- Comedy
- Action & Adventure
- Historical
- Children

Source: Murray and Beilby 1980

As will be seen, this listing is less expansive than that of several other writers, suggesting either that there are fewer genres at work in the new Australian cinema or that in the first nine years there were insufficient films to call other genres into play. In any case, Murray and Beilby's categorization raises doubt as to whether the editors and the contributors have not in some cases confused subject matter with genre. For example, two of the last three types – Personal Relationships and Sexuality, and Loneliness and Alienation – seem to be film themes rather than genres. Both types might, arguably, belong to a larger category already indicated, namely that of social realism. Several other familiar genres appear to miss out altogether, including the art film, crime, and the erotic film, even though by 1980 there was a good deal that could be written about these different types.

A similar problem involving another private, idiosyncratic schema arises with a more recent morphology of Australian feature films (Stratton 1990). The intention of this volume was to collect a series of the author's reviews of Australian feature films that appeared between 1980 and 1990. These are grouped into 11 different genre-like categories as follows:

- True Stories
- Lovers & Other Strangers
- Author! Author!
- Gun Crazy
- Come Up Smiling
- The Children Are Watching Us
- The Big Country
- A Walk on the Wild Side
- And Justice For All
- Them!
- The Kid Stakes

Source: Stratton 1990

Unfortunately, despite the thoughtful insights provided at the level of individual films, this categorization turns out to be less useful than that of Murray and Beilby. The reversion to authorial categorization (Author! Author!) can be put to one side, thereby reducing the list to ten film types. In addition, the last two seem to concern children, suggesting that these might be grouped together, thus yielding a breakdown of nine types. While some of these might be translated into more familiar generic classes such as Crime for Gun Crazy and Comedy for Come Up Smiling, one is hard put to understand common elements operating with other categories such as The Big Country and True Stories. Indeed, Stratton's cinematic archness and referentiality in using past film titles as names for his categories would seem to be self-defeating. This impression is reinforced when one examines any particular chapter, where there is little general analysis and argument to support a particular label.

The most ambitious and sustained attempt to discuss Australian feature films in terms of type or kind is that represented by Dermody and Jacka (1987, 1988). Their work is an industry-based genre account of output where the major strategy is to see film types as derivatives of particular government agencies and policies. Hence, in their investigation of the Revival, these authors stress the period from 1975 up to 1988 as one in which the principal film agency, the Australian Film Commission, helped create a kind of mainstream or paradigmatic film which they define as the AFC genre film (1987: 49). In turn, several other types are then identified next to this kind including the social realist or social problem film, the 'purely commercial', and a large group of others. Among the latter, they further identify the

Australian gothic, films portraying sexual identities including the male ensemble film, 'interiors', and a rump that they label as 'eccentrics'. This final kind includes generic hybrids, isolates, films sensitive to local settings, as well as others not easily accommodated within their other types (1988: 28–74).

There is no doubt about the completeness and the intelligence of this analysis. Dermody and Jacka bring together an exhaustive list of features made over a twenty-year period and offer useful accounts of very many films. Some of their analytical groupings and discussions, such as those concerning the Australian gothic and 'interiors', are highly suggestive and valuable. However, from the point of view of this book, the designation of their two main types of film, the AFC genre and the 'purely commercial', is, in its own way, a private set of categories, like those chosen by Stratton. And although Dermody and Jacka's genres are not as arbitrary as Stratton's, nevertheless these types are most intelligible and accessible only within the context of the author's prior examination of the Australian feature production industry. In other words, even though this book refers to particular points in their inquiry in the pages that follow, nevertheless, one is forced to go elsewhere in terms of developing a repertory of useful and practical genres for the investigation of Australian films.

Genre in Hollywood

Hence, to overcome this lack of foundation for this study, this chapter turns briefly to the generic investigation of the American film industry. This is so not because of any bias on the part of the authors suggesting that Australian cinema necessarily reproduces the genres operating in Hollywood, but rather because there is more of an English-language tradition of genre study in relation to Hollywood cinema. In fact, as has been pointed out, the scholarly inquiry into genre in Hollywood begins on the other side of the Atlantic. Despite incidental essays concerning specific film genres by US writers such as Warshow and Ferguson in the 1940s and early 1950s, the systematic generic analysis of Hollywood films began in France as early as the 1940s and had spread to the UK by the 1960s (Anderson 1988: 346; Neale 2000: 9–13). It comes as no surprise then that of four studies of Hollywood examined, two are British in origin while a third draws in part on the work of French and British writers.

Of the four, Pirie's analysis (1981) occurs in the more general context of a study of the Hollywood film industry in the present and in the past. To handle box-office data and other materials, he restricts himself to the following nine dominant genres of feature production:

- Westerns
- Romance
- Musicals
- Science Fiction
- Drama

- Thrillers
- Comedy
- Horror
- Action-Adventure

Source: Pirie 1981: 204–94

These are all general kinds and might be seen as corresponding to Todorov's labelling as complex rather than elementary genres. Indeed, Pirie's last genre, Drama, carries a name that is so sweeping as to present particular problems so far as setting generic boundaries is concerned. In other words, Pirie's listing seems restricted and conservative and there is worth in developing a more extended taxonomy.

More specialist genre studies of Hollywood commend themselves to one's attention. Three recent inquiries are especially relevant. First, beginning in the mid 1970s, Grant (1977, 1986) established an anatomy of major genres that consists of twelve types as follows:

- Comedy
- Disaster
- Erotic
- Horror
- Science Fiction
- War

- Crime
- Epic
- Gangster
- Musical
- Sports
- Western

Source: Grant 1977, 1986

In addition, his bibliography furnishes references for at least a further dozen more minor genres including adventure, mystery, romance, black, paranoia, exploitation, hot car, prison, *film noir*, kidpix, romantic drama and women's films (1986: 370–92). Clearly, what is happening is that the editor is operating with both smaller and larger, lower-order and higher-order, minor and major genres. This is a very useful path that will be followed even though Grant's taxonomy must be varied for application to Australian cinema.

Gehring has been even more liberal in his analysis, identifying eighteen different genres at work in the American cinema. His group is comprised as follows:

- Adventure
- Gangster
- World War II Combat
- Populist Comedy

- Western
- *Film Noir*
- Screwball Comedy
- Parody

- Black Humour
- Horror
- Fantasy
- Melodrama
- Biographical

- Clown Comedy
- Science Fiction
- Musical
- Social Problem
- Art Film

Source: Gehring 1988

Again, like Grant's, such a listing runs the gamut from the very specific (such as the World War II combat film) to the much more general type (represented by adventure). Gehring also suggests that there are a number of super or meta genres that comprise several of the more specific genres listed. (One is reminded again of Todorov's useful distinction between elementary and complex genres.) These more expansive types enumerated by Gehring are action-adventure, the fantastic, comedy, and song-and-soap. There is also a kind of left-over grouping that he labels non-traditional (1988: 305).

Although there is some overlapping of names among the more local and the more global of these genres, nevertheless Gehring's conceptual point is clear. He would, for instance, insist that in a real sense the genre of comedy is a higher-order one, an abstraction, perhaps a theoretical genre (1988: 105–210). His point is that it makes sense only to speak of the type in the plural and in terms of a series of more specific genres such as screwball comedy, black humour comedy and parody. All the same, Gehring's example is extremely useful in alerting one to the potential variety of generic kinds in general, thereby helping to expand the range of genres to be looked for in the case of Australia.

Most recently, Neale has listed a total of 16 major genres currently operating in Hollywood feature films (2000: 51–151). In his discussion, he devotes the greatest amount of attention to two especially problematic genres, those of *film noir* and the women's film/melodrama. His list runs this way:

- Action-Adventure
- Comedy
- Detective
- *Film noir*
- Musical
- Social Problem
- Teenpic
- War

- Biographical
- Crime/Gangster
- Epic
- Horror
- Science Fiction
- Suspense/Thriller
- Women's Film/Melodrama
- Western

Source: Neale 2000

Again, this anatomy is an expansive one and taken in conjunction with Grant's and, Gehring's inventories, considerably expands the range of possibilities that might exist in the case of Australian cinema. Like the other two authors, Neale is careful not to include sociological categories and thematic concerns that might masquerade as genres. Instead, all of the types named in this list have won recognition as genres (to a greater or a lesser extent) so that these have considerable analytical history that will be drawn on below. More generally, this book follows the broad example of these three researchers, believing that it is especially productive to veer in the direction of identifying more rather than fewer genres. Accordingly, as a glance at the table of contents of this book will reveal, this book investigates thirteen different genres in relation to Australian cinema. However, before beginning this exploration, some further remarks about this kind of analysis are in order.

Undertaking Genre Inquiry

A first point to note is that Grant, Gehring and Neale agree and disagree on what are the most important genres in current cinema. It is not a case that one is right and others are wrong. Rather, they have chosen to highlight some genres and have ignored or marginalized others. Secondly, genres can be approached at different levels and this has a bearing on the number of types that might be identified. And, again, no particular level is right or wrong. At least two considerations come into play here. First, for purposes of analysis, genres should be approximately commensurate in terms of level. Hence, this book attempts to concentrate on genres at the mid range. None of the types treated here are elemental but neither are they of a highly complex, higher-order kind. The second consideration is that, collectively, the genres assembled should furnish a reasonably complete inventory or taxonomy of the kinds of narrative film found in Australia.

The qualifying adverb in the last sentence points up another consideration. For the fact is that a typology of genres may strike one as arbitrary: why, for example, is the medical film not listed as a genre by any of these authors nor adopted in these pages? The fact is that genre analysis proceeds by deduction. As Todorov notes, 'we do not observe every instance of a class or kind but rather describe it on the basis of a limited number of cases' (1975: 155). In turn, a hypothesis concerning genre is verified by other cases, causing its modification or even abandonment as needs be. So while both authors of this book have attempted to view and review many films for this study, there are many that have not been investigated. The hope is that those

11

using this book will complement rather than simply duplicate the inquiry by applying ideas concerning a range of genres both to other existing Australian films not discussed in these pages and to new films as they appear.

One could put this another way by noting that what is vital when one does genre analysis is the logical coherence of the generic models assembled rather than the number of films watched. The models are important in grasping an understanding of the films just as the films are critical in comprehending the system. So the strategy employed is empirical and inductive rather than theoretical and deductive. Following Todorov, one might say that the basis of the method is structural not scientific (1975: 160). And yet the classifications used here, like those cited in other volumes, are not entirely logically coherent even if that is the ambition held out (Bordwell 1989: 249–54). Not only could this book end up describing genres (and therefore films) that have not yet come into existence, even more paradoxically, every work modifies the sum of possible works, each new example alters the species. There is a movement from abstraction to the concrete and back to the abstract.

Generic designation is therefore a postulation or a hypothesis rather than a description or a classification. Anderson, quoting the historian Haydn White, puts this well:

> 'The same set of events can serve as components of a story that is tragic or comic, as the case may be, depending upon the historian's choice of plot structure that he considers most appropriate for ordering events . . . into a comprehensible story.' Thus, the biographical genre could be divided by tone, with the hagiographic bio-pic offering a model of achievement . . . at one extreme, and a satire . . . at the other'. (Anderson 1988: 345)

A hypothesis has no need of proofs; but its effectiveness can be measured by the results achieved by accepting it. Since the formal organization that is Australian cinema cannot be apprehended on the level of particular films, all that one can say about the latter will remain only approximate. As Todorov puts it: 'We must be content with probabilities, instead of dealing with certainties and impossibilities' (1975: 18).

The definition of Australian narrative film genres is, therefore, a continual oscillation between the description of specific films and abstract theory. Every investigation of this kind must involve itself in a double movement: from film to genre and from genre to film. This book intends to kick start this investigation by providing conceptual tools for its undertaking rather than to fix and foreclose such a study.

2
The Adventure Film

Poetics of Adventure

Depending on the context, Australian cinema is either littered with many examples of adventure or may be populated with very few. Recognizing adventure is the crux of the matter. Ian Cameron has asserted that there is no such genre as the adventure film (1974: 2–5). Instead, various segments that answer to the name of adventure are to be found in a wide range of film types including the jungle film, the swashbuckler film, the military combat film, the epic, science fiction and the horror film. Cameron's point is that adventure has not only to do with what is on screen but what is engendered in audiences as they watch particular elements of many different kinds of films. As such, adventure is an affective term, akin to others such as entertainment and suspense. Cameron's position is an extreme one and has not been supported by other writers on the type including Cawelti, Sobchack and Neale.

Hence, it is more useful to start with Sobchack's assertion that it is meaningful to talk about such a genre (1988: 1–5). The notion of adventure is the obvious place to begin. As Neale following Nerlich (1987: 3–4) suggests, the term is an old one and has to do with unexpected and extraordinary events. In medieval times, the adventurer was a figure bent on seeking out such situations in the cult of the courtly knight. Following the development of merchant adventuring and state-supported piracy in the West after 1500, and especially the expansion of empire in the nineteenth and twentieth centuries, the figure of the adventurer developed intimate ties with colonialism, imperialism, racism and masculinity (Neale 2000: 57). As part of this thematic, the adventure story frequently involves a good deal of mobility in terms of setting and situation. It is often episodic in structure as its protagonist encounters a variety of tasks, challenges and trials. The form allows for a good deal of variation in incident, setting and character (Marchetti 1989: 188).

Given this pedigree and expansiveness, it is no wonder that one encounters an initial difficulty in grasping adventure as a genre. Indeed, the adventure story – whether in written or in filmic form – seems to live at a higher or macro level alongside other larger generic groupings such as comedy and romance. In the case of Australian cinema, adventure has various subgenres that include the war film but exclude others such as the disaster film. In between are more occasional forays into such types as westerns, aviation, kung-fu and prison films. To these can be added some other more local variants, including the road movie, the vendetta film and the bush/outback film. These various subgenres are distinguished by recurring narratives, settings, character patterns, icons, and ideological themes and issues that mark these off from one another and from other broad genres of the screen. In addition, segments of spectacle, action, suspense and thrills reassert the family connections of this type with other genres treated in this book including the crime film and the suspense thriller.

Following Frye (1957) and Cawelti (1976), Sobchack suggests that all genre films, apart from those in the comic mode, are descendants from medieval romance literature. The basic structure of such an archetypal story involves a hero who has or acquires special skills and uses these to overcome impossible obstacles in extraordinary situations to achieve a particular goal or outcome (1988: 1–5). This may involve the restoration of order, the defeat of a superhuman foe, the completion of a quest, the ending of a journey and so on. The protagonist may be ordinary and everyday or may be near god-like, and the confrontations may occur with powers that again run the gamut from the natural to the supernatural. Whatever the type of forces arrayed against the protagonist, the adventure hero will manage to thwart or defeat them. Such an abstract trajectory, although recurring in other genres including the suspense thriller and the horror movie, is most obviously manifest in the films bracketed as adventure films.

In this class, the world is represented as existing in a situation besieged with dangers and threats of all kinds. Nevertheless, through the noteworthy energy, cooperation, and courage of individuals and groups, the social order, without which society would disappear, is upheld against all dangers to its continued existence. At the same time, it is the central feature of the adventure film that it gives unbridled rein to actions which are outside the boundaries of the ordinary, the normal and the everyday, happening as they do in circumstances and locations in which social restraints upon the characters are in many ways suspended, if not dispensed with completely. To put this another way, a defining characteristic of the adventure film is that the characters and their conflicts are found in a mythological past or in an alien and dangerous setting in the present or in isolated circumstances from the world of the everyday. This situation of danger and adventure is necessary in order to create the conditions and the necessity for special powers and abilities to come into play in order to free the individual or the group from the threat that has come upon them. In effect, then, the world of the adventure film may be obviously or subtly different from the ordinary natural one in order to prompt the display of both danger and peril and their defeat.

The romantic, often flamboyant settings and extraordinary actions, including fights, chases, explosions, crashes, fires, natural disasters and so on, typically contained in the adventure film make so many of these so good to look at (Neale 2000: 52–60). The frequent use of unusual locations, employing colourful costumes and settings, often using relatively large casts, plus special effects and cinematography all combine to highlight the extraordinary world and situation in which the adventure film takes place. Whether it is the sight of British and French sailing ships lunging through the waters with cannons booming and recoiling on their decks, the thundering sight and sound of a herd of wild horses plunging down the side of mountains, or two great motor convoys, rigs, bikes and so on sweeping across the desert at breakneck speed with extraordinary crashes and collisions, or exciting chases on planes, trains, cars and boats, the adventure film constantly yields striking sequences of action and spectacle that are as characteristic of this genre as are, for instance, segments of song and dance in the musical or scenes of funny business in comedy.

A Local Tradition

However, in Australia, the adventure film has often had to struggle to get made. The perilous state of film finance, production and distribution in the period up to World War II is sufficiently well known not to need retelling here. Suffice to say that at the time when Hollywood was elaborating some of the main subgenres of the adventure film, including the swashbuckler, the Biblical epic, the western, the jungle picture and the suspense-thriller movie, Australian film makers were hampered not least in being able to afford some of the locations, special effects, sets, costumes and so on required for this kind of genre (Pike and Cooper 1980; Shirley and Adams 1983). The one notable exception so far as following an urge towards adventure both in his projects and in his film subjects was director/producer, Charles Chauvel. Making a successful transition to sound recording, Chauvel in his 1930s films, including *Heritage* (1935) and *Uncivilised* (1936), offered strong elements of adventure mapped into epic subjects (Routt 1985: 55–71; Cunningham 1991).

15

All the same, it was in war and the post-World War I period that the Australian adventure film first came into its own. In particular, the advent of Chips Rafferty as a major Australian film star celebrity enabled several directors to follow their bent towards adventure with a virile Australian as their central figure. As might be expected, a number of these films are war films, films wherein one of the principal narrative motors is martial combat. The first, released in 1940, was Chauvel's *Forty Thousand Horsemen*, a filmic embodiment of the Anzac legend as immortalized in the Desert campaign of that war. As its title suggests, the film did not want for those scenes of action and spectacle that are a hallmark of the more important subgenres of the adventure film. The heroic figure of Rafferty was again to the fore in *Rats of Tobruk* (1944), another narrative of Australian soldiers at war, this time in World War II. And indeed, further adding to the mythological stature of the Rafferty figure, his character is killed in action. A final combat film of Rafferty's in this decade occurred in 1949 with Harry Watt's *Eureka Stockade*. In the latter, Rafferty, as the Irish rebel leader on the Victorian goldfields, leads his men against the tyrannous military forces of the Crown in an ill-fated but courageous rebellion.

With its historical setting and costume, this last linked Rafferty with another subgenre of the adventure film, namely the western. Although most famously associated with the US, the western has in fact long been an international genre, made as wide afield as Argentina to Japan, Spain to Iran. A seminal film in the local output was another feature of visiting English director, Harry Watt, *The Overlanders* (1945). Hailed by French critic André Bazin as an Australian western (1971: 140), this concerned an epic cattle drive across the top of Australia with Rafferty as leader of the stockmen. By the early 1950s, Rafferty had teamed up with a younger director, Lee Robinson, and their first film was again a kind of western, *The Phantom Stockman* (1952). Meanwhile, another British production company was responsible for *Robbery Under Arms* (1957), a reminder that the Australian western also existed in the bushranger subgenre. Two other films of the postwar period of the Rafferty/Robinson partnership should also be mentioned (Cunningham 1989: 53–72). First came *King of the Coral Sea* (1953) followed by *Walk into Paradise* (1956), both of which reworked elements of the safari/jungle films in such exotic locations as the Great Barrier Reef and New Guinea.

Noticing adventure films in this period is not to say that the genre in its classic form has not been a viable entity since the Revival. In 2003, for example, Peter Weir made the film *Master and Commander* with Australian Russell Crowe and Briton Paul Bettany in the principal roles. Based on the novels of Patrick O'Brian set in the era of the Napoleonic Wars, this was a fine example of the swashbuckler or swordfighting film in a tradition dating back to Errol Flynn as Captain Blood and Gregory Peck as Captain Horatio Hornblower. Similarly, *The Lighthorsemen* (1987) was a serious homage both to the military charge at Beersheba in Palestine in 1917 and also to its representation in the Chauvel film of 1940. In other words, various film makers continued to find the adventure film to their liking as the occasion arose and proceeded to treat its forms and style without parody or irony.

This is not to say that the genre is beyond mockery and caricature on the part of local directors and writers. Certainly, as the chapter on comedy notes, there have been several anti-heroic mock adventure films. On the other hand, there also remains an important place for a more serious and sober approach. Accordingly, one might follow Sobchack in examining the standard form of the adventure film, to grasp its structure of action and character networks in order to discover how the genre works, and then see what elements in the standard formula lend themselves to irony and parody (1988: 4–9).

Defining Action-Adventure

As noted above, the adventure genre is actually a grouping of several more well-defined subgenres including the swashbuckler, the war film, the spy film and the survival film. Although each of these exhibits superficial variations in terms of setting, costume, period and imagery, two distinctive, frequently overlapping, plot structures are characteristically deployed. The first concentrates on the single lone hero, the adventurer *par excellence*, the soldier of fortune, the knight errant, the wandering champion, the road warrior. Such a figure is god-like to a greater or a lesser extent, often an outsider to the group or circumstances that s/he enters and must leave after the situation has been righted, the foe vanquished. In fact, the adventurer has usually been male. However, as both Tasker (1993) and Jeffords (1994) have noted, Hollywood has recently cast women as adventure protagonists. As Neale points out, this reworking recalls a much earlier tradition in adventure films of the 'serial queens' (2000: 184–8).

The second adventure pattern, labelled the survival narrative, focusses on a small band in an extreme situation of distress and danger (Sobchack 1988: 10–15). The disaster film constitutes a favourite reconstruction of the type (Keane 2004). To escape from this peril and to reach safety, the group must embark on a journey that is also an ordeal of endurance, suffering and courage. Again, the journey and the task throw up many different challenges and dangers and very often members of the ensemble are struck down and fail to survive. On the other hand, usually one or two of the band prove to

17

have exceptional powers and abilities that come to the fore in this extremity. Hence, with one or more new leaders, the group finally reaches a place of security and safety. At this point, the exceptionality of the leader is not needed and s/he may revert to a more unexceptional manner of life.

Several Australian adventure films can be mapped onto these schemata. Coincidentally, both these patterns were deployed in the *Mad Max* trilogy (1979–85). Significantly, the lone hero structure was deployed in *Mad Max* (1979), especially its first half, while *Mad Max: The Road Warrior* (1981) and *Mad Max: Beyond Thunderdome* (1985) follow the survival pattern. There, with director George Miller influenced by Joseph Campbell's *The Hero With A Thousand Faces*, this futuristic adventure's meta narrative follows the figure of the title from policeman insider to an outsider, one set to roam the wilderness. *Mad Max* traces a rising pattern of violence, vendetta and revenge. Although already marked as exceptional in his control of car and road, Max Rockatansky is an insider, happily married with a young wife and child, a professional law officer, respected and admired by both superior and fellow officers. However, he inadvertently provokes the Toe Cutter and his gang and they slaughter his loved ones. Enraged by this loss, Max turns his back on his profession and exacts a bloody revenge on the gang.But, this is not without terrible personal toll as it turns him into someone who no longer belongs within society.

Instead, as the saga is resumed at the beginning of the second film, he has become a road warrior, a wanderer destined to roam the wilderness, his only companion a dog and his only concern to ensure that he has fuel and food. In the second and third part of the trilogy, Max is this kind of outsider. These two films are tales of the survival adventure; and although Max is instrumental in ensuring that the bands reach safety it is also due to the efforts of others including the Feral Kid, the Gyro Captain, Warrior Woman and Pappagallo. And although in these two films he goes to the rescue of the innocent and the peaceful as they are at the mercy of the violent and the savage, he cannot himself settle again in the company of people. He must, instead, continue his wanderings. Although this knight errant can restore the social equilibrium, he cannot himself be integrated into the civil or the communal order. His fate is a sacrificial one that restores and saves the society even as he finds no final redemption, peace or resting place himself. In a real sense, the *Mad Max* trilogy is the most radical and uncompromising rendering of the adventure film. As personified by Mel Gibson, who later went on to a Hollywood career in other action films including the *Lethal Weapon* quartet (1987–98) and *Braveheart* (1995), Max is truly exceptional in both his powers and in his fate. The films make no attempt to reincorporate him into the society but rather underline that this kind of hero pays the ultimate price of remaining outside the community that he saves.

Not all Australian adventure films assign their heroes to this level of exception and sacrifice. In the other great Australian cycle of adventure films of the 1980s – the western subgenre of *The Man from Snowy River* (1982), *Cool Change* (1985) and *The Man from Snowy River 2* (1988), the hero has less grandeur and more everyday qualities so that he can be reconciled to society rather than remaining unable to find integration. Although the protagonist wins his manhood, he also effects an improvement in the social order. In the 1982 original, for instance, the physical adventure of the horse chase is matched by a kind of moral struggle that has the effect of displacing the brutal, greed-driven values of the patriarch, Harrison (Kirk Douglas), in favour of those displayed by his twin brother, Spur. With the Man of the title, Jim Craig (Tom Burlinson), graduating into this reformed society, the film exhibits a recurring tendency in many adventure films to finally affirm traditional social patterns and values, including broad political ones (Cawelti 1976: 29–44; Sobchack 1988: 4–12).

Other Modes and Figures

Like the other high genres such as comedy and crime, adventure can embrace a wide range of tones and modes. This includes parody and comedy. Such an observation is hardly surprising given that the adventures of a god-like hero can always border on the absurd and the ridiculous. And even 'serious' adventure films can occasionally stray into tongue-in-cheek archness, as Martin notes (1995a: 78) in connection with the middle sections of *Mad Max: Beyond Thunderdome*. Even beyond such occasional elements, several other films considered in the chapter on comedy also have claims to be adventure films. Among those answering to the label of caricature are *The Return of Captain Invincible* (1983) and *Sons of Steel* (1987). In both, there are global conspiracies afoot that are defeated by a comical superhero despite the various villainies abroad. As noted in other relevant chapters, music is also present in these adventure spoofs as part of their comic effect.

However the four comedies made by Paul Hogan – *Crocodile Dundee* (1986), *Crocodile Dundee 2* (1988), *Lightning Jack* (1993) and *Crocodile Dundee in Los Angeles* (2001) – have more claim to be considered under the name of adventure. In particular the *Dundee* films are variants of the jungle film while *Jack* is a western. For despite the fact that the main figure is undoubtedly a trickster and a joker, not surprising given Paul Hogan's background in television stand-up and sketch comedy, Dundee/Jack is also very

19

much the embodiment of the adventure hero. Indeed, part of the attraction and appeal of the best of the quartet, *Crocodile Dundee*, is the fact that the hero is at home and equally skilled and able in both the Northern Territory and in New York. As mentioned, the films are the embodiment of the jungle subgenre of the adventure film with the hero being a kind of modern-day Tarzan or Jungle Jim, two fictional heroes referred to in the film. Like the former in the original story, Dundee is brought to the most overwhelming city in the world but proves to be adept, skilful, resourceful and cunning in meeting its various challenges just as he is equally adroit in the more rugged landscapes of outback Australia.

Over and above its links with comedy, *Crocodile Dundee* is also important in highlighting another feature of the adventure film. This has to do with the innately democratic spirit of the adventurer. For while Mick Dundee is not of noble or aristocratic stock, as is a Tarzan or a Robin Hood, nevertheless he is instinctively a man of the people. In the Northern Territory, he is friendly and well liked among his companions. Equally, in New York, he remains affable and befriends various inhabitants, including a policeman on traffic duty, a hotel doorman, a cabdriver and even the crowds on a subway station. In other words, like the classic hero of adventure, he is a man of the people, one of the masses, a dimension that O'Regan notes in connection with the protagonist in *The Man from Snowy River* (1985: 242–51). And yet, of course, the adventure hero – including Mick Dundee – is never completely a part of the crowd. This is, of course, one of the paradoxes of the adventure genre. Such a figure never fully assimilates themself into the common herd; the adventure subject is always flamboyant and marked by a superior intelligence, grace, physical prowess and fighting skills. But, all the same, s/he continues to express 'the idea that all men can treat each other equally, that distinctions between men based on rank, privilege, and birth are outmoded and unjust in themselves' (Sobchack 1988: 12–8).

Besides the explicitly comic adventure film, one can also include mention of another variation of the tale of the gallant hero who deals with adversity and cruel circumstance as these come along but often in a less than totally heroic mode. Again, this kind of subtype may also be found in the area of comedy – witness the title of the first ocker film of the 1970s, *The Adventures of Barry McKenzie* (1972). Here, though, this chapter is particularly interested in a kind of ironic or parodic variation of the picaresque tale of adventure. Less than god-like in terms of physical prowess and moral rectitude, the picaresque hero has a long lineage in literature running from as early as Don Quixote down to at least Huckleberry Finn. This mode is alive and well in Australian cinema. Two examples of this kind of ironic adventure are *High Rolling* (1977) and *Buddies* (1983). As the latter's title implies, both are 'buddy' films which trace a series of episodes involving two male principals who despite external differences are, nonetheless, united by their desire to defeat a common enemy. By duplicating the central protagonist, this variant obviates the need for romance even while it is able to share qualities of both superiority and ordinariness across the two figures.

Mention of the substitution of a second male hero reminds one that another traditional figure present in the adventure film is the romantic heroine. Sobchack, following Cawelti, notes that frequently the hero's democratic instincts create one of the stumbling blocks to successful union with the heroine, who is often aristocratic (Sobchack 1988: 14). In this respect, the romantic subplot of several adventure films is surprisingly like the main plot of a romantic comedy – the male and female meet, dislike each other after an initial attraction, but finally realize their love and come together. But unlike a romantic comedy, the adventure film creates different barriers to the union of the two, such as physical danger or peril, in addition to other obstacles such as those of class and comic misadventure. Again, *The Man from Snowy River* is a notable example of this pattern in action. As embodied by actor Sigrid Thornton, Jessica Harrison is an aspirational object for Jim Craig. However, she comes to understand that worth is not equivalent to class and that despite his background, he possesses a high nobility, a natural superiority among men. In due course, Jessica falls in love with him and their union is seen to represent the coming together of the best of two worlds of wealth and property and of democratic ideals and ability.

Although its origin lies in US newspaper comic strips of the 1930s, nevertheless the namesake of the film made in north Queensland, *The Phantom* (1996), is the epitome of a galaxy of superheroes to be found across a wide variety of adventure modes, including Biblical and knightly epics, crimefighting, spies and conspiracy tales, jungle stories, martial arts encounters and pirate movies. Like many another adventure champion, the Phantom is a loner, self-reliant, the mysterious being who calls on no one except himself. To do otherwise would mean putting the secret of his own identity in the balance. Such a type is therefore the opposite of the second kind of adventure story already mentioned, that of the survival film.

In the latter, the protagonist is one of a group whether through choice or circumstance and has abilities, strength, courage and intelligence that are of the same order as that of others in such a band. In this kind of adventure tale, the narrative action turns not on proaction but on reaction. The objective is not necessarily to achieve great victory but rather to survive and overcome a calamitous and deadly circumstance and situation. Heroism in the survival film arises as the result of accident with one or perhaps two individuals managing to help themselves and others to avoid perishing. And after their ordeal, their instinct is to step back into anonymity and ordinariness, to again become part of the crowd. One can see this pattern in action in a handful of Australian war films.

Survival – Four Australian War Films

Although as mentioned, the disaster film has been one recent favoured location for the adventure survival genre, a more traditional subtype for this mode lies in the war film. For example, not all war films are concerned with combat. Both *Breaker Morant* (1980) and *Blood Oath* (1990) although set in time of war are, nonetheless, focussed on other related matters – a courtroom drama in the case of the first and a group of Australian soldiers held in a Japanese prison camp during World War II in the second. Others are, however, concerned with combat and four in particular produced in the 1970s and 1980s can be used to help pinpoint achievements in this mode. The films in question are *Attack Force Z* (1979), *The Odd Angry Shot* (1980), *Gallipoli* (1982) and *The Lighthorsemen* (1987).

Although having to do with war, the quartet differ in terms of their mode and orientation. At the time of its release, the first was seen as deliberately commercial in intention so that it most conforms to the conventions of the war combat genre. By contrast, the second and third films are more artistic in orientation. In fact, this disposition led those making *The Odd Angry Shot* to concentrate on a group of soldiers behind the lines in the Vietnam War who are not caught up in any major action of danger, desperation, death and survival. Instead, their situation is more futile, thereby justifying the film's ironic tone and narrative enervation. *Gallipoli*, by contrast, manages to achieve a more interesting accommodation between the demands of the art film and those of the combat survival film. Hence, on one level it is seen to function as a Boy's Own Adventure although it also works to artic-ulate matters concerned with fate and determinism (Rohdie 1985: 194–7). Finally, *The Lighthorsemen*, although a dramatization of an actual war inci-dent and situation, manages to combine its historical celebration with very solid action and adventure in yet another combat film.

Chance abounds in the adventure film whether one is considering the unexpected turn of incident and setting in both the heroic and the survival variants or even the chain of circumstances that have made the quest or task necessary in the first place. This is as true of the group under threat as it is of the lone errant adventurer. Consider, for example, *Attack Force Z* where the mission to rescue the VIP whose plane has crashed in the jungle in enemy territory comes about because of this chance event. In

The Odd Angry Shot, Bung's (John Hargreaves) unit has been cut to pieces under enemy fire so that he joins another platoon, that of the Special Air Squadron 21st Regiment in Vietnam. *Gallipoli* stitches together the fact of Archie's (Mark Lee) running ability, the encounter and friendship with Frank (Mel Gibson), the volunteering for duty, shipping to the Dardanelles and his employment as a military runner. Meanwhile, in *The Lighthorsemen*, it is the British artillery's inability to overcome their enemy and the need to gain access to precious wells that leads to the decision to have the Light Horse cavalry charge the enemy.

However, even more than the larger external forces shaping the narrative of these films is the repeated emphasis on the accidental nature of the group under threat. As small as two and no larger than six members, a group is frequently a microcosm of the society at large. Hence, its members are different and individual, complementing each other not only in terms of ability but also in terms of attitudes, age, experience, ethnic background, social class and so on.

And, of course, a film such as *Attack Force Z*, in keeping with the fact that it concerns a war mission, is able to draw on other films of this particular type in terms of making considerable play of the rituals of selection, initiation and training of the group for the particular task in hand. However, in the other films, in common with the usual circumstances of the survival film, the individuals are simply thrown together. No matter what the situation though, the important point is the internal composition of the group, the balances and checks that get put in place. This is most evident in the deliberate system of contrasts that *Gallipoli* constructs around Archie and Frank. Hence, there is a careful overlapping, contrasting and balancing of a string of qualities including idealist/cynic, blond/dark, virgin/sexually experienced and patriotic/pragmatic. Commenting on the action of *Gallipoli*, McFarlane offers a designation of the thematic movement that not only applies to the relationship of the central characters in that film but by extension pinpoints the coming together of the group in the survival film: 'Beside these, Archie's mindless patriotism and Frank's pragmatism in response to Britain's war diminish in importance as their friendship is strengthened in exotic places and dangerous engagements' (1995: 74).

However, unlike the tale of romantic adventure, the survival film frequently reminds its audience that heroism is not one of the qualities distributed beforehand across the group. Instead, it is only under fire and in dire situations that heroism begins to emerge. Extremity, whether in the shape of disaster or war, has the effect of reducing those involved to the same level; but it also triggers the assertion of a leadership that is seen to be natural, spontaneous and democratic. In at least three of the four films,

23

the name given to the human value that facilitates survival is that of mateship. Courage, skill and endurance are only means to an end and have little place beyond the situation of war whereas the stronger values of loyalty, friendship, sacrifice, endurance and so on are seen to be the essential human values that need to survive. The death of Archie in *Gallipoli*, of Bung in *The Odd Angry Shot* and the fall of several of the cavalry in *The Lighthorsemen* are testimony to this dramatic proposition.

As this litany of loss suggests, there is a far more sombre emphasis at work in the survival film generally and in the combat film in particular. The possibility of death is ever present. To underline this point in *The Lighthorsemen*, several letters anticipate the mortal cost of what is to come on the field of battle. For this is not the arena of the superhero, a world where extraordinary feats of strength, courage, endurance and skill become the order of the day. There are few if any opportunities to indulge in the wide-eyed heroics of the heroic adventure tale. This is particularly the situation in the sardonic *Odd Angry Shot* where boredom is a bigger challenge than the enemy, although Bung still dies under fire.

Despite this overall grimness in the combat film, there is yet a visual pleasure, a frequent sumptuousness to the physical action that threatens to shift it back in the direction of the Boy's Own adventure. Hence, for example, the last frozen shot of Archie's body ripped open by enemy bullets or the cavalry charge at Beersheba in Palestine are true moments of grand spectacle, thrilling passages of action cinema. In other words, the combat film oscillates between the theme of 'war is hell' and that of 'action is fun'. How else to understand reviews of *Gallipoli* by Rohdie and McFarlane, which although diametrically opposed end up admitting the same elements (1985: 174–8; 1995: 74).

Finally, it is worth pointing out the oscillatory pattern at work in the survival combat type. Again *Gallipoli* is the purest expression of this tendency. The film begins with Archie running in the outback of Western Australia and ends with the frozen shot of him running under Turkish gunfire.

More generally, as already mentioned, there is in this type an action which sees a motley group of individuals, unconnected apart from sharing a common situation and setting. However, circumstances conspire to force them to come together for a common good. Acting on one's own is likely to lead to defeat and disaster. They shed identities conferred by everyday life. In the process, some are recognized as having natural qualities and outlook that entitle them to lead, to become responsible for the group even if enemy action is causing the size of the group to shrink. With the task accomplished, the mission at an end, the threat overcome, the exceptional individual who has come forward melts back into the throng, into anonymity.

More generally, in consonance with the heroic adventure mode, the survival type also ends with the restoration of order, the subjugation of threat, the reemergence of a social equilibrium.

Women Heroes

The four war films discussed in the last section are all films entailing what Dermody and Jacka have dubbed 'the male ensemble film' (1988: 97–105). Indeed, while the great majority of adventure films are masculinist, depicting exemplary instances of male strength, courage, know-how, cunning, endurance, prowess and so on, nevertheless, there is the possibility of role reversal that would see a woman as hero of the adventure film. Earlier mention was made of the work of Jeffords (1994) and Tasker (1993) on contemporary heroines in recent Hollywood action-adventure films and Neale's discussion in linking this to much earlier cycles of 'serial queens' (2000: 184–8). So, the case of the adventure heroine is not completely exceptional. While Australian cinema since the Revival shows little affinity to this tendency in American films, nonetheless at least two examples of gender reversal in Australian action films come to mind. The two examples are instructive in that the substitution takes place in adventure films that are generically mixed. This hybridity has been recognized in one case but ignored in the other.

The first of these two films is *Shame* (1988), in several ways a reworking of some of the conventions of the western (Crofts 1993: 1–44). As though to underline the connections, the heroine is a stranger to the place that she enters at the beginning of the film. Astra (Deborah-Lee Furness) rides a motor bike and wears jeans and a black leather jacket. Like the Hollywood 'town' westerns of the 1950s, the Australian town in *Shame* proves to be one where some, principally women, are oppressed by others. Astra takes on these oppressors on behalf of the victims and overcomes them with the help of those who were previously helpless. Her task at an end, she rides off. In the best tradition of 'town' westerns including the similarly sounding *Shane* (1952), the outsider is central in the community's process of overcoming oppression and stimulating regeneration. Always a selfless champion of others, helping them to help themselves, the stranger is compelled to move on. To settle would mean surrendering the power of righting wrong, overcoming oppression, helping the weak. To settle would mean breaking an unvoiced vow, turning one's back on a noble calling. Further adventures await this kind of protagonist in another place, down the road, around the next bend, so that Astra's riding off at the end of the film is necessary and inevitable.

The survival mode of the adventure film: Rabbit Proof Fence *(2001). Image courtesy of Rumbalara Productions.*

Meanwhile, a second very different example of the woman adventure film, this time in the survival mode, is to be found in *Rabbit Proof Fence* (2001). At first glance, such an identification might seem arbitrary, a sport. But the relevance of the genre to this story can be understood in several ways. Based on a true incident in Aboriginal–white relations that occurred in Western Australia in 1931, *Rabbit Proof Fence* is biographical. The film is also very much one in the mode of social realism. At the same time, such placings by no means exhaust ways of understanding *Rabbit Proof Fence*. For like *Shame*, the film is generically mixed, hybrid, a mongrel, so that it is worth exploring the suggestion that it can be related to the survival adventure film.

The film is again one concerning courage and endurance, on the part of three young girls – the fourteen-year-old Molly (Evelyn Sampi), her ten-year-old sister Daisy (Tiama Sansbury) and their cousin Grace, who is eight years of age (Laura Monaghan) – who are half-castes forcibly taken from their Aboriginal mothers to what amounts to indentured servitude 1,500 miles away. They escape and led by Molly begin a trek north following the fence that keeps rabbits out of white settlements. Not only must they rely on their own wits and determination in walking the 1,500 miles to reach home, they are also forced to elude the tracker and regional police sent by government officials under orders from the chief protector of Aborigines, A. O. Neville (Kenneth Branagh). Altogether the story is deeply moving, concerning as it does an important moment of resistance in Aboriginal–white relations.

More to the purpose here is the fact that despite its status as historical document, biographical memoir and politically sensitive story, *Rabbit Proof Fence* is clearly also a survival adventure film. Unlike the more overtly heroic mode in the genre, the journey of Molly and the other two girls involves no colourful battles with great monsters or overwhelming technologies. Nevertheless, their trek is truly epic with them walking over 1,500 miles without any provisions or aids, relying only on their own knowledge of the land, endurance and determination to return home. All they can call upon are tenacity, ingenuity and each other. As the oldest, Molly takes on the necessary role of leader, a task wherein she proves to be truly remarkable. As Moodoo (David Gulpilil) the Aboriginal tracker remarks: 'This girl is clever – she wants to go home'. Thus, despite the best efforts of white officials to capture them and return them to the government camp, the children succeed in their quest.

Finally

In short, women protagonists can certainly be found at the centre of different Australian action-adventure films. And while Astra in *Shame* is something of a fantasy figure, be that as it may, the general attitude imposed by the tendency towards social realism has ensured that there has been a marked absence of women warrior heroes. In any case, whether focussing on an individual hero or a microcosmic group's survival, the adventure film tends to play out the mythic ideal of social unity. All the abnormal, exotic, excessive activity of individuals is a necessary component of social unity.

In the course of such films, all kinds of aggression, violence, cruelty, prejudice, intrigue, greed, cowardice, ignorance, prejudice, lust and madness are displayed and these in turn prompt equally extraordinary feats of endurance, courage, physical prowess, imagination, energy, knowledge, subtlety and so on to come into play. And, of course, there is great vicarious pleasure for audiences not only in the contestation of these forces but in the narrative patterns punctuated by spectacle of one kind or another through which this is presented. This kind of cinema sanctions the viewer to indulge in fantasies regarding the identification and engagement with social actors and the solution of social situations and problems. Above all, an adventure film labours to persuade the viewer that the social order can be restored to equilibrium. Given this broad action, some writers have been led to suggest that the adventure story is at base a highly conservative genre (Cawelti 1976; Sobchack 1988). While there is a good deal of truth in this charge, the bald assertion leaves no room for the kinds of displacement and problematizing that have been noted at different points in the present chapter. In any case, the adventure film is only one way of approaching form and meaning in Australian film subjects. The next chapter therefore adopts a very different stance towards its cinematic materials.

3
Art Film

Boundaries

Although Pirie (1981), Maltby (1995), Grant (1977, 1986) and Neale (2000, 2002) in their discussion of Hollywood genres afford no space to this kind of cinema, in other quarters a strong case has been made for the art film as an international genre of cinema (Lev 1993; Tudor 1974). Bordwell (1985), for example, has specifically included Australia as one of several film industries that has seen a 'new wave' output in this class in recent years. Although not popularly recognized as a distinct genre in such domains as film reviewing or in video and DVD retailing, nevertheless 'arthouse' is a term increasingly recognised in other parts of the trade. In fact, the art film has had a steady presence in Australian cinema ever since the Revival. For mainstream audiences, its most characteristic form was what was registered in the historical or period film cycle between 1975 and around 1982 (Dermody and Jacka 1987, 1988). However, to reduce Australian art cinema to this kind of historical film is to ignore some of the more interesting and varied tendencies that exist within the genre.

That said, it must still be admitted that there have been relatively few films produced that can be understood in this particular way. While some other film genres discussed in these pages are also minor forms of the Australian cinema, art cinema is even more minuscule, guaranteed a place here only because of this period cycle. In addition, the art film as genre lacks a very specific imagery or iconography. Whereas other types such as suspense thrillers and even musicals have recurring bodies of imagery having to do with situation and setting, this type lacks specific visual grounding. Instead, the most useful way to characterize art film is in terms of yet another label – that of the 'puzzle film' (Holland 1964: 71–96).

Films of this type frequently offer their viewers an enigma or a riddle that besets their characters. Of course, part of the narrative strategy of the detective film is precisely to present and then solve a puzzle, to clear up a mystery. In the crime genre, baffling mysteries and enigmas are capable of solution and explanation within the narrative chain of events.

What happened and why it happened is answered by the detective usually towards the end of this kind of crime film. However, the puzzle in an art film is of a different order. Frequently, it is not resolved during the course of the narrative action with either an explicit avowal of failure, of continued perplexity; or else whatever answer or explanation that is provided is inadequate to the full circumstances of the enigma. Even more often, explanation and solution are seen to be beyond the capability of the characters so that they continue to ask questions up to the end of the film. The audience is also involved in attempting to solve the puzzle and is highly likely to carry this attempt at puzzle-solving well beyond the end of the film. What in *Citizen Kane* (1942) is meant by the dying Kane's last word 'Rosebud'? Did a murder really take place in the park in *Blow Up* (1966)? What happened to the missing woman in *L'Avventura* (1960)? With this kind of 'puzzle film', viewing is constructed in such a way that the audience plays the game of interpretation even after the viewing situation itself is concluded. Put another way, this puzzle construction is part of the textual strategy of the art film. The aim is to encourage explicit explication and hypothesizing as part of the total viewing situation.

Taking this audience effect on board, both Bordwell (1979: 56–64, 1985: 205–32) and Siska (1988: 331–54) have argued that any definition of the art film must start with its narrative strategy. Just as Todorov locates the literary genre of the fantastic at a border between two other genres, the uncanny and the marvellous, so Bordwell has suggested that the art film is a mode of cinema narration that hovers between two other modes of narration (1985: 205–14). These are, on the one hand, the more conventional and familiar form of classical film narration associated with Hollywood (Bordwell, Staiger and Thompson 1985) and, on the other, a type of filmic exposition that may, variously, be called modernist or avant-garde (O'Pray 2003). These delineations are very pertinent to Australian art cinema and help suggest some of the subtypes of the genre. Before looking at these, however, it is useful to offer a more sustained definition of art cinema.

Identifying Art Cinema

This section begins by recording certain of the more external features of European art film first evident in the 1950s and 1960s, particularly as these help in the identification of such a genre in the local context (Bordwell 1979: 56–9; Lev 1993: 1–16). As Siska and Lev have suggested, this mode has also been embraced by particular film makers in Hollywood from the 1970s onwards, including Robert Altman and Woody Allen, so that art cinema and Hollywood narration continue to have a lot in common. More to the point, as Bordwell (1985) has observed, despite various surface differences, the overall function of style and theme remains remarkably consistent in art cinema. Generally, the narrative and stylistic principles of these films form a logically coherent mode of cinematic discourse. Here, it is worth recalling that the art film is still, for the most part, oriented towards narrative and it rejects those elements of experimental, modernist or avant-garde film making that distracts from or destroys the project of narration. In other words, one can introduce a distinction between what might be called a soft and a hard filmic modernism. Hence, for example, Australian feature-length films such as *Sketch on Abigayl's Belly* (1968), *Marinetti* (1969) and *Sunshine City* (1973), which are artistic and experimental films, more concerned with perceptual play and investigation of visual and sound qualities than with story telling, can be seen as instances of a determined avant-garde practice, a hard modernism (Hodsdon 1985: 288–94; O'Pray 2003: 1–14). As such, these and many others with shorter running times are not considered part of an Australian art cinema. Instead, they belong to a local avant-garde form of cinematic practice whose analysis is beyond the scope of this book.

At the same time, and more paradoxically, art cinema frequently defines itself against conventional narrative, most especially in disrupting the tighter, cause-effect linkage of a Hollywood-like cinema, in favour of a looser, more sketchy relationship between narrative events (Bordwell 1985: 205–18; Siska 1988: 331–8). Two different kinds of reality are seen to bring about this outcome (Bordwell 1985: 314–18). On the one hand, an objective reality of time and place is felt to work with its own logic and effect. In *The Plains of Heaven* (1982), for instance, one of the two workers at the satellite tracking station, Cunningham (Reg Evans), suddenly appears naked, as though awakening from sleep, and smashes equipment before plunging outside and disappearing. The event is phenomenal and inexplicable. However, some kind of explanation can be mustered by the viewer. For the film has repeatedly dwelt on the landscape, distant hills, eagles circling overhead and so on, suggesting that place has its own, perhaps ominous, presence that has somehow brought about Cunningham's outburst and his (subsequently discovered) death. Put another way, one of the familiar tropes of art cinema has to do with general conditions besetting characters and shaping actions, and sometimes this kind of presence – as in *The Plains of Heaven* – is detected in terms of setting and locale.

A second kind of reality at work in this cinema is more personal, individual and subjective. Like Hollywood narrative, the art film continues to rely on psychological causation although often the characters lack defined desires and goals (Bordwell 1979, 1985; Siska 1988). Protagonists frequently lack purpose and drift towards goals and situations rather than pursuing them in the active, determined manner of protagonists in particular Hollywood genres. In fact, the reasons for action may be inconsistent, fluid and even contradictory. Characters may question their own reasons while choices are often vague or non-existent. *In Search of Anna* (1978) with its deliberate invocation of Antonioni's *L'Avventura* is a case in point. Like a character from the Italian predecessor, Tony (Richard Moir) is a typical enough protagonist of the Australian art cinema. In flashback, he is seen to eschew the opportunity to take revenge for betrayal and imprisonment against a former friend and accomplice. In fact, the film's main structuring principle for its narrative is a familiar one found in art films as well as in more conventional cinema, namely that of the journey. Much of *In Search of Anna* is occupied by Tony travelling north from Melbourne to Sydney and from there to the Gold Coast to find a former girlfriend. Like *L'Avventura*, this Anna, too, is not re-encountered even though at the end of the film, Tony has the means at his disposal. Instead, he continues a liaison with another young woman, Sam (Judy Morris), who is as unmotivated and aimless as he is.

Over and above these two kinds of reality – whether objective or subjective – there is another fundamental principle providing motivation in the art film. This has to do with authorial expressivity. It is no accident that both *The Plains of Heaven* and *In Search of Anna* are films displaying *auteur*-like credentials, having been written and directed by Ian Pringle and Esben Storm, respectively. Of course, film culture has long been in the grip of a directorial *auteurism* so that feature films constantly parade a name above the title – this is a Peter Weir film while that is a film by Bruce Beresford, for instance. However, art cinema appears especially prone to registering the presence of a teller in attendance in the tale being told, an artist apparently detectable in the art of the particular film. Very frequently, the genre of art film is seen to be the outcome of a cinematic personality whose artistic shadow is sensed in various textual features of the film. One can therefore take this matter a little further, considering it not only in terms of parody but also in terms of its institutional setting.

Auteur, Auteurism and Art Cinema

Yackety Yack (1974) is an excellent (and very funny) instance of the artist explicitly present and apparently at work in the art film. Like various European predecessors, such as Fellini's *8½* (1963) and Truffaut's *Day for Night* (1973), the film concerns a film maker and university lecturer Maurice making a film in the basement of a building, in this case at La Trobe University, Melbourne. Although the script for *Yackety Yack* was carefully and fully written, the film deliberately presents itself as an improvised work-in-progress where aesthetic choices are evidently spontaneously taken by the comically megalomaniac director. In turn, this Russian doll effect allows *Yackety Yack* to reference and parody many different film directors ranging from Sam Fuller to Jean-Luc Godard. More particularly, many of these different elements come together in the comically dictatorial figure of Maurice, played by David Jones who also wrote, directed and produced the film. On the surface, the film appears to engage in long *vérité*-like takes so that the criticisms and objections of two film critics caught up in the film-within-the-film are taken on board. In fact, these on-screen objections are only left as it suits the fictional director. Rather, the intervention of Maurice/Jones is comically everywhere from the many intertitles to jokey jump cuts comically suggesting the film maker's determination to leave his mark on every last frame of the film being made. Put another way, *Yackety Yack* is hilariously constructed to support the project of art cinema as a cinema of the *auteur*.

And while the excessive *auteurism* represented by this film is not repeated within the oeuvre of Australian cinema, nevertheless a good deal of the institutional apparatus for an *auteurist* reading strategy remains in place. Take the following reviews of *The Plains of Heaven* and *In Search of Anna*, both taken from the canonical 'survey' of theatrical features produced between 1978 and 1994 (Murray 1995a). Writing of the former, Marcus Breen shows himself to be, finally, more preoccupied with the teller rather than what is being told in that film. He notes:

> The Europeanization of Australian films, rather than a concentration on everyday American life, has not had an easy time. Pringle (the film's director) is something of an unsung hero for his pursuit of big themes. At the time it was made, *The Plains of Heaven* represented a bold attempt to examine psycho-social issues in a European style of film-making in an Australian context. (Breen 1995b: 108)

Similarly, in writing about *In Search of Anna*, Anna Dzenis describes the film as:

> a poetic moment in Australian cinema . . . The significance of this reference (to *L'Avventura*) lies in the European art-cinema traditions that it invokes, the cinema of filmmakers such as Antonioni and Alain Resnais. It is an auteurist cinema of poetic images whose preoccupations with time, memory, history and the struggle for self are also concerns central to Storm's film. (Dzenis 1995: 32–3)

33

In other words, a favoured reading strategy promoted at many different institutional sites in Australia, including the pages of the journal *Cinema Papers*, various related books published by Oxford University Press and the AFI's annual film awards, constructs Australian feature films in terms of a series of expressive personalities, authorial presences that implicitly, if not explicitly, support the project of an Australian art cinema. Nonetheless, one of many ironies of local feature film output since the Revival is the fact that government film policy has deliberately turned its back on the more experimental edge, the more artistic tendencies in art cinema, in favour of much more conventional forms of narration. One can gain a sense of a path not pursued if one turns briefly to a film of the very late 1970s which while championed at the time as a more interesting and venturesome kind of art film than many others being produced at the same time seems, in retrospect, to stand alone.

Aesthetic Adventure on the Side

Palm Beach (1979) is a good example of one of the more aesthetically significant art films that have been produced within the genre. As its title suggests, the film is set in a Sydney beach suburb but also takes the opportunity to follow up to a dozen different characters along the chain of water neighbourhoods from Manly to Palm Beach on Sydney's north side.

Like a European predecessor such as *Cleo de 5 à 7* (1962), the film traces an itinerary across this world of beach, sand, fast-moving cars on highways, surf shop, houses, school, club, flats and so on over two days. And although some of the characters cross the paths of others, nevertheless there are a good many segments that turn out to be incidental and only loosely episodic. Various of the plot strands do reach some kind of narrative point – Joe (Ken Brown) turns out to be a police informer and seems to have succeeded in helping find a drug dealer, while the frustration of Paul Kite (Bryan Brown) at being unemployed builds to the point where he bungles a store robbery and kills a security man. On the other hand, other narrative strands remain open and without resolution – especially the attempt by the private detective, Larry Kent (John Flaus), to trace a missing teenager. Equally, the film is also marked by a good deal of movement on the part of the characters, from the opening extended long take from behind Joe at the driving wheel of his car to the bravura and celebratory helicopter shot that traces the northern tip of the suburb from Pittwater around to and down the Pacific coastline that ends the film. Again, though, much of this turns out to be inconsequential and to little apparent purpose. For the most part, the characters drift towards their various goals rather than actively and determinedly pursuing these.

And indeed, in terms of *Palm Beach*'s strategy of (mostly) resisting the psychologizing of character, the film engenders a documentary-type detachment and an observational stance in dealing with the world of the setting. The soundtrack is particularly important in helping to achieve this effect. For the latter combines the sounds of radio, the incidental conversations of characters, many apparently accidental noises and several rock-and-roll numbers. Moreover, segments containing different characters are frequently linked together by a continuous radio program. This is especially evident in segments in the first half of the film. Even more significant is the fact that diegetic sound appears to be violated, seeming to spill over and compete with diegetic sound in the following segment. Again, the effect is to shift the viewer into a more detached, contemplative mode as well as to direct attention to the more general setting and human types than a particular engagement with specific characters. In other words, *Palm Beach* belongs to a more aesthetically adventurous, more experimental tendency within the Australian art cinema. For while the film works within the broad conventions of mainstream narrative cinema, it is – all the same – prepared to suggest a more objective reality that lies beyond any of the specific characters and yet it is one in which they are all caught up.

Looked at twenty-five years later, *Palm Beach* remains as interesting, accessible and engaging as when it first appeared. It more than confirms some perceptive discussions that appeared at the time of its first release (Hodsdon 1980: 6; Purdon 1980: 660; Gardiner 1995a: 65). However, it is a tragedy of Australian cinema that its director Albie Thoms was denied government funds that would have enabled him to continue his film making career. Instead, the Australian Film Commission (AFC) was determined to promote another subtype of the Australian art film.

The Period Art Film

Writing about what he calls the 'Euro-American art film', Lev notes that this kind of variant of the genre 'attempts a synthesis of the American entertainment film (large budget, good production values, internationally known stars) and the European art film (*auteur* director, artistic subject and/or style) with the aim of reaching a much larger audience than the art film normally commands' (1993: 1). Some generic options are more likely at certain points in time than are others. The late 1960s and early to mid 1970s, one might suggest, represented a particular moment of fluidity so far as a potential Australian art cinema was concerned. The impact of the international art cinema was at its height in terms of influence even if that was always a minority taste (Lev 1993: 1–15; Bordwell, Staiger and Thompson 1985: 339). Hollywood cinema appeared to have lost its way in terms of a changing feature film market (Balio 1990; Maltby 1995). Meanwhile, Australian government production funding was, briefly, more liberal and catholic in the kinds of projects that it would support than would be the case later on (Moran and O'Regan 1985: 110–19). Dermody and Jacka (1987) have drawn attention to the genre of the 'interior' film and certainly by the early 1970s, various films had been undertaken in this mould including *2000 Weeks* (1968), *Matchless* (1974) and *Between Wars* (1974).

However, it was the commercial and critical success of *Picnic at Hanging Rock* (1975) that catapulted art cinema into the mainstream of Australian feature film production. This film was that rare creature that appeared to unite cultural respectability (literary source, haunting musical soundtrack, visual sumptuousness) with a contemporary aesthetic register that simultaneously united the categories of quality, art cinema and Australian-ness. Based on a literary forerunner and with impressive emphasis on period *mise en scène*, cinematography and soundtrack, the film secured its nationalist credentials with its 'look', its story and its music. The textual system of the film was sufficiently accommodating to allow for the sense of an objective realism, encountered in the portentous presence of the rock, a less emphatic inner realism involving the inner psychology of various characters, and an *auteurist* registration of Peter Weir as a director concerned with the numinous and the inexplicable.

In fact *Picnic* is the quintessential Australian period art film, the marriage of a muted commercialism with a foregrounded aesthetic textual surface that was seen as a guarantee of 'quality'. Above all, the film had a powerful 'puzzle' (Holland 1964) or raised-problem (Siska 1988) at its centre, concerning what happened to the girls and teacher who disappeared. This, too, helped guarantee *Picnic*'s status as art film. Unlike the matter of the 'lived' problem of the whodunit constructed in the detective film, where the interpretative problem is one besetting the characters of the film, the raised-problem in this kind of film is one that centrally involves audience as well as characters. How was one to make sense of the story event of the disappearance, how to interpret enigmatic or puzzling details such as the fact that two of the girls are left behind or the subsequent impact of the disappearance on Miss Appleyard and the others? The art cinema deliberately invokes such a puzzle as one means among others of supporting its aesthetic credentials. In the case of *Picnic*, the hermeneutic problem is how to read or understand the disappearance. As Hunter (1985: 190–3) recognized at the time, part of the novelty of the film that cemented its claims for high seriousness was precisely to do with the fact that a generic device common in other genres, including the fairy story, was here translated into a period Australian setting. The puzzle is not resolved but left open-ended. Like some of the characters who attempt to offer conclusions to what has happened, the audience is explicitly invited to continue to ponder the fate of the characters and the reasons behind this.

Here, then, *Picnic at Hanging Rock* helps pinpoint the nub of the art film. The genre is defined as those narrative films in which abstract issues are dealt with overtly in dialogue and by direction of the viewer to symbolic or metaphorical images (Siska 1988: 331–45; Lev 1993: 1–28). In this kind of film, the puzzle or enigma is an abstract question that invites discussion and exploration. Where this kind of problem cannot be solved by a singular solution, the dilemma is turned into a broader, more abstract matter for contemplation. As a seminal film in the Australian cinema, *Picnic* can be seen to have forged a strong connection between landscape and film art. For physical nature is seen as beautiful, picturesque, fascinating, haunting, tantalizing and inviting. As part of an ideological discourse having to do with colonialism as well as romanticism, nature can be dangerous as well as beautiful, annihilating as well as exhilarating, having terrors as well as charms. *Picnic at Hanging Rock* provided a kind of template of how elements of landscape, period setting, Australian history, and themes of identity and nation might be brought together in the project of a 'quality' cinema, an art cinema thinly disguised with a period look, which had international as well as national valency (Murray 1975: 264–5; McGuinness 1985: 188–9). Over the next seven years or so, there tumbled out a string of features that attempted to use this format, including *Caddie* (1976), *Break of Day* (1976), *The Picture Show Man* (1977), *The Getting of Wisdom* (1977), *Summerfield* (1977), *The Irishman* (1978), *My Brilliant Career* (1979) and *We of the Never Never* (1982). And although these films in this period cycle were able, as David Bordwell once put it (1985: 205–12), to link narrative and nation, they were, for the most part, unable to construct as potent a formula as had been derived in *Picnic*. Put another way, the Australian period art cinema constituted the most conventional form of narration with very little of the ambiguous reality outlined above.

There is, however, at least one film in this cycle that partly defies this latter characterization – *My Brilliant Career*. Here, the audience can identify a raised-problem but one given a more conventional narrative grounding. The film concerns a young woman growing up in rural Australia in the late nineteenth century, so that the narrative is, at one level, a *Bildungsroman*, a journey towards maturity and emotional self-discovery, identity and full adulthood. Sybella (Judy Davis), the heroine, comes of age, is courted by two men – Frank (Robert Grubb), an expatriate Englishman, and Harry (Sam Neill), an Australian – and is particularly drawn towards the latter. However, the film has both a feminist and an artistic project. Although she is attracted to Harry, Sybella realises that marrying Harry would lead her into a life of constant procreation and housework that would rule out any artistic ambitions. She finally rejects his offer of marriage in favour of devoting her life to art, including writing. The film ends with Sybella posting off to a publisher the manuscript for her first book. The audience can infer that the manuscript is her account of growing up, and may in fact be entitled *My Brilliant Career*.

In other words, despite its period setting, the film hints at a degree of reflexivity that edges it in the direction of a modernism frequently found in art cinema. *My Brilliant Career* also discloses its credentials as art cinema in terms of the raised-problem of its ending. For it is open-ended in the familiar mode of many art films, with the audience wondering whether Sybella was right to reject the marriage offer and also pondering if her book will be accepted for publication. There lingers a strong likelihood that such a book is highly autobiographical, is in fact the basis for the film so that the fact of the film vindicates Sybella's decision. In addition, as a feminist project with a female author (Miles Franklin), screenwriter (Eleanor Whitcomb), producer (Margaret Fink), director (Gillian Armstrong) and star (Judy Davis), *My Brilliant Career* further vindicates Sybella's choice of an artistic career.

Modernist Interiority and Art Cinema

Despite the popular and critical success of *Picnic at Hanging Rock* and *My Brilliant Career*, the period art film cycle generally was deemed worthy but dull. By 1983, it was clear that this particular output was at an end. The brief union between historical drama and the art film was dissolved. Thereafter, the Australian art film has had a more fugitive existence. Following earlier contemporary excursions into the genre such as *2,000 Weeks*, *In Search of Anna* and *The Plains of Heaven*, the small handful of art films that have appeared over the past two decades have adopted present-day settings. Hence, the remainder of this chapter examines two of these more contemporary works in the genre. The films in question are *Lantana* (2001) and *Alexandra's Project* (2003).

Beginning as a stage play written by Andrew Bossell before becoming a feature film that won Best Feature Award at the AFI Awards in 2001, *Lantana* is best thought of as an art film. Although marketed as a crime thriller and even described by Harrison as a 'psychological thriller' (2005: 82), the concern of the film has more to do with a series of relationships of four married couples. (In fact, if one also includes another married relationship, recounted to Valerie the psychiatrist by her single homosexual patient, Alex, who is having a clandestine affair with an unidentified husband, then the number of heterosexual relationships put under the spotlight expands to five.) *Lantana* concentrates on these eight figures. As might be anticipated from its theatrical origins, there are only a handful of other incidental characters in the film – the children of two of the couples, a female detective, Claudia Wiss (Leah Purcell), colleague to Detective Leon Zat (Anthony La Paglia), and the male patient. Admittedly, in the second half of the film, when Dr Valerie Somers (Barbara Hershey), wife to a law professor John Somers (Geoffrey Rush) goes missing, the audience's suspicion is briefly aroused to the possibility that Steve Valdez (Jon Bennet), a house husband, may be responsible for this disappearance and possible death. One of her shoes is discovered in a clump of lantana by Jane O'May (Rachel Blake), an estranged neighbour who, earlier, had a brief affair with Leon. In turn, his wife Sonia (Kerry Armstrong) happens both to be a patient of Valerie, the missing woman psychiatrist, and to attend the same dancing school as Jane. In fact, what *Lantana* has in abundance is coincidence, with each of the principal eight characters crossing the different paths of most of the others. In this sense, one sees the point of Leon being a detective. Like Valerie, he has a professional reason for speaking to and getting to know strangers. When Valerie disappears, Leon is one of a number of detectives assigned to the investigation. This allows several conversations between him and John the husband, as well as a re-encounter with Jane and her husband, who appear to have reconciled, as well as with Steve Valdez and his wife Lisa (Melissa Martinez), their neighbours, with Steve being brought into custody. Most importantly, the investigation also enables Leon to discover in Valerie's files recordings of his wife Sonia's psychiatric sessions with her, wherein she reveals the poor state of their marriage.

And, in turn, while the film is prepared to heap coincidence upon coincidence so far as relationships are concerned, it is not prepared to do so when it comes to the matter of Valerie's disappearance. The married man with whom Alex the homosexual is having an affair turns out not to be Valerie's husband John. Steve did give Valerie a lift on the night of her disappearance, but was not responsible for her death which turns out to have occurred through accident and misadventure.

Were *Lantana* attempting to be a crime or detective film then these would be highly untidy narrative elements so far as the film's narrative resolution is concerned. This is not, however, an issue when the film is understood as an art film. Hence the raised-problem or puzzle operating here is the fragility of long-term relationships between wife and husband in contemporary society. *Lantana* is, above all else, an examination of modern marriage with three of the four married couples witnessing to particular disaffection and alienation. Leon confesses to emotional numbness, Valerie and John are traumatized with grief over the death of an only child while Jane and her husband are estranged. It is only the working-class neighbours, where husband Steve briefly falls under suspicion, who have a happy and sustaining relationship. For each of the other more middle-class couples, marriage is seen to be alienating and disaffecting. In other words, in line with much art cinema, *Lantana* suggests that existing among the three couples is a more pervasive condition of modern life. This is amply supported by the *mise en scène*, which recalls films of Antonioni and others. And, in the case of the most central of the characters, Leon, there is a further inner psychological trauma that has resulted in an emotional deadness. In turn, these 'realisms', both subjective and objective, reach out to affect other elements in the film. In this sense, the reference to the tangled lantana clump is introduced as a portentous symbol that we, the audience, are meant to both witness and attempt to interpret.

Alexandra's Project is even more recent, although it lacks both a stage predecessor and the prestige associated with AFI awards. Continuing the divorce between period and the art film evident in *Lantana*, the film is contemporary and urban in setting. Although its video cover refers to it as a thriller, it is more useful to focus on the fact that, like a detective story, the film begins with a situation and proceeds to, retrospectively, reinterpret this from the point of view of the female protagonist, Alexandra (Helen Buday). While the enigma or puzzle is not as overt or as explicit as it is in a film such as *Picnic at Hanging Rock*, nevertheless there are early intimations on the soundtrack (that continue through the film) that all is not as it first seems. Instead, Alexandra's husband, Steve (Gary Sweet), is forced to listen and watch a video he finds waiting for him in his empty house on the night of his birthday. However, instead of disclosing some sexual threat that is in store for him, Alexandra gives vent on the video to her frustration in her marriage and her plan for revenge. By having Steve as well as ourselves view the birthday videotape, the film opens up a reflexive dimension. This is, of course, more than an aesthetic touch because this film within the film becomes a means of signalling the shift in power in the domestic relationship, most especially when the source of the television image ceases to be a pre-recorded videotape and becomes a live telecast from outside the home.

40

In other words, even putting aside any attempt to derive *auteurist* meanings in the text of the film that might be associated with director Rolf

"AS POWERFUL AS PAINT-STRIPPER
.as a psycho-sexual thriller it's compelling." *Vicky Roach, Marie Claire*

Gary Sweet
Helen Buday

a Rolf de Heer film

ALeXandra's
ProJECT

Not everyone loves surprises

MA 15+ PERSONS UNDER 15 YEARS MUST BE ACCOMPANIED BY A PARENT OR ADULT GUARDIAN
ADULT THEMES, HIGH LEVEL SEX SCENES, MEDIUM LEVEL COARSE LANGUAGE

PALACE FILMS
DVD

Art cinema as women's film: Alexandra's Project *(2003). Image courtesy of Palace Films.*

de Heer, there are sufficient qualities there to anchor *Alexandra's Project* firmly within the domain of art cinema. In the course of the film, Steve, the male protagonist, is rendered passive, impotent, helpless. At the same time, the film's ending is open so far as the fate of the character is concerned. In fact, if the conclusion is equivocal, it is only one of the many

41

ambiguities deliberately cultivated in *Alexandra's Project*. Most especially, there is the intense subjective realism of the wife's situation and emotions that are progressively revealed to the husband and to the audience. The film's opening credits are superimposed over a travelling shot of middle-class houses in an anonymous suburb accompanied by a high-pitched wailing sound and it is only as this wail returns several times through the film that the audience learns to connect it with Alexandra, with her situation, and finally too with Steve at the end of the film. Meanwhile, on a thematic level that would link *Alexandra's Project* with *Lantana*, there are also intimations of a more objective reality having to do with the impossibility of the marriage relationship itself. Finally, the film's self-consciousness about cinema, voyeurism and spectatorship, power and sexuality is also in evidence, again helping to secure its credentials as a contemporary Australian art film.

Epilogue

Bringing together the different concerns of this chapter, one can reiterate the fact that 'art cinema' is a meaningful genre label in itself and of continuing importance in the Australian feature film output. Unlike some genres, such as war and combat and crime, the art film is not distinguished in terms of familiar recurring imagery nor is it usefully thought of in terms of particular structures or patterns of narrative. Instead, it is best thought of in affective terms involving audience engagement and response. Hence, this chapter has been at pains to explain the centrality of the 'raised-problem', including the variety of forms and settings wherein the art film puzzle can be deployed. Art cinema stands at a crossroad between conventional mainstream narration film on the one hand and more experimental and modernist compositional practice on the other. Briefly, in the guise of the period film, Australian film makers in the late 1970s and early 1980s attempted a wholesale commitment to this class of film. Where such films as *Picnic at Hanging Rock* and *My Brilliant Career* succeeded in terms of box office and critical reception, the local transmutation of the art film seemed to offer a permanent domain in which Australian cinema might dwell. However, the films soon turned dull and worthy with little in the way of conceptual enigma or puzzle to engage audiences. There followed a shyness towards this class of film, one that is still with us.

As the chapter has also shown, taking the cases of *Yackety Yack* and *Palm Beach* as examples, film makers and film funding agencies were more adventurous and imaginative in the past, so that the art side of art cinema has not been entirely neglected. All the same, such films are now rare and the conditions that brought them about do not look like being repeated, at least not in the near future. However, the health of the genre is not entirely terminal. Recent films such as *Lantana* and *Alexandra's Project* suggest that there remain marginal opportunities for contemporary stories in this vein.

4
The Biopic

Aussie Lives

Like the genre of the musical, the biographical film or biopic seems at first glance to be ill-suited to the local film appetite. While Australia may be seen to have many national heroes (and villains), nevertheless, the very great majority of these have not been significant on the world stage. From a film distribution and marketing point of view, it would seem as though there are few internationally famous Australian figures worth becoming subjects of feature films. Fame is not, though, an immediate requirement for either biography or even a biographical film (Anderson 1988; Custen 1992). Instead the real criterion is whether the personage to be depicted in a film was historically real, a living human being. In other words, did such a subject have a beginning, a life's span, and have they died or will they die? Even more importantly from both a textual and a marketing point of view is whether the figure was interesting or important (or even infamous) in some way. Can the biopic recreate its human subject on the basis of curiosity and significance, noteworthy in some kind of way?

Here, the media itself functions as an important intervening element in the process of deciding which lives are important and worth recounting. (And, of course, the biographical film is itself part and parcel of that operation.) Take two otherwise very unremarkable Australians, namely Albert Facey and Brendan Abbott, and consider the circumstances of their becoming biographical subjects on the small and the large screen respectively. Facey grew up in poverty in Western Australia before the First World War. He enlisted in the Australian armed forces, served at Gallipoli, returned, married and had several children and grandchildren. Towards the end of his life, he was persuaded to write down elements of memoirs. These were edited, posthumously published and the book *A Fortunate Life* became a best seller. Given this literary fame, the book was subsequently adapted for television and appeared in the form of the mini series *A Fortunate Life* (1986). The same form of intervention was at work in the case of Brendan Abbott, a clever bank robber who spread his criminal activities across several Australian states. After an earlier capture and imprisonment, he joined a large prison breakout and remained free and on the run for several years while all the other escapees were caught. Abbott won a good deal of notoriety and newspapers, radio and television gave him a large amount of media space over this period. It was claimed that he sent postcards to police from different places so that he became known as the postcard bandit, a kind of modern Australian larrikin-figure, if not a Robin Hood. After his recapture, trial and imprisonment, the Nine Network produced a feature telemovie, *The Postcard Bandit* (2003). Taken together, these two instances make the point that a biopic does not demand a historical figure, merely a famous one – a point confirmed elsewhere (Anderson 1988; Neale 2000; Anderson and Lupo 2002). Whatever public recognition the biographical subject might have in the first place is considerably enhanced by a subsequent biopic.

Given this degree of latitude in the modern biographical subject, it might be anticipated that, just as the biopic has become increasingly favoured in Hollywood recently (Neale 2000: 60–5; Anderson and Lupo 2002: 60–5), so the opportunity is emerging for more work in this genre in Australia. After all, there is an ever-increasing interest and market for life stories both on the part of commercial publishers and also on the part of do-it-yourself publishers (Davison 1991: 5, 2003: 11–12).

Television has also seen sustained interest in the type in the form of documentary series such as the ABC's *Australian Story*, and also in a stream of mini series over the past twenty-five years ranging from *The Last Outlaw* (1980) to *Dynasties* (2003). All the same, this burgeoning of interest in the life story has had only a limited impact in Australian cinema. Less than two dozen biopics appear to have been produced here both in the period before the Revival and more recently. A listing of these biographical films would include the following: *Smithy* (1946), *Sister Kenny* (1946), *Wherever She Goes* (1951), *Ned Kelly* (1970), *Dawn!* (1978), *Breaker Morant* (1981), *Squizzy Taylor* (1982), *Tudawali* (1983), *Phar Lap* (1983), *The Slim Dusty Movie* (1984), *Annie's Coming Out* (1985), *Hostage: The Christine Maresch Story* (1986), *Evil Angels* (1988), *The Story of Damien Parer* (1988), *Mary* (1994), *Shine* (1996), *Molokai: The Story of Father Damien* (1999), *Chopper* (2000), *Ned Kelly* (2003), *Swimming Upstream* (2003), and *The Postcard Bandit* (2003).

Several points are worth making about such a group. First, this list is a relatively short one, emphasizing the point that the biopic is not a favoured genre among Australian film makers. This is somewhat surprising given developments in television during the last thirty years. Apart from a very early cycle of four ABC TV dramas to do with different historical figures in the life of the early colony of New South Wales ranging from *Stormy Petrel* (1960) to *The Hungry Ones* (1963), dramatic biography was ignored by television producers for over twenty years. The only exception was provided by very occasional forays by ABC Drama into the form, such as occurred in 1974 when it produced both *Behind the Legend* and *Ben Hall* (the latter being a co-production with the BBC). On the other hand, the form was embraced with a vengeance in the 1980s. In the period from 1982 to 1992 no fewer than thirty-one biographical mini series appeared on Australian television ranging from the ten-hour *The Dismissal* (1982) to the four-hour *Bligh* (1992) after which the output of biographical screen stories fell off rapidly, not least due to important shifts in the production industry (Turner and Cunningham 2000).

However, to return to the scarcity of output in the film biopic, the listing above is somewhat opportunistic. For instance, three of the films mentioned were produced as telemovies. *Sister Kenny* was a Hollywood film even though it concerns an Australian-born woman later active in health matters in the US. *Phar Lap* has to do with a famous racehorse rather than a person. Although the production originated in Australia and employed many Australians before and behind the camera, *Molokai* had to do with a Belgian-born Catholic priest, Father Damien, and his work in a leper colony in the Pacific. Mention of this figure as well as that of Mary MacKillop in *Mary* also reminds us that the range of biographical figures can run from saint to sinner with a large number of protagonists who are both extraordinary and ordinary appearing in between. Before looking at elements of this output in more detail, it is necessary to move the discussion from subject matter to the more formal, stylistic and discursive elements at work in the genre.

Defining the Type

The Australian biopic has not received any sustained analysis from film researchers or historians. This is hardly surprising given both the small local output and the fact that there is a more general lack of analysis of the type among film researchers in the English-speaking world. There is only one book-length study of the subject (Custen 1992), although both Gehring and Neale have devoted chapters to the topic inside larger concerns with the Hollywood genre (Anderson 1988: 331–52; Neale 2000: 60–5; Anderson and Lupo 2002: 91–104). From Custen is borrowed the definition that the biopic is 'one which portrays the life of a historical person, past or present' (1992: 5). The term calls attention to the fact that the figure depicted did or does live so that their biography in film form may have a kind of documentary component. Frequently, such a film recreates actual people, places, events and time. In fact, this historicity often finds support and verification of a kind in the incorporation of such elements as archival film footage and written intertitles. This 'actuality' does not, though, mean that imaginative licence is not taken with the life story. Rather, as Anderson notes, a biopic may engage in great liberties with a personal history including creating various related fictions. She quotes the case of Warner's *Night and Day* (1946), a biopic concerning popular composer Cole Porter (1988: 340). In the film, the latter is heterosexual whereas the actual figure was openly homosexual, a fact readdressed in the more recent biopic of Porter's life *De-Lovely* (2004).

Secondly, the biographical subject must have a degree of fame so that the biopic acts to expand and elaborate the source, background, circumstances and consequences of this public recognition. However, as already noted above, this matter of noteworthiness is more complicated than it may first seem. Fame may be a consequence not of any particular acclaim or public recognition gained during a subject's lifetime, but may arise because of subsequent events including the publication of autobiography, memoir, life story and so on. What matters is not the historical importance of the life but rather that the life itself actually happened. Beyond that, generic form and style intervene to ensure that the biographical subject becomes a screen subject. And, of course, fame may be ill-repute so that the lives of infamous figures also form part of the genre.

In the case of Australian biopics, there are so few titles in the cluster that it is difficult to apply some of the broad findings of Custen with any degree of real conviction. Be that as it may, it is worth noting his claim of a marked preference on the part of Hollywood towards males as biopic subjects (1992: 1–25). The Australian output tallies with this although women subjects are in a sizeable minority. Further, Neale suggests that the Hollywood genre has addressed an audience as consumers of popular culture (2000: 62). While several Australian films such as *Dawn!* and *Phar Lap* conform to this pattern, by dramatizing the career of figures immensely popular in their lifetime and still alive in folk memory, other films including *Annie's Coming Out*, *Shine* and *Molokai* vary this by bringing less well-known figures to the attention of a contemporary public.

Anderson makes some related points that also seem potentially applicable (1988: 334). Print biographies display a penchant for featuring the lives of literary figures, as is indirectly evident in *Annie's Coming Out* and *Swimming Upstream* which are based on autobiographies. More importantly, she notes the recent centrality of performers in the Hollywood biopic (Anderson 1988, Anderson and Lupo 2002). This is certainly relevant to Australian cinema, whose biopic subjects have attracted attention in the domains of sport (*Dawn!*, *Swimming Upstream*), film acting (*Tudawali*), popular music (*The Slim Dusty Movie*) and concert pianist (*Wherever She Goes* and *Shine*). What unites these particular subtypes is the emphasis on the physical body as the site on which the subject's significance emerges (1988: 334–8). Once one grasps the centrality of the human form as the location of effort and struggle, then one might even begin to see *Molokai* as part of the modern biopic, with its emphasis on the forced submission of Father Damien (David Wenham) to a medical examination to verify that he has not broken his vow of chastity and is succumbing to leprosy towards the end of his life. Equally, in *Chopper*, Mark Read's (Eric Bana) upper body is revealed as the site of extraordinary physical markings including tattoos and scars. And indeed, in the course of the film, it is further subjected both to repeated stabbing in the stomach and the voluntary hacking off of one ear.

The reference to submission in *Molokai* prompts mention of a further general point of Custen to do with a recurring thematic in the biopic. This has to do with a continued struggle between the unique individual and established institutions and traditions (1992: 47–79). In *Dawn!*, for example, this struggle is embodied in an antagonism between the swimmer and sporting officials; in *Tudawali* between the Aboriginal actor and government officials; and in *Molokai* it is between Father Damien and both the Governor of Hawaii and later his bishop. However, there is no obligation on the genre to trace an ever-upward path on the part of its central figure. Triumph and affirmation may only be incidental moments in the biographical film. Although it concerns a champion swimmer, the actual clash in *Swimming Upstream* is more domestic and inward. Although its protagonist, Tony Fingleton, wins his most publicly important race at the end of the film, this is staged without the intensity and competitiveness that has marked many of his other races. He abandons competitive swimming shortly afterwards, implying that winning a silver medal at the Commonwealth Games was only of limited importance in his own maturation.

The pattern of an ever-upward path is varied by the nature of the protagonists in some of the other films. Four of these examine notorious criminals (two concern Ned Kelly). These films end with a downward or at least a more indeterminate resolution. So, too, does another – *Tudawali* – which follows the rise of the Aboriginal film star and his tragic death. Moreover, several of the films on the list, including *Squizzy Taylor*, *Chopper*, *The Postcard Bandit*, *Annie's Coming Out* and *Shine*, are also hybrids that overlap other genres treated elsewhere in this book. However, to gain a sharper sense of the Australian biopic, it is necessary to look at some of these films in more detail so that in the remainder of this chapter three films are given extended analysis. Coincidentally, two of these happen to have parallel situations and figures and it is with these that the account begins.

Sons and Fathers

Not all biopics need be concerned with the struggle of a historical individual and an institution. In line with recent biographical films elsewhere, such as *Angela's Ashes* (1999) and *The Life and Death of Peter Sellers* (2004), at least two recent Australian excursions into the genre – *Shine* (1996) and *Swimming Upstream* (2003) – have also concerned the damaging psychological effects on children of an emotionally disturbed and disturbing parent. Put another way, although both these films deal with actual childhoods and the historical figures' fathers – such emotional monsters as Sam Helfgott and Harold Fingleton really did exist – nevertheless, there is more point in claiming them as belonging to the genre of the biopic rather than aligning these films with that of social realism. (It's perhaps worth noting that David Helfgott's sister claimed that the film's portrayal of their father was grossly exaggerated, due in particular to the influence of David's wife, who of course never knew his father. Her contention potentially implies that the film thus provides a more satisfactorily 'dramatic' story trajectory than a more 'truthful' portrayal would suggest.) The crucial consideration is the fact that neither film claims to be representative and revelatory of a social problem or issue but rather are part of the elements that their respective protagonists, David Helfgott and Tony Fingleton, had to struggle to overcome. Put simply, although all four of these films have something in common in terms of family situations, each film is all the same focussed on the matter of personal biography rather than universal social tale. In the two Australian instances, *Shine* and *Swimming Upstream*, the struggles of their central characters are not public but private and domestic. To succeed in their calling, they have to overcome the emotional effects of an abusive father for whom children are a means of somehow gaining the recognition that they feel was denied them when they were younger. At the same time, it is important to consider each of these films in turn in case their various differences are forgotten.

Shine begins *in medias res* with the adult David Helfgott bursting into a restaurant where there is a piano and beginning to play. A long flashback then proceeds to trace parts of his childhood as a pianist and his subsequent training and breakdown. The work at the restaurant is part of a process of recovery that sees him, at the end of the film, married and resuming his career as an international concert pianist. In effect, like many biopics, *Shine* focusses not on a full life but on a period preceding public fame. Typically,

49

what emerges is the sense that David, like many other biopic heroes, is at the behest of forces over which he has little control. In David's case, it is not only a tyrannous father but also a fragile inner self that precipitates his breakdown. And, again, representative of the genre, there are several forebodings and omens of the disastrous emotional rapids that are ahead.

In this biopic, the conflict between protagonist and institution noted by Custen is more muted. If it emerges at all, it is to be found in the misguided actions of the mental hospital in locking David out from playing the piano. Overall, the point of this kind of conflict in the biopic is – as Neale, following Custen suggests – to show that the hero frequently devotes 'as much time fighting those who police their fields of endeavour as they do pursuing those endeavours themselves' (Custen 1992: 54). If one recalls that David must primarily overcome the ghost of his past if he is to triumph then such an antagonism is necessary.

When it comes to narrative patterning, *Shine* is again a characteristic example of the genre. While voice-over is not used, there is nevertheless a typical instance of montage as David plays 'Rach Three' for his graduation performance at the Royal College of Music in London. The musical piece holds together the sequence of shots, climaxing in silence as David's breakdown becomes clear even in this moment of triumph. The segment itself also highlights two other narrative moments of the genre. First, this performance constitutes a trial scene or its various analogues. For David, there are a string of testings, auditions that begin with him publicly performing in competition when he is a child of ten. Perhaps the most important of these trials is not the one at the Royal College of Music but rather his happy improvised access to the piano in the restaurant. He wins the approval of diners and staff which leads to a job there that becomes part of his recovery. Hence, unlike the performance of 'Rach Three' which he has been warned against and which finally lets loose his demons, this restaurant performance witnesses both to his musical genius and its continued capacity to make for pleasure and joy. But the playing of 'Rach Three' also illustrates another common feature of the biopic, namely a pull towards visual spectacle that also results in a concentration on moments of physical suffering (Anderson 1988: 339). The iconography of the playing of 'Rach Three' resembles that in many melodramas, but the visual power of the pain is intensified by the audience's knowledge that David's life has been lived rather than simply imagined (Anderson 1988: 339).

For both protagonists, David Helfgott in *Shine* and Tony Fingleton in *Swimming Upstream*, the body is the human instrument through which they achieve fame. The first's ability lies in his piano playing while the second reaches champion status in the domain of backstroke swimming. In fact, as *Swimming Upstream* suggests by including a fictional Dawn Fraser (and a cameo appearance by the historical person), this biopic might be linked with the other Australian swimming film, *Dawn!*. However, to note this connection is to realize some of the shifts in social values in the period since the 1950s and 1960s when these swimming champions were at their peak, to 1978 when *Dawn!* appeared, and 2003 when *Swimming Upstream* was released. Not only did Tony Fingleton have a much shorter swimming career but the more recent film indicates that the protagonist's desire to win a medal arose because of domestic rather than public pressures, to impress an uncaring father rather than a general public. Indeed, anticipating his later turning his back on competitive swimming, Tony is attracted to more cultured activities such as literature and the piano. However, his father has no regard for these – he flicks Tony's copy of the play *Hamlet* into a swimming pool and refers to piano practice as 'poofta stuff'. Finally, though, Tony moves beyond the pool to other things. Swimming becomes the means for him to win a bursary to Harvard University and so escape the emotional rollercoaster life at home, most especially at the hands of his father. What he achieves is referred to in a seaside conversation with his mother. There, sitting looking out at the blue water, Tony asks Dora whether she thinks that he could swim to America. This is precisely what he does achieve, metaphorically if not physically.

Nevertheless, *Swimming Upstream* is a biopic. Tony Fingleton and his brother John were excellent competitive swimmers in Australia in the early 1960s. The film is centrally concerned with many pool sessions as well as a total of eight swimming race meetings, beginning with a district championship in Brisbane and the Australian Swimming Championships in Sydney and ending with the Commonwealth Games backstroke race in Perth in 1962. Documentary-type verifications of time and place are further corroborated by the fictional appearance of several historical figures as well as the use of archival film footage. At the same time, the conflict between protagonist and institution noted by Custen (1992) and present in *Dawn!* is absent. Officialdom is missing. Instead, it is domestic strife that is amplified when the father deliberately encourages the competitiveness of the younger brother John against Tony.

But the general point remains the same as it does in other biopics – to show that the hero frequently devotes as much time overcoming the obstacles created by authority figures as they do pursuing their goals. If one recalls that Tony must primarily overcome not only the general emotional abuse of his father but the fact that swimming has been turned from an enjoyable leisure activity into an arena of competition and attempted wilful dominance, then the same kind of broad challenge lies there for the biographical protagonist.

In terms of narrative strategy, *Swimming Upstream* is another equally characteristic example of the genre. Tony's voice-over is heard at the very beginning of the film and returns at various points so that the film can engage in both telling and showing. But unlike *Shine*, it is organized in a more linear, conservative pattern, beginning with the protagonist as a young boy and ending with him on the edge of manhood, leaving the place where he grew up in favour of new places. In a postscript title, the film notes that Tony married the day after graduation and has continued to live in New York ever since. Significantly, the intertitle informs us about his domestic life thereafter rather than his public life, thereby suggesting that the biographical representation of *Swimming Upstream* is complete and almost self-contained.

As mentioned, the various races, whether against the stopwatch or against competition, highlight two other narrative moments of the genre. For Tony, there is an obvious string of testings, trials and races that begin with him publicly performing in competition when his father first times him and his brother John at a local swimming pool. Perhaps the most important of these trials is not his win at the Australian Swimming Championships in 1961 or his defeat of John in a local swimming championship but rather his win in the Commonwealth Games. None of the family are present and the compositional style of the film at that point suggests that Tony is under none of the pressure that he has been under in other races. But his actual final swim is in an empty pool, suggesting that he is no longer involved in competition and that swimming has reverted to the pleasure it had been when he was young. All the same, there have been several signs of this capacity so that Tony's disavowal of competitive swimming comes as little surprise.

The poetics of the races in *Swimming Upstream* illustrate a second common feature of the biopic, namely a pull towards visual spectacle especially in the scenes of testing and trial. As Anderson has noted, this engagement results in a concentration on moments of physical endurance and even suffering (1988: 339). As Tony's voice-over chants at one point: 'Training and racing, training and racing' – as the film offers a montage of images of water and swimming bodies. The style of filming of the various races, including split screen and multiscreen images, wipes, mobile camera, soundtrack and so on, catches the viewer up in thrilling sequences of spectacle and movement every bit as exciting as comparable segments in the action-adventure film.

As noted above, *Shine* and *Swimming Upstream* are two examples of a heroic biographical subject. Both David Helfgott and Tony Fingleton win out against many odds, particularly those set in train by abusive fathers who seek to gain through the younger man the kind of fame that has eluded them. Put another way, what is operating in these films is a kind of muted or not-so-muted social realism, repeated many times over in recent feature films in Australia, where the historical triumph has been internal and private as much as it is external and public. All the same, biographical tales can be exemplary in ways other than the triumph of virtue. Sinners are just as useful in terms of offering cautionary tales as are saints. Hence to complete this account of the biopic, this chapter turns to the cinematic life of an Australian ne'er-do-well.

The Criminal Biopic

Although *Chopper* (2000) begins with an intertitle warning that narrative liberties have been taken and the film is not a biography, any biopic might carry such a disclaimer. As already indicated, every biography – whether written or on screen – will necessarily and inevitably take particular liberties so far as narrative, character, setting and situation are concerned. Put another way, there is no need to respond to this warning and not treat *Chopper* as a film biography. Although it supplies little in the way of a background story, the film's plot covers a series of events in the criminal life of Mark 'Chopper' Read (Eric Bana) between 1978 and 1991 and this is supplemented by titles and (fictional although representative) archival footage to amplify the plot account of the criminal life still further. However, the film is anything but conventional in terms of being a partial life history. Late in *Chopper*, two detectives remind Chopper that he is a 'bullshit artist' while the film ends, as it began, with Chopper in his cell with two guards who he informs that he 'never lets the truth get in the way of a good yarn'.

And indeed there are several intimations not only that Chopper does lie but, more radically, that in this world of criminals, drugs, murder, jail and courts, it is frequently difficult to know what is true. This is suggested in Chopper's initial murder of veteran top dog criminal Keithy George in Pentridge Jail in 1978. When guards come to drag the bleeding man out, they appear to accept Chopper's and his cell mates' explanation that Keithy 'did himself a mischief', including stabbing himself in the eye. More radically, *Chopper* constantly juxtaposes one version of events against another. Hence, even when Chopper is interviewed in connection with the stabbing by officers from the Prisoner Liaison Office and claims that no one saw the incident, a slow motion flashback shows prisoners going about their business, apparently confirming his version of events.

Nonetheless, two incidents that are much more tangled and complicated in terms of what happened and who is telling the truth occur in the second half of the film. The first of these incidents involves Chopper shooting Neville Bartos (Vince Colosimo), the Albanian-Australian drug dealer. He is on friendly terms with two detectives led by Downie (Bill Young) and in what appear to be two different pub discussions offers to help them rid Melbourne of drug dealers and claims that there is no truth in the story that he drove Bartos to hospital. All the same, the next scene seems to immediately contradict this when, at Bartos' house, Chopper and the latter's henchmen load the wounded man into a car to be taken to hospital by Chopper. The next scene again returns to the pub and the two detectives, who reiterate to Chopper that he should stop claiming publicly and inaccurately that he has been authorized by the police to kill Melbourne drug dealers. There is a similar indeterminacy surrounding the killing of Sammy the Turk (Serge Liistro) outside Bojangle's nightclub. The first disclosure involves Chopper going outside with the Turk and demanding to know which team he is on. When the latter is confused, Chopper shoots him. Immediately, in another version of events, Mandy, the junkie girlfriend of Loughman (Simon Lyndon), a former cell mate of Chopper, sees the incident and goes screaming to Loughman. However, Chopper's version of events soon becomes one wherein the Turk tried to sell him some guns. In yet another version, the Turk tries to ambush him and Chopper fires in self-defence. This is told to the detectives but the latter point out that the murderer has already been caught with the murder weapon. Chopper is accused of being a 'bullshit artist'.

Lest the reader is led into thinking that *Chopper* is an art film to do with epistemological problems regarding truth, there is certainly enough in the film to place these complications and multi-perspectivism in relation to the biographical subject of Mark 'Chopper' Read. The point is that the film is at pains to present three indisputable facts concerning its criminal hero. First, Chopper is strikingly brave to the point of having no physical qualms concerning his body. Hence, in an extraordinary example of the trial or testing incident so common in the biopic, Loughman unexpectedly stabs Chopper while the two are in the cell at Pentridge. Blood flows after the second time the knife is thrust into the stomach of the bewildered Chopper. The latter responds as if Loughman has merely nudged him with an elbow. After several more thrusts, Loughman appears to apologize only to resume the stabbing, causing the victim to exclaim that '. . . if you keep stabbing me, I'll die . . .' . This is a remarkable segment but quite in keeping with the portrait of Chopper as a phenomenal being, one apparently without interiority or psychology. How else to understand the quite radical shifts of attitude and behaviour on the part of the protagonist that recur in the film beginning with the sudden, unexpected stabbing of Keithy George (David Field)?

All of this has a frequently surreal, comic effect, and this is the last element that needs to be registered in this biopic. 'Don't Fence Me In', sung by Frankie Laine, accompanies the film's opening credits and implies that this biography has an often funny, at times ironic dimension. So much of the story is sourced to Mark Read's very probably unreliable memoir that *Chopper* insists that in part what it is recounting may indeed be a 'tall tale'. Above all else, Chopper appears endlessly fascinated at his own image as it is mediated by television interviews and other forms of public attention. As he points out to the guards after they have watched one of his current affairs interviews, he is an artist of sorts in relation to his own history and exploits, committed to the needs of a 'good story'. This is a suitable epigraph for the biopic of the Australian criminal subject.

Last Words

Altogether, then, the biopic is another example of a genre that has not, for the most part, engaged the imagination and energy of Australian film makers or audiences in any sustained way. While there was an astonishingly prolific output in the television version of the genre in the 1980s and early 1990s, feature film makers have mostly not followed suit. Of the three films discussed in this chapter, *Shine* sustained a good deal of critical and popular interest and engagement, winning the 1996 AFI award as Best Feature, possibly because the real-life protagonist is still alive and performing. Geoffrey Rush's work as David Helfgott won him an AFI award as Best Actor. All the same, when the same actor came to play a leading role in another biopic nearly 10 years later, much less attention was lavished on the result. Hence, although *Swimming Upstream* received good reviews and attracted incidental attention (not least because the real-life sister of the protagonist was herself embroiled in a legal controversy in Queensland), nevertheless the film did not spur any great investment in the genre by film makers or audiences. Probably because it involved less acting bravura and because Rush played a far less sympathetic role as Harold Fingleton than had been the case with David Helfgott, Rush received no nominations at the annual round of AFI awards. More generally, in the immediate future at least, the genre of the biopic seems set to be a minor one so far as Australian cinema is concerned.

One might speculate as to this dearth. After all, the increasing need of producers and directors to market films internationally may have an inhibiting effect on the promotion of local heroes as suitable subjects for feature films. Regardless, this kind of recognition factor may not be all that important. After all, the biopic as genre frequently chooses obscure historical subjects with the case for their dramatic importance being made in the course of the film. In any case, biopics also deal with anti-heroes, so factors other than recognizability must be considered.

5
Comedy

Comedy and the Comic

According to a recent posting on an Australian Film Commission (AFC) website, Australian film makers are highly disposed towards the production of feature comedies (AFC 2004).This master list offers a breakdown of 35 different film genres in which Australian directors and writers are currently specializing, a highly catholic labelling that includes such disparate genre types as action, adventure, gay, satire, prison and political. However, comedy seems to be king, easily outstripping all these other types. The website lists a total of 191 feature comedies out of a film total of 795. Put another way, one in every four films produced in Australia in recent years is claimed to be a comedy.

This is a highly inflated figure and suggests a deal of confusion about matters of definition and identification. After all, even though films have comic moments, they are often better understood in terms of other genres. Hence, for example, although both *Don's Party* (1976) and *The Odd Angry Shot* (1979) feature television host and comedian Graham Kennedy, it is rather straining the definition to regard either film as a comedy. In addition, it is also necessary to recall that comedy can be found outside as well as inside narrative. On television in particular, gags, jokes, spoofs and so on frequently attach themselves to a series of other forms, including the variety show, sports programs, sketch and stand-up comedy, that are not based on the integration of comedy and narrative (Neale and Krutnik 1990: 4–15). Even in the cinema, comedy means more than funny moments, episodes, jokes and gags. Instead, the class is a meta genre, rather like other broad types such as adventure and crime. Gehring insists that comedy can only be thought about in terms of specific types such as the screwball comedy, popular comedy, parody, black humour and clown comedy (1986, 1988) and Neale echoes this general sentiment (2000: 69). Historically, the term comedy indicates a kind of story that stands opposed to tragedy (Neale and Krutnik 1990: 11–17). In opposition to this latter type which tends to concern itself with characters of high standing who suffer a fateful downfall, comedy involves everyday life and a happy ending (Bordwell 1982; Horton 1991). The latter frequently entails the arbitrary and the coincidental playing a role that is denied to them in so-called serious genres. Frequently, too, in comedy casual motivation and narrative integration are abandoned for the sake of humorous effect (Karnick and Jenkins 1995: 4–11). The genre therefore becomes a prime site for all manner of unlikely actions and all manner of unexpected and even implausible justifications for their occurrence. Comedy often introduces the audience to the illogical, the impossible and the absurd (Palmer 1987: 1–14; 1995: 9–44). Coincidence can also play an important role both in an ending and throughout. Hence, it is worth taking note of an Australian film such as *Dallas Doll* (1993), which failed to gain an exhibition release. While some would put this down to conservative taste in the face of a bisexual central figure who seduces all members of the same family, others might put this distribution misadventure down to the film's awkward blend of modes. The central figure is undone in her designs not least because she is trampled to death by a herd of cattle, an ending that highlights the extent to which the narrative of *Dallas Doll* has strayed from a basic tenet of comedy.

Further complicating this definition is the fact that comedy has a capacity to take over or reanimate most if not all other genres in terms of parody and satire (Neale 2000: 62). In the chapter on the adventure film, the figure and narrative of *Crocodile Dundee* is discussed. Clearly, Dundee is an adventure hero. However, as embodied by popular television comedian, Paul Hogan, the figure of Dundee is also a funnyman, joker and trickster. And, indeed, the fact that it is Hogan in the leading role inclines viewers to want to categorize the film as a comedy rather than an adventure film. With its capacity to infect, satirize and parody all other forms, the genre of comedy stands on a kind of different plane to other genres. Understanding this, one should not be surprised to realize that there are several types of comedy at work in Australian cinema.

Narrative and Subgenres

One way to comprehend this range is in terms of different subgenres. Overlapping types of Australian film comedy might include the following:

1 **Adventure comedy** – This traces the path of a comic hero and the different situations and succession of events that befall such a figure. The loose, episodic, picaresque structure of *The Adventures of Barry McKenzie* (1972) and the first half of *Alvin Purple* (1973) represents one pole, while the

tighter, double narratives of *Crocodile Dundee* (1986), set in the Northern Territory and in New York, constitute another. Whatever the case, the comedy adventure film follows its central figure through a series of loosely connected episodes and encounters wherein there is frequently a doubling or rhyming of the first and last of these. Hence, for example, in both of the Barry McKenzie films, the hero leaves Australia at the beginning and after many escapades returns home at the end.

2 **Social comedy** – In this subtype, the central figure enters another world where conventions, behaviours and even language are different so that there is a clash of codes and social conventions. In such an environment, the hero is comically out of joint so far as norms and expectations are concerned (Neale 2000: 61–7; Barr 1977: 44–69; Horton 1991: 1–19). Obviously, there are connections between this type of comedy and the first. Nevertheless, the narrative structure and setting of this kind of comic tale are those of the world upside down, with the 'fish out of water' character. The clash is one of values, behaviours and social expectations and opposes the initial codes of the central figure with those in operation in the world s/he has entered. This type owes a lot to the comedy of manners or genteel comedy, including the famous Ealing comedies of the 1940s and 1950s (Barr 1977) and can be found in several Australian films including *Spotswood* (1992), *The Castle* (1997) and *Crackerjack* (2002).

3 **Slapsick or zany comedy** – This type is less frequent. Here gags, puns, slapstick and other forms of comic craziness abound, often breaking patterns of verisimilitude and emphasizing absurdity, the ridiculous, gags, jokes, pratfalls and so on. There are far fewer examples of this type but any list would have to include *Malcolm* (1986), *Pizza* (2002), *Takeaway* (2003) and *He Died with a Felafel in His Hand* (2004). Especially in the second of these, craziness, absurdity and illogicalities of setting, situation and language are very pronounced even to the point of keeping the world of ordinary everyday reality and verisimilitude at bay.

4 **Satirical comedy** – A subgenre that derives its motivation from deliberately and sustainedly making fun of another genre and narrative, whether it be such historical send-ups as *Eliza Fraser* (1976) and *Wills and Burke* (1985) or such generic parodies as *Yackety Yack* (1973), *The Return of Captain Invincible* (1983) and *The Roly Poly Man* (1994) where, respectively, the art film, the action-adventure film and the detective genre are lampooned. Such comedy is founded on caricature, comic exaggeration, satire and mockery, and depends in part on audiences' familiarity with the history or genre being held up to ridicule.

5 **Caper comedy** – Yet another comedy type that cross-fertilizes another genre is the caper comedy. Here, the type being imitated is that of the

robbery film. However, instead of treating the subject in a serious straight-forward fashion wherein things often go astray with disastrous and often murderous consequences for those involved, the film maker chooses to portray the robbery or chain of robberies as comically unrealistic and even fantastic. *Touch and Go* (1980) and *Malcolm* both belong to this type while others such as *Ricki and Pete* (1988) and *Gettin' Square* (2003) also share some of its elements.

6 **Romantic comedy** – Again, like the last, this type verges on a kind of generic hybridity and may not seem so unfailingly funny as other types, such as the zany comedy. A recurring subgenre, nonetheless, the type involves a comedy of the sexes wherein male and female must adjust and learn to live with the other. Disguise and masquerade may well be resorted to in this process. The romantic comedy uses humour to interrupt and complicate its romance, and romance to extend and amplify its comedy. A few of the many titles found in Australian film output include *They're a Weird Mob* (1966), *The Big Steal* (1990), *Green Card* (1990), *All Men Are Liars* (1995), *Brilliant Lies* (1996), *Dating the Enemy* (1996) and *Paperback Hero* (1999). Frequently, too, cycles or subgenres occur within the type. Neale and Krutnik, for example, have referred to a comic Hollywood romance type involving the wooing of a boss lady (1990: 116–20). Such a pattern seems to be in operation in Australian cinema comedy in a group of films extending from *They're a Weird Mob* to at least *Paperback Hero*.

7 **Women's comedy** – Again, this subtype spills over into several of those already mentioned (Rowe 1995). However, Collins has called attention to a surge of Australian features written and/or directed by women that subtly subvert heterosexuality and mock images of Australian masculinity, most especially within the genre of the romantic comedy (1999a: 74–6). Such a cycle of comically satirical films include Jane Campion's *Sweetie* (1989), Shirley Barrett's *Love Serenade* (1996), Emma-Kate Croghan's *Love and Other Catastrophes* (1996), Megan Simpson-Huberman's *Dating the Enemy* (1996), Clara Law's *Floating Life* (1996), Cherie Nowlan's *Thank God He Met Lizzie* (1997), Sue Brook's *Road to Nhill* (1997) and Monica Pellizari's *A Fistful of Flies* (1997).

A Comic Tale

The identification of different subgenres is not meant to imply that specific narrative schemes are unique to these comic plots. Rather, Australian film comedies, like those produced elsewhere, use different narrative strategies at different points in their development. In effect, they can weave in and out of several different story schemata. This point is well demonstrated in the narrative structure of *Alvin Purple*, so an examination of that film's structure highlights the flexibility of narrative types at work in comedy. The film's plot can be represented as follows:

1 Precredit segment – Alvin in a Melbourne tram fantasizes about women.
2 A young woman neighbour borrows sugar which leads to sex. Film titles.
3 Alvin as schoolboy. Mrs Horewitz, his teacher's wife, saves him from chasing schoolgirls and begins an affair.
4 At his 21st birthday party, Alvin declares his affection for Tina, his childhood sweetheart.
5 Alvin and Spike work as waterbed salesmen. Spike works in a store demonstrating to customers. Meanwhile, Alvin makes more sales by installing the beds and sexually satisfying the women buyers.
6 Tina explains to Alvin that she does not trust him because of his sexual attraction. She suggests that he see a psychiatrist.
7 A clinic where Dr McBirney and Dr Liz Sort share a practice. She will take Alvin on as a patient.
8 His therapy has begun. Whenever sexual opportunities come his way, Alvin must sublimate by running around the block, taking cold showers and so on.
9 Liz is sexually attracted to him. However, her therapy is working so that he does not respond.
10 McBirney is aware of Alvin's erotic attraction for women. He sets up an arrangement whereby Alvin becomes a sex therapist serving women sent by McBirney.
11 Liz has discovered this arrangement. She begins visiting Alvin as a customer, threatening exposure if he does not satisfy her sexual demands.
12 McBirney is puzzled as to why Alvin is always tired and increasingly unable to do his work.
13 Visiting his friends, Alvin confesses that he is unable to get out of the situation with Liz, McBirney and the women patients.
14 The media obtain information on the secret goings-on. McBirney flees but Alvin is put on trial.
15 While Liz is an unfriendly witness, it is disclosed that McBirney had been filming Alvin's sex sessions and selling these in the porn film market. The judge sees various of these encounters. However, the jury acquits Alvin.

16 Fleeing from the media after being discharged, Alvin is chased to an airstrip. He evades his pursuers by dressing as a parachutist and jumping from a plane.

17 Dressed as a hippie Indian, he ends up in a city park. There he discovers McBirney disguised as a preacher, haranguing the crowd about sin. McBirney spots Alvin and turns the crowd's attention in that direction. Alvin is pursued along Melbourne streets almost completely naked.

18 Alvin finds that Tina has left her job. She is becoming a nun. He visits her at the convent and finds a job there as a gardener. The film ends with him working surrounded by women who have taken vows of chastity.

What this breakdown reveals is the variety of narrative strategies at work in this representative Australian comedy. The early episodes are highly temporal and picaresque and establish the point about Alvin's attraction for the opposite sex. This episodic scheme is at work in miniature in the segment that involves Alvin and Spike working as waterbed salesmen, the one going about it in the store while the other operates in the homes of women customers. Not only is there the comic contrast between the two but Alvin's meetings with customers are arranged as a series of short, comically sexual encounters. Clearly, too, this picaresque pattern is revisited in segments 15–18 at the end of the film. However, in segment 6, the romance with the virginal Tina becomes the narrative motor for much of the rest of the film.

In fact, what *Alvin Purple* is doing here is borrowing from another comic narrative source. In its time of first release in 1973, the film was billed as a sex comedy indirectly highlighting its connection with a British sex comedy with a more historical setting, *Tom Jones* (1960). The Australian comedy owes much of its overall structure, most especially in its second half, to the 'mock epic' structure of both the British film and the Fielding novel on which it was based. The latter followed Fielding's *Joseph Andrews* and was a kind of further riposte to the novel *Pamela* by Samuel Richardson. *Tom Jones* inverts the melodrama of the latter, which has its heroine constantly in danger of her chastity being violated by a nobleman holding the young woman as a kind of prisoner. *Tom Jones* jokingly inverts this situation by having a young man who is sexually irresistible to women so that he is constantly being seduced, often even against his will. In turn, *Alvin Purple* owes much to this broad narrative scheme. Dr Liz Sort is the haughty boss woman comparable to Lady Bellaston in the Fielding story, sexually demanding and even threatening. Alvin himself is in the great tradition of comic heroes, being naive, a gull or

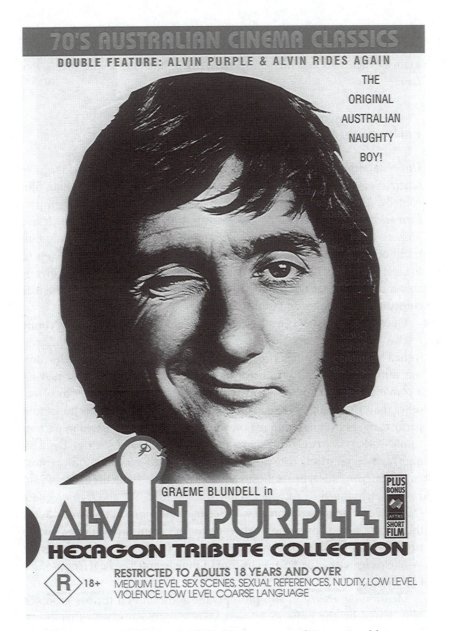

70'S AUSTRALIAN CINEMA CLASSICS

DOUBLE FEATURE: ALVIN PURPLE & ALVIN RIDES AGAIN

THE ORIGINAL AUSTRALIAN NAUGHTY BOY!

GRAEME BLUNDELL in

ALVIN PURPLE

HEXAGON TRIBUTE COLLECTION

PLUS BONUS AFTRS SHORT FILM

R 18+ RESTRICTED TO ADULTS 18 YEARS AND OVER
MEDIUM LEVEL SEX SCENES, SEXUAL REFERENCES, NUDITY, LOW LEVEL VIOLENCE, LOW LEVEL COARSE LANGUAGE

Comedy adventure: Alvin Purple *(1973). Image courtesy of Warner Roadshow.*

dupe, the object of others' conspiracies and secrets. It concludes that it is far better to have a fiancée who is chaste, modest and physically undemanding, again a conclusion that *Alvin Purple* shares with the 'comic epic' that is *Tom Jones*.

Performers and Performance

Understanding the genre in terms of its generic subtypes and narrative schemata is only one way to get a handle on the subject of Australian film comedy. Another approach might be in terms of performers and their performance (Fisher 1977; Neale and Krutnik 1990; Rowe 1995; Karnick and Jenkins 1995). Seidman has directed attention to one kind of comic film tradition that he calls 'the comedian's comedy' (1981). The phrase refers to the fact that many films feature well-known funnymen (it is almost invariably a male) so that the film becomes in part a vehicle for the particular comedian's gags, jokes and funny business.

Of course, comedies can also feature 'straight' performers playing comic roles. When Colin Friels, for instance, played the central figure in *Malcolm*, he had had no history of performing in comedy. Neither in radio, television nor film had he been funny. Instead, Friels was a (serious) actor playing a comic role. Put another way, the film had to find its comedy in places other than this actor's persona. On the other hand, many films do feature performers, both minor and major, who have reputations based in part on comic work, very frequently occurring in other media and settings. Displaying a high degree of self-conscious reflexivity and self-mockery, the foremost embodiment of this type are those comedies associated with the figure of Paul Hogan, including the *Crocodile Dundee* trilogy (1986–97) and *Lightning Jack* (1994). For many Australian viewers seeing these films on the large screen, there was a direct connection between Hogan's comic appearances on the small screen in such outlets as *A Current Affair* (1974–76), commercials for Winfield cigarettes, the Australian Tourist Bureau and *The Paul Hogan Show* (1977–84).

Mentioning television also prompts the addition of a further group of films based on the presence of well-known comedians, who first established themselves elsewhere including vaudeville, radio and television. These comprise: George Wallace – *His Royal Highness* (1932), *Harmony Row* (1933), *A Ticket in Tatts* (1934), *Let George Do It* (1938) and *Gone to the Dogs* (1939); Roy 'Mo' Rene – *Strike Me Lucky* (1934); Cecil Kellaway – *It Isn't Done* (1937) and *Mr Chadworth Steps Out* (1939); Graham Kennedy – *Don's Party, The Odd Angry Shot, The Club* (1980) and *Travelling North*

(1987); John Clarke – *Death in Brunswick* (1991) and *Crackerjack* (2002); and Mick Molloy – *Crackerjack* and *Bad Eggs* (2003).

Other films deserve a place alongside this type. One of the earliest films of the Revival featured another funny although fictitious figure. Thanks to his portrayal in the comic strip in *Private Eye*, Barry McKenzie was already relatively well known before Barry Crocker played the role in the two *Barry McKenzie* films (1972–75). Mention should also be made of comedian Barry Humphries, who has singularly failed to import his comedy to the cinema. Unlike those mentioned above, who worked in popular outlets where they developed their comic art, Humphries' early stand-up comedy was almost exclusively confined to university revue and the theatre in Australia so that figures such as Edna Everage could only play comic second fiddle in the two *Barry McKenzie* films. When Humphries tried launching another of his comic creations in the shape of fictitious politician Les Patterson in *Les Patterson Saves The World* (1986), the film sank without comic trace. Others capable of comedy on the small screen, including Bert Newton, Gordon Chater, Garry McDonald/Norman Gunston, Paul Chubb, Eric Bana and Stephen Curry, have often appeared in comedies in roles which if not cameos nevertheless do draw on their funnyman persona disclosed and developed on television.

Finally, a further extension of the comedian's comedy is represented by the crossover from television series to comedy films exemplified by *Number 96* (1974), *The Box* (1975) and *Pizza*. All of these were successful and very popular television programs before they appeared as feature films. (Meanwhile, the pendulum could swing the other way, as occurred when the *Alvin Purple* films also gave rise to an ABC TV series of the same name.) What is important here is not the crossover itself but rather the fact that with the release of the films a kind of comic repertory company made famous in the three television series was being brought to a cinema audience.

Overall, it is important to recognize the intertextual connection between comedies and comedians in relation to both the big and the small screen. With the singular exception of Paul Hogan, there has been no continuing link between an Australian comedian and Australian film comedy, as there has been in Hollywood with figures such as Jack Nicholson, Jim Carrey and Adam Sandler. Nevertheless, the occasional comedian's comedy reminds us that on-screen faces, voices and bodies are often as important to this genre as they are to other types of cinema. And just as elsewhere in this book discussion pays attention to such icons as Chips Rafferty in relation to early Australian action-adventure films and to Bryan Brown in connection with the genre of crime, so it is necessary to remember this extra textual dimension in relation to film comedy.

Comic Types

Over and above well-known performers who have carried their comic reputations and *personae* into feature comedies, there is the fact that the genre
needs the presence of particular character types. While comedy often attacks
verisimilitude, it also draws on stereotypes for its own effects. Hence, it makes
sense to talk of a comic hero or type while recognizing that many comedies
may be exceptions to such a generalization. Nonetheless, there are several
different ways of describing such a figure including the innocent, the naive,
the trusting, the fool, the dim-witted, the childish, the stupid, the credulous,
the obsessive, the eccentric, the crazy, the grotesque and the ugly. Hence, in
Spotswood, Errol Wallace (Anthony Hopkins) stumbles into a world of these
different character types; while in *The Castle* the entire eccentric community of the Kerrigan family and their neighbours and friends, especially in
the person of Dale Kerrigan (Michael Caton) himself, finds itself in conflict
with powerful institutions of the public world, most especially in the shape
of capital and law (Lloyd 2001: 171–84). Other types that confound notions
of normality also abound in Australian comedy including the aged (*Crackerjack*), aliens, scatty females and others (*Pizza*) and the foreigner (*They're
a Weird Mob* and *Wog Boy* (2000)). Further compounding this effect of
eccentricity, confusion and even deviance is a repertoire of masquerades,
disguises, dressing up, cross-dressing, lookalikes and the playing of dual
roles which, among other films, can be found in *Barry McKenzie Holds His
Own, Alvin Purple Rides Again, All Men Are Liars, Paperback Hero* and *Wog
Boy*. These films can also have elements of childishness and infantilism that
registers in naivety, an apparent lack of coordination, and a tendency towards
daydreams and fantasy.

    Pizza is a case in point. Among the comically outrageous, absurd types
that pass through the film are delivery boys Pauley and Sleek and shop
owner Bobo, and these are followed by Mama, Bobo's Italian mother, Shaza,
the sexually frustrated single mother, the Supermodel, Rupert Packer the
media owner, Big Yobbo, a Rastafarian gang, the Lebanese home boys, aliens
from space, police bent on harassment and entrapment, Habib's uncle in
Lebanon, Sadam from Iraq and the lascivious Big Helga. In turn, these
comic eccentrics and types help to ground the comedy in the hilarious and
riotous world of the outer western suburbs both as a site for Bobo's Fat
Pizza shop and as it is encountered in the course of pizza deliveries. This
became mythologized as Hashfield, formerly Ashfield, a white, Anglo-Saxon
middle-class inner western suburb of Sydney, but now comically contested
by other ethnic cultures and subcultures. *Pizza* discloses a hilarious and
absurd cross-section of multicultural Australia inhabited by such ethnic

types as Chokos, Lebanese, Indians, Vietnamese and, more occasionally, Australians of white Anglo-Saxon background. In other words, the film is cheerfully and outrageously complicit in stereotypes of the West. Life on the streets is jokingly brutal. Hence, comic robberies, violence and even homicide happen in the background. Like a good deal of comedy, *Pizza* is not afraid to be ethnically insulting and outrageous about whichever groups fall within its sights (Palmer 1987; Neale and Krutnik 1990). By turn, it is farcical, slapstick, absurd, funny, humorous and satirical about such social problems as unemployment, dole bludging, crime, robbery, cheating and drug peddling.

Talking about types and characters also serves to highlight yet another orientation of Australian film comedy. This subgenre has, mostly, favoured not sophisticated comedy or romantic comedy but rather the comedy of the innocent, who is translated into an unfamiliar social situation but soon discloses himself (it is almost invariably a male) to finally be more than a match for these conditions. This kind of social comedy accurately underlines such 'rural' cycles before World War II as that concerning the Hayseeds – *The Hayseeds* (1933) – and those featuring Dad and Dave, comprising *On Our Selection* (1932), *Grandad Rudd* (1935), *Dad and Dave Come to Town* (1938) and *Dad Rudd MP* (1940). Equally, despite differences in time, film production infrastructure, audiences and general outlook, the same kind of designation also covers the 'ocker' cycle of the 1970s and 1980s (Moran and Vieth 2005: 261). This cycle is particularly pronounced and, arguably, includes *The Naked Bunyip* (1970), *The Adventures of Barry McKenzie, Alvin Purple, Number 96, Alvin Purple Rides Again, Stork* (1974), *Barry McKenzie Holds His Own, The True Story of Eskimo Nell* (1975), *Fantasm* (1976), *The Great McCarthy* (1975), *The Box, Don's Party, Fantasm Comes Again* (1978), *Dimboola* (1979), *Pacific Banana* (1981), *Melvin, Son of Alvin* (1984), *Les Patterson Saves the World*, the *Crocodile Dundee* trilogy and *The Castle*.

Comic Surprise and Suspense

The presence of this general comic type, the involvement in a world turned upside down, and the incidence of such narrative features as masquerade, deception, plots, conspiracy and intrigues alert the reader to yet another feature of comic narrative. This has to do with the fact that some of the same narrative elements found in other genres are also present in comedy. Hence, comic surprise and suspense often serve as engines for standard plots in comedy. In *Malcolm*, the central figure (Colin Friels) initially appears oblivious to the fact that Frank (John Hargreaves) is a bank robber. However, when he takes the latter for a drive in a new car that he has built, Frank as well as the viewer is surprised to discover that Malcolm is in fact aware of his lodger's line of work and has already designed a getaway car for a future robbery. Equally, comic suspense can also come into operation. Later in the park, Frank is persuaded by Malcolm and Judith (Lindy Davis) to show how he confronts bank officials in a hold-up. Wrapping his hand in a jacket, he menaces them with an imaginary gun. They notice that a passer-by is creeping up behind him, apparently to save them from robbery. Frank, however, refuses to heed their warning, believing that it is a trick to have him turn around. For Malcolm and Judith as well as for the viewer, the comic joke momentarily carries a good deal of suspense. All the characters as well as the viewer are surprised when Frank is hit by the shovel.

Gags, jokes, and local comic moments within larger narratives are extreme examples of a particular tendency and pattern within generic narrative. This is the inclination for specific generic segments to become semi-independent modules, stand-alone sequences within a larger narrative whole. Hence, the musical contains the performance of the song or dance, the action-adventure film offers the spectacle of violence or action while the comedy film offers the clowning, the gag or the piece of funny business. However, even while appearing to be one-offs or to stand alone, these latter segments can be seen to observe their own principles of structure. As Neale and Krutnik point out, such segments have their own minute patterns that both construct and then undermine reality and verisimilitude (1990: 90–112). They also provoke laughter. The funny moment or humorous event is dependent on narrative. Hence, in *Alvin Purple Rides Again*, the comedy of the sexual encounter of Alvin with May (Abigail), the waitress in a roadside cafe, helps illustrate this patterning. Her mechanic husband and Alvin's friend Spike are outside attending to a malfunctioning car. As a sexually comic performer who rose to fame through the television series *Number 96* (1972–78), Abigail is nonchalant in making him a cup of tea, her famous breasts appearing to burst the buttons of her blouse. She is sexually turned on as Alvin goes cross-eyed trying to thread a needle, and he falls obligingly to the floor beneath her. All this is intercut with the two outside commenting on the performance and condition of the car. Meanwhile, the sexual encounter has caused all the shelved items in the shop to shake and finally fall in a climactic gag of colours and shapes cascading on the couple on the floor.

In fact, as this instance suggests, jokes, wisecracks and gags are, like their counterparts in musicals and action-adventure films, often digressive to a narrative and not integral to it. Special motivation is therefore often pro-vided for this kind of comic episode. Here, for instance, the comic sexual encounter is motivated not in terms of any verisimilitude of character or incident. Rather, the tendency of Alvin towards an inevitable sexual attraction for women coupled with the stereotypical figure of Abigail, based on her role in *Number 96*, propels them both towards this encounter. Of course, some of these short comedy sequences also lead outwards to larger narrative constructions. Take, for example, the matter of the double plot. In *Alvin Purple Rides Again*, Alvin meets a lookalike in the shape of American gangster Balls McGee. But the latter accidentally and comically kills himself with a loaded gun and his gang force Alvin to masquerade as Balls. In turn, to allay the suspicions of a house detective that Alvin has been rubbed out, the latter is required to alternate as Alvin and as Balls.

A second kind of comic plot structure involves accident and coincidence replacing scheming as the main motivation of the narrative. Hence, for example, in *Dating the Enemy*, it is a moment of magic, an inexplicable accident associated with the moon, that causes the swapping of gender that triggers the comedy of the film. In *The Castle*, it is the circumstance that the Kerrigan house is situated next to an airport that is wanting to expand that sets the story in train. In turn, this general kind of narrative premise may trigger comic narrative suspense. Such accidents and coincidences can motivate different schemes on the part of different characters such that their interaction across the pattern of events comically ensures that each of their goals fails or else must be modified. Although less than outstandingly funny as a comedy, *The Nugget* (2002) is a good example of this type of structure. After the surprising discovery of the very large gold nugget, the three central characters connive to hide it. Subsequently, various others in the town learn of their luck and become involved in different schemes surrounding the gold. Not unexpectedly, surprise and even the arbitrary also occur in this comedy both in terms of the gold and in the way that the gold finds its way back to the trio.

Gags and Jokes

From the observation that there are many non-narrative elements in a comedy that make the audience laugh, one can pass on to a more careful pinpointing of the action and function of the joke. As the example from *Alvin Purple Rides Again* suggests, the joke can in miniature function as 'time out', much like the musical number in a musical or even a sexual encounter in an erotic film. In comedy, the comedian constrains the fiction just as the fiction constrains the comedian. Even a sense of playing for the sake of play itself can come into operation. In any case, the joke or gag has a structure. It is, then, necessary to consider how it works as well as how it functions within the flow of comic narration. Palmer has analysed the structure of the joke, affirming that the latter has a discernible and distinct structure and order of progression (1987, 1995).

These include an opener or premise stage and a climax stage (frequently delivered in the form of a punchline of sight or sound). In turn, the topper is one of the intervening stages of the unexpected or the surprise, all of which is orchestrated by an apparent logic that is yet absurd. Here:

> ... the plausible and the implausible always combine, but in unequal measure: while plausibility is always present, implausibility is always dominant, and it is this dominance that allows us to perceive the events, actions and utterances with which we are presented in comedy as comic rather than poetic or tragic. (Neale 2000: 69)

Jokes may, of course, be cast in story or in more rhetorical form. In turn, the build-up may contain further elements of the story or various attempts at solving a puzzle or answering a question. This stage of the pattern may be deliberately elongated by repeating various steps of the situation or introducing further variations in the story or the puzzle. Comic suspense may come into operation at this point in terms of the deliberate creation of a gap between what the listener or viewer knows and what a protagonist is aware of. Finally, the punchline delivers the comic climax, frequently containing both comic surprise and release from the situation.

Hence, in *Crocodile Dundee*, there is the gag that occurs when Dundee and Sue (Linda Kozlowski) in New York are confronted by a would-be robber. Sue is scared and warns Dundee to hand over his wallet as the thief has a knife. But Dundee is unmoved. His inertia causes Sue and the audience a kind of comic tension. But then comes Dundee's famous punchline, 'That's not a knife – this is a knife' wherein he produces his own weapon which is bigger and more threatening than that of the thief, causing the latter to flee. This is a rich and well-constructed gag that depends in part on the comic persona of Hogan as Dundee. The episode might be seen to further the romance of the two in that the male protects the woman and thus further draws her to him. However, there is a stronger case for affirming that the joke does in fact suspend the narrative flow of the segment. It is an opportunity for Paul Hogan to engage in some funny business, thereby affirming his reputation as comedian. Up to a point, the jester is in conflict with the conventional laws of the genre with a suspension of narrative in favour of the progressive disclosure of the joke. The sudden appearance of the thief and his brandishing of a knife are both a surprise and a threat and we, along with Sue, react as such. However, Dundee is unmoved and his lack of compliance in being apparently slow to hand over his wallet increases her suspense and anxiety. The cap on the gag when he produces his large knife causing the thief to flee brings comic relief for Linda and the audience as both realize that Dundee was master of the situation rather than being at its mercy. In short, gags constantly tend to digress from a narrative succession of events. Or more precisely, one can think of the operation of different degrees of integration or degrees of transgression involved in jokes as opposed to comic narrative. Hence, it becomes necessary to stress the different kinds of integration operating in different types of film comedy (Gehring 1986, 1988; Neale and Krutnik 1990).

Towards an Australian Film Comedy Tradition

This chapter has had, of necessity, to skirt over a series of topics that deserve more attention. There is, for example, a need for more sustained investigation of the historical poetics of Australian film comedy and on the sociocultural forces at work in the genre, most especially in the past thirty years. Film comedy is one of the very few genres that existed in the period from the coming of sound up until the 1960s, so that this tradition was renewed rather than invented in the period after the Revival. More obviously than some other genres, film comedy relies not only on what is happening elsewhere in the Australian cinema but what is happening elsewhere in other arenas where laughter matters, including the popular stage, live theatre, radio, television, bars, clubs and cafes. Over the years, these different circuits have produced a large number of comedians and this has been to the general benefit of film comedy.

In terms of a starting point for a poetics of Australian film comedy, research might look to two different traditions first proposed by Neale (1980). These involve what has been described above as social and zany comedy. For the most part, Australian comedy tends towards the first type although, as noted, the second crazy, disruptive type is also present at a variety of levels and in so many different ways. Here, it is important to note the necessity of both types and to avoid elevating one above the other. All comedy involves the disruption of the social and the everyday. Laughter and humour come about through the transgression of verisimilitude as well as the verisimilitude of transgression.

In the ocker cycle and elsewhere, Australian film comedy, like comedy in general, constantly deals with a humorous troubling of the familiar. A beer-drinking Aussie innocent is loose among the British, a young man is lustily pursued by women, an unemployed tram mechanic turns to robbery,

71

an Australian bushman finds himself in New York, a family man fights to save his home next to an airport and under a flypath, a pizza shop owner and delivery boys encounter a crazy succession of homicidal police, ethnic gangs, aliens and so on. In comedy, order is turned upside down as craziness and misrule become the order of the day. Although some have argued that this kind of transgression (albeit in relation to television comedy) is politically progressive and subversive (Turner 1989: 25–38; McKee 2001: 17–32), the fact is that this kind of action and effect is a regular part of comedy and complemented by a familiarization of transgression as the comic film orients its viewers to the particular conditions that operate in any of its specific worlds (Neale and Krutnik 1990: 83–94). In fact, it is likely that, as is the case with most genres, comedy's thematic effects oscillate from film to film, cycle to cycle, and audience to audience. Put another way, Australian film comedy's impact must finally be traced in terms of its specificity rather than in any gross abstraction.

6

Crime

Poe's Triangle

This is the first of three chapters having to do with the general matter of law and order. In turn, Chapter 7 deals with the detective film and Chapter 12 examines the suspense thriller. Hence, although this book is arranged alphabetically, these chapters should be read with reference to each other because of the general interrelations between these parts of the meta genre of crime. The impulse for this breakdown comes from a model first proposed by Edgar Allan Poe, the early nineteenth-century American writer of horror and detective stories. Poe pointed out the connection between three figures that are integral to stories of crime and mystery (Cawelti 1976: 80–8). These are the Criminal, the Detective and the Victim, with the three standing in a triangular relationship with each other.

Commenting on Poe's Triangle, Derry notes that each figure can vary in terms of having more dynamic or more passive roles in different stories so that different kinds of fiction relating to each type become possible (1988: 55–68). Moreover, focussing on the relationship between any two of these figures may also have the effect of diminishing the importance of the third.

The matter of this chapter is that of crime and the criminal. It is necessary to insist on this double subject because the criminal frequently manifests herself or himself in carrying out a crime. Law-breaking is what the criminal is all about. This double focus is important because of a common tendency to equate crime with the gangster film. Even Derry, whose work on the suspense thriller is exemplary, rather misses the point in reducing the crime film to that of the gangster film and, in turn, understanding the gangster film following Cawelti (1976) and Kaminsky (1974) as inherently American (Derry 1988: 55–61). Deriving their cultural argument from Warshow (1962), these authors see the gangster film as one that follows a rise-and-fall narrative action and thus equates the genre with tragedy. Moreover, the possible national terms of potential reference are restricted by seeing the Hollywood gangster film as an ideological critique of the American dream.

Such a thematic reading of the genre is not especially helpful when it comes to considering crime films made elsewhere.

One of the most useful interventions in the discussion of this type is that provided by Neale (2000: 76–9). Its significance has to do with his extending understanding of this genre well beyond that of the Prohibition gangster film. Hence, instead of accepting claims that such films as *Little Caesar* (1930), *The Public Enemy* (1931) and *Scarface* (1932) initiated the 'classic' gangster film, Neale points to surveys of the numerous films of different types concerning crime and criminals produced in the 1910s and 1920s as a means of underlining the point that the crime film had many precursors (2000: 76–82). Equally important for the discussion here is the related point that the so-called 'classic' gangster film had many forerunners in the earlier silent period as did several other types of crime film. Among the variants noted by Neale are the underworld/overworld narrative, the rise-and-fall pattern, the gangster-as-cop variation, the Cain-and-Abel prototype, the syndicate film, the caper film and the cop film (2000: 76–9). Put another way, Neale sees the crime or gangster film not in terms of some inner core or essence but in terms of a series of different subtypes that vary, parallel, repeat and even discard different elements to be found in the genre as a whole. Therefore, in what follows, the chapter begins not so much with a definition of the genre but rather with an awareness of its variety and subtypes. At its core, this kind of film is concerned with crime and with criminals and the subcategories derived are empirical ones. Starting with the very activity of crime, at least two particular kinds of criminal behaviour and enterprise on film might be suggested. The first has to do with theft while the second involves killing.

Theft as Business

Apart from murder, one of the principal pieces of criminal activity is that of armed robbery, usually of a bank or some other money-holding operation. Of course, the bank robbery or heist is something of a defining action in different law-and-order stories so that hold-ups take place in several other crime films where they are incidental to the main action, a means of generating particular plot complications. In both *Heaven's Burning* (1996) and *Two Hands* (1996), for example, robberies take place early in each film which, in part, helps pave the way for another kind of climax involving death. Armed robberies also occur with ex-prisoners in both *The Hard Word* (2002) and *Gettin' Square* (2003). But in each case the crimes are integrated into comedies so that the tone of each film is more akin to that of the caper film. Instead of looking to these more recent examples of the heist film, the benchmark for the classic Australian robbery film, *The Money Movers*, which appeared in 1979, will be considered.

In such a film, the recruitment of personnel, planning and execution of the robbery is a chain of actions that occupy much of the plot. The emphasis falls on this kind of activity as a mode of work, clearly criminal in intention but entailing a good deal of care, patience, specific skills, organization, timing, rehearsal, practice and execution. This is obviously labour even if it is criminal labour. Derry even suggests that this sort of crime film is a kind of mirror opposite to the police film involving the routines of investigation, the business of police work. In effect, the robbery film might be described as the criminal procedural, both of them being variations on the process-thriller (1988: 67–8). In the archetypal pattern of such Hollywood predecessors as *The Asphalt Jungle* (1950), *The Killing* (1956), *Thunderbolt and Lightfoot* (1974) and *Reservoir Dogs* (1992), *The Money Movers* concerns a deadly serious robbery that yet goes astray.

Hence, early scenes in the film place a strong emphasis on the routines in operation at Darcys Security Services, particularly the system of safeguards involving the orderly arrival of the trucks and the automated high-security gates and other electronic checks that make the headquarters almost impregnable to an attempted robbery from outside. All the same, trucks making their rounds are vulnerable to attack and theft – witness the violent robbery that occurs early in the film. Jack Henderson (Charles Tingwell), an underworld crime boss, derives the profits from this heist and through a bent detective, Sammy Rose (Alan Cassell), gets wind that an inside robbery at Darcys is also being hatched. The trail leads to a senior supervisor, Eric Jackson (Terence Donovan), who with his brother Brian (Bryan Brown) and a crooked union leader at the company, Gallagher (Ray Marshall), are already well advanced with their plans. By dint of some bloody toe-cutting of Jackson, Henderson buys in as a partner. Meanwhile, various other narrative elements are in play including an anonymous tip that an inside job is underway, a young new guard who seems suspicious but turns out to be an undercover insurance investigator, and an older, honest ex-policeman, Dick Martin (Ed Devereaux), who takes the rookie under his wing and is increasingly suspicious of the supervisor. In a fast-moving climax, the thieves swing into action but things go wrong. Martin's truck is the last in and he is shot. However, he manages to wound Jackson who is then savagely shot to pieces by Griffiths, a plain clothes security figure at the company.

As a crime procedural, *The Money Movers* is rich in the detail of how things work at Darcys. The opening segment in particular offers an extended sense of how the operation proceeds and this forms a highly relevant prelude to the mechanics of the actual robbery late in the film. In addition, the thieves themselves are there in part because of special knowledge or abilities – Jackson to operate the control room, Gallagher to call a stop-work meeting at a crucial time in the operation and Brian for his muscle in physically moving the money. Emphasis also falls on other activities and detail, including gaining false number plates, building elements of a truck and coming up with a scale model of Darcys as part of the planning. Equally, though, small things go wrong – in particular, a cage falls, causing wads of money to scatter across the floor and making the whole operation unravel. The bloody, bullet-ridden body of Jackson at the end of the film is a reminder not only of the credo that crime does not pay but also that fate strikes down those who overreach. At the same time, the fact that the underworld boss and the crooked cop are still in business also allows *The Money Movers* to suggest a more cynical view of a deeply corrupt world.

Robbery as Fun

Theft and swindle may occur for other, more personal and less mercenary reasons. Here, an element of adventure is at work, frequently wedded to a Robin Hood impulse of robbing the rich to give to the poor. The motivation is to seek to turn the tables on others, to outwit and outdo those in authority and in control, to administer a kind of rough justice. Such films very frequently have a lightness of tone and often verge on comedy. Additionally, the robbery or fraud may also turn out to have unexpected and surprising results, not so much to enforce the lesson that crime does not pay but rather as an absurd or comic climax to events that nobody fully comprehends or controls.

To mark out such a type from its sibling in the robbery or heist film, the former is sometimes labelled as the caper film. McFarlane (2004: 48–52) quotes several US and British forerunners of this class including *The Lavender Hill Mob* (1951), *Topkapi* (1964), *Ocean's Eleven* (1960, 2001), and *Ocean's Twelve* (2004). The first Australian venture into this particular genre, *Touch and Go* (1980), appeared within a year of the definitive robbery film *The Money Movers*. Produced in the wake of the very successful US television caper series, *Charlie's Angels* (1976), the film substituted a female trio of Eva (Wendy Hughes), Fiona (Chantal Contouri) and Millicent (Carmen Duncan) for the male ensemble of the robbery film. The film is not easily available but has been described as follows: '(A) comedy . . . thriller concerns three attractive young society sophisticates working for charity, who turn to robbery at a luxurious island resort on the Great Barrier Reef to keep a special primary school for underprivileged children in operation' (Harris 1995: 67).

While only one full example of the robbery film exists in the post-Revival period, various Australian film makers have produced caper films. One recent example of such a film, albeit in a darker, less comic vein, is *The Bank* (2001) which is discussed in the chapter on the suspense thriller. Meanwhile, McFarlane has drawn attention to a recent cycle of Australian films in this class, that consist of *Two Hands* (1999), *Dirty Deeds* (2002), *Bad Eggs* (2003) and *Gettin' Square*. Robberies certainly occur in the first, third and last of these although the first three are better considered in terms of different prototypes. *Dirty Deeds* does not involve a robbery but instead a trick or sting that Barry Ryan (Bryan Brown) plays on two American emissaries of the Mafia. Instead, there is more point in bracketing *Gettin' Square* with another film released around the same time, *The Hard Word* (2002), as recent examples of the caper film.

The Hard Word is a light thriller with many comic moments, which concerns a trio – Dale (Guy Pearce) and his brothers Shane (Joel Edgerton) and Mal (Robert Taylor) – who are highly experienced in the art of robbery. Not content with small-scale theft while they are on day release, their crooked lawyer Frank (Sam Neill) sets them up as part of a team to pull a large bookie robbery in Melbourne on Cup Day. The brothers, who forswear guns and violence, manage to escape even though the robbery comes undone and the money disappears. However, Frank sets up yet another job although he finally gets his deadly deserts from Carol (Rachel Griffiths), Dale's wife, who has also been his mistress. *The Hard Word* ends with the gang complete with women companions embarking on yet another robbery. Brief as this synopsis is, it is sufficient to indicate the comically cyclical nature of the robberies in the film. The brothers are experts at theft although they do not get to keep the proceeds of their crimes. As part of the caper element, another robbery is always necessary and becomes a defining element in the brothers' existence. In addition, in keeping with the requirements of this mode, the trio are good 'bad men' who are never armed or violent. Instead that is left to criminal thugs and corrupt figures of law and justice. Additionally, the film allows space for Shane and Mal to form new romantic relationships between robberies. And indeed, *The Hard Word* is at pains to emphasize the criminal integrity of the brothers as against the corruption and violence of others.

Robbery also figures in *Gettin' Square* but as part of a much larger caper. The credit sequence shows the beginnings of this robbery with four gunmen in overalls and masks comically attempting (in the manner of *Reservoir Dogs*) to keep their identities from each other as they speed to the crime. An extended flashback then presents the many interests and figures who will be caught up in the caper. There are good cops, bad cops, a drug lord, gambler and money launderer, a former criminal now going straight (apart from ill-gotten gains hidden everywhere including his backyard), a randy accountant turned in by his wife, several ex-prisoners attempting to go straight, as well as henchmen, other petty crooks, a corrupt councillor and a sympathetic policewoman probation officer. Barry Worth (Sam Worthington) is one of the ex-prisoners, who not only turns around the restaurant business of Darren Barrington (Timothy Spall), the former criminal, but in a comic variation of the robbery that comes undone, this heist goes magically right. Barry surprises the audience by masterminding an operation that delivers the crooked cop and drug lord to justice while paying out personal scores in the process, restores the money seized in the backyard and at the accountant's, gets the other ex-prisoner to a successful drug program out of the country, and sees the restaurant doing a roaring trade.

Loners

Robbery and fraud are only one kind of criminal calling or business. Even more prolific in film, including Australian cinema, are crimes against the person, most especially in the form of wounding or killing. One character type offering this kind of service in the criminal world is the hit man, the professional assassin, the lone killer. Two individual types can be noted. The first is the professional killer. Like the investigator in the detective film, the professional killer has a fixity of purpose, a professional commitment that makes other figures in the world of crime seem venal and lazy. Among many Hollywood examples that might be cited are *This Gun for Hire* (1942), *The Killers* (1964), *Le Samurai* (1973) and *Collateral* (2004). Meanwhile, in Australian films, both after and before the Revival, there is no comparable subgenre. Even in *Squizzy Taylor* (1982), the anti-hero of the title is intent on becoming a criminal boss rather than remaining a hired gun. While in classic gangster fashion, Squizzy (David Atkins) kills on his way to the top, he is without the professional dedication and specialization of the lone-wolf hit man.

One of only two Australian examples of the type is *Sensitive New-Age Killer* (SNAK) (2001). A film with a light touch and plenty of comic moments as well as plenty of gunfire and bodies, it clearly is indebted to Quentin Tarantino and his impact on the hit-man subgenre. The plot concerns Paul

Morris (Paul Moder), a small-time gunman, who aspires to become a top killer like his idol, Colin 'The Snake' Adder (Frank Bren). Although a good family man to wife Helen (Helen Hopkins) and their child, Paul is being doublecrossed by his best friend George Hartley (Kevin Hopkins) as well as being forced into a sexual relationship with a policewoman. Finally, though, he meets the Snake, who he is forced to kill and then, in a gruesomely hilarious climax, takes out a Chinese underworld boss complete with a large number of henchmen and also accounts for George. In reviews at the time of its release, the film was linked to *Pulp Fiction* (1994) as well as the films of John Woo and David Lynch, suggesting that this first venture into this particular subtype of crime by Australian film makers had to be played for comedy rather than anything approaching any kind of realism.

A more black-humoured version of this type is *The Magician* (2005), filmed mainly in the gritty streets of Melbourne. The main character, Ray Shoesmith (Scott Ryan, who also wrote and directed this, his first film), is a lone hit man in this sardonic 'mockumentary', being filmed by a friend, Max (Massimiliano Andrighetto), as he goes about his deadly daily business. Ray is bemused at Max's interest in him as a filmic subject and amused at Max's innocence about the nature of Ray's 'trade'. The film had a limited theatrical release and was popular at the Melbourne and Sydney film festivals in 2005, so perhaps the lone-wolf hit man subgenre is a fruitful area for future exploration by Australian film makers.

The ageing renegade, the good 'bad man' is a variant on this figure of the lone gunman. Usually, the crime film as a whole tends to equate the world of crime and the world of the criminal, to suggest a taken-for-granted fit between the criminal and the milieu in which he operates. However, *Blood Money* (1980), a fine crime film hailed by Adrian Martin, varies this by taking as its central figure an ageing gangster, Pete Shields (John Flaus), who re-enters the criminal world only to discover that it has changed irrevocably (1995a: 52). Crime is no longer individual, a personal test of intelligence and courage, even honourable in its own way. Instead, it has become corporate, often sloppy and lazy, peopled by scheming businessmen, muscle-bound thugs and petty criminals. The hero himself is tired, ageing, dying of cancer and determined to settle the account books before he goes. The scores to be settled are in both the public and the private domains, which come together in the film's ambiguous title. The anti-hero kidnaps the daughter of the criminal Mr Big – Curtis (Peter Stratford) – and elaborately stage-manages his own death. Meanwhile, the money will help stabilize the future of his brother and the latter's wife and daughter. It may also, possibly, be a settlement for a past relationship and pregnancy.

Fugitives

The hit man must hunt his quarry. Equally, the tables may be turned so that the criminal finds himself fleeing from those who he had sought to capture or kill. Hence, a further variant of the crime film has to do with the criminal on the run. Such a tale of outlawry may or may not concern a lone-wolf outlaw or may be about a couple, usually male and female. Hollywood forerunners of the first type include *High Sierra* (1941), *I Died A Thousand Times* (1955), *One Perfect Day* (2004) and, to a lesser extent, *The Fugitive* (1993), while examples of the criminal couple include *You Only Live Once* (1937), *Bonnie and Clyde* (1967) and *The Getaway* (1972). Some Australian incarnations of this subtype include *Freedom* (1982), *Heaven's Burning* (1996) and *Kiss or Kill* (1997). *Freedom* is discussed in Chapter 11 on social realism and taken up again in Chapter 13 on the teen film, so here the discussion is limited to the second and the third of these films.

Heaven's Burning and *Kiss or Kill* can be identified as suspense thrillers cast in the form of road movies. Both involve car journeys-cum-chases that begin in a big city but soon give way to deserted highways and country roads. In both, the protagonists have a series of encounters with others along the way. Among those that Colin (Russell Crowe) and Midori (Hyouki Kudoh) meet in *Heaven's Burning* are a man in a wheelchair, the blind owner of a second-hand shop and Colin's father on his drought-stricken farm (recalling the retreat-like visit to Bonnie's mother's farm in *Bonnie and Clyde*). Meanwhile, Al (Matt Day) and Nikki (Frances O'Connor) in *Kiss or Kill* encounter motel owners and isolated dwellers in out of the way places. Such meetings bespeak more than a picaresque adventure but are instead part of a suspense-thriller structure. In both cases, the couple are outlaws on the run because of crimes that they have perpetrated or are committing. In *Heaven's Burning*, the crimes are robbery and murder, while in *Kiss or Kill* the couple have committed robbery and killed a victim with a drug overdose. Hence, compounding the chase by law enforcement officials – detectives helped by local uniformed police – is the fact that others have other reasons to hunt the couple. In *Heaven's Burning*, Colin is pursued by an Iraqi gangster whose sons were killed by Colin as they attempted to murder Midori, who happened to be in the bank at the time of the robbery. Meanwhile, Midori herself is also on the run being pursued by her new husband, Yukio (Kenji Isomura), who wants revenge for a perceived violation of his honour. In *Kiss or Kill*, the couple are also wanted by a child molester because a video of his exploits has fallen into their hands after they shake down a drunken businessman who was blackmailing the pedophile.

Hence, an inevitable part of the two films is a rhyming of encounters, firstly that of the pursued with incidental situations and figures and secondly that of the pursuers with many of those same elements. In addition, there is other recurring imagery to do with cars, highways, high-speed chases, road blocks, police stations, computer screens, and helicopters that constitutes part of the vocabulary of the pursuit. There is also an inevitable outcome in terms of the three conflicting forces and the final resolution of events. First, the police are there as secondary figures to witness the end of the chase and to ensure (although it turns out to be unnecessary) that the protagonists go no further. On the other hand, the truly criminal pursuers have been destroyed. Colin and Midori kill the Iraqis in a motel room and also kill Yukio, not least to protect themselves from being killed. Meanwhile, Zipper, the pedophile, is killed in the car driven by Al.

In a variation of the pattern, Al and Nikki survive and are given suspended sentences because of their assistance to the police in cracking a ring of pedophiles. Colin and Midori, on the other hand, have peaceful romantic deaths as foretold to Midori. Shot by Midori's husband, they manage to drive to the ocean's edge thus fulfilling a boyhood dream of Colin's. In short, what the films suggest is that although the protagonists are criminals, they yet have a higher moral and heroic stature than those who have helped to strike them down.

Street Life

The settings and narratives of the outlaws, the mavericks and the hit men are all part of the milieu of the crime film. So, too, are the mean streets of the criminal world populated by thugs and standover criminals, drug pushers and addicts, prostitutes and pimps, bent police, unsavoury club owners, ex-convicts and others. On screen, this world only really springs to life at night, in such locations as King's Cross, Bondi and St Kilda where casinos, gambling joints, pubs, clubs and brothels become synonymous with the criminal world. Many of the souls inhabiting this setting are losers, victims, frequently even ex-convicts, who are not so much committed to going straight but rather to nonchalantly assuming that they can do as they like.

Two recent films offer vivid pictures of this underclass of the criminal world – *The Boys* (1998) and *Chopper* (2000). The former, derived from a stage play, is loosely based on the Anita Cobby murder and the subsequent insight into the situation and lifestyle of the gang of brothers who committed the abduction, rape and killing of the Sydney woman. The film begins with the release from prison of the older domineering brother, Brett Sprague (David Wenham), after serving a sentence for assault with a deadly weapon. He returns to the poor, squalid suburban house where he grew up with his mother and brothers. Back in his home territory, he again asserts his dominance and is intent on paying back those who have offended him in one way or another. Above all, *The Boys* is concerned to show the link between social environment, personality and crime and to suggest that Sprague has derived nothing from his time in jail other than a general anger with the world that is waiting to be unleashed.

Meanwhile, *Chopper* also concerns another thug, Mark 'Chopper' Read (Eric Bana), who has also done time. In fact, the film – like both *The Hard Word* and *Gettin' Square* – begins in jail and serves to remind us that cells, workshops, prison yards, wardens' offices and so on are part of the extended imagery of the crime genre. There is both novel as well as recurring imagery. The film, for instance, begins with the protagonist in Pentridge Jail where he cuts off his ear in order to be moved to a country prison where he is in less danger from other inmates. Chopper, too, visits a parent when he is out of jail – in this case his father who appears to live a meagre existence. These scenes, together with the fact that he cannot read or write, suggest the lowly socioeconomic circumstances of the anti-hero's upbringing. Equally, life on the outside brings him no obvious level of wealth or material comfort. Instead the choice of what to do appears to lie between the dangerous environs of a seedy St Kilda or the comparative safety of some remote place in Tasmania. *Chopper* also strays into the environs of the prison film with its visual invocation of a series of settings including cells, walkways, prison yards and visiting areas, and the registration of a series of character types including guards, fellow prisoners and wardens. This milieu also reinforces the sense of criminals as a part of the underclass of society.

High Life

In the various strands of the crime film discussed to this point, honest police and law enforcement agencies frequently have only a marginal role. These are often highly ineffective in stopping or even curtailing crime. Indeed, one recurring figure in the genre is that of the bent policeman or public official, sometimes involved in petty graft or bullying but more usually working for corrupt masters including politicians and businessmen. In such a world, crime is organized, a business enterprise intended to make money even if the means adopted are against the law. However, if the law has been bribed, then organized crime can go about its business in peace. Therefore, this part of the discussion is concerned with the world of organized crime, the setting for a range of illegal activities and the various pleasures and luxuries that accrue because of these.

Two films in the cycle of period costume narratives made an early contribution to the milieu of the Australian crime film. *Kitty and the Bagman* and *Squizzy Taylor* both appeared in 1982, and focussed on the Australian underworld earlier in the century. The two films portray a world of corruption and crime, a setting wherein the rule of law and order is in abeyance. Instead a kind of ordered disorder is in evidence. *Kitty* is characterized by a light tone which, although it touches on a series of venal actions and situations, determinedly insists that crime is for the most part simply fun, a way of having a nice time (Gardiner 1995b: 130). Thus, although Kitty (Liddy Clark) is an honest seamstress newly arrived in Sydney with her new husband, she is momentarily surprised to discover that he plans to have her work as a prostitute. She drifts into the criminal world and is set up by the Bagman (John Stanton) as a manager of her own brothel. The latter was a thuggish policeman who shortly becomes an organizer of the prostitution trade on behalf of powerful but unseen politicians and businessmen. In between the developing rivalry between Kitty and another brothel manager, Big Lil (Val Lehmann), there is an opportunity for plenty of light often comic action including an attempted train robbery that goes wrong and a vicious gang war. Finally, Kitty and the Bagman, by now her lover, leave for a quieter life together.

On the other hand, *Squizzy Taylor* purports to document the Melbourne underworld in the same period of the 1920s. Probably a minor hoodlum in real life, Taylor (David Atkins) in this biopic is lionized in the rise-and-fall pattern characteristic of the classic gangster film. The anti-hero gets his start by engineering a war between two criminal gangs which creates the power vacuum wherein he rises to influence and wealth among the underworld. Caputo draws attention to elements of story and imagery at work in the film: ' . . . gangland vendettas, guns blazing from speeding vintage cars, gambling dens, brothel houses, dance halls, and so on' (1995: 111). If the film has a weakness, it is surely the fact that the central figure is mostly passive in the face of events, often a pawn in the power struggles of others, such as the two very different detectives. Like many other protagonists embodied in the Australian historical costume dramas of the period (Ryan 1980: 113–37), this czar of crime is reactive in the face of events, a spectator of history rather than one attempting to make it over in his own image. It is necessary to turn the clock almost twenty years forward to find Australian crime bosses on film who realize that aggression and energy are necessary if one is to continue to enjoy the high life. Two films made within a short time of each other, and starring the same actor in what is to all extent and purposes the same role, are particularly relevant.

For while there are no Australian crime films or TV programs such as *The Godfather* trilogy (1972, 1974 and 1990) or *The Sopranos* (1999–) that show the family life of the gangster in all its domestic detail, nevertheless both *Two Hands* (1999) and *Dirty Deeds* (2002) go some distance towards representing the criminal boss as a businessman, albeit a 'Mr Big', and the fact that he lives a kind of normal suburban existence. In the former Pando (Bryan Brown) is represented as a kind of businessman, seen sitting in his office with his gang, passing the time with Scrabble and chess even while others are on the streets and elsewhere conducting money drop-offs on his behalf. When a complication occurs, Pando phones his wife to announce that he will be late home and also to talk to his young son before the latter goes to bed.

Set in Sydney in the late 1960s, *Dirty Deeds* amplifies this sense of the criminal boss as a suburban house-owner, husband and father. Barry Ryan (Bryan Brown) controls the slot machine business in pubs and clubs across the city. Asked by wife Sharon (Toni Collette) one morning as to what he is doing that day, his answer is ' . . . a busy day . . . bibs and bobs'. And indeed it is. After a kitchen breakfast with his son and wife, he and his henchmen visit a club where the owner has broken ranks and installed slot machines of a business rival; so that these must be destroyed and the owner taught a lesson. Coins from the slot machines must be collected each day and taken to an anonymous-looking suburban house that operates as a counting house where a group of middle-aged suburban women are employed to organize and count the money. The law is kept at bay by dint of the fact that Barry has a senior detective, Ray (Sam Neill), on the payroll. Meanwhile, other criminals who want to muscle in on Barry's business all have to be dealt with.

The Rake's Progress – An Endnote on Bryan Brown

The last two films discussed star Bryan Brown and indeed no discussion of the Australian crime genre would be complete without some account of 'the boy from Revesby', and his iconic presence in the genre. Harrison describes him as 'rugged and tough looking' (2005: 520) but the matter can be taken further by considering how various physical attributes of the performer connect with and reinforce specific themes and discourses in his films, especially those relating to crime.

First, the physical toughness of body. In early roles including *Palm Beach* (1979) and *Stir* (1980), his physique was muscular and taut like a coiled spring while in more recent films such as *Dirty Deeds* and *Risk* (2003), it is wiry but still rugged. When the shirt is off revealing the torso, there is never a hint of softness or flabbiness. Several films suggest why this is the case – the largely working-class male activity of boxing is mentioned in *Stir* and shown in *Dirty Deeds*, although in *Far East* (1982) the character keeps fit by the more modish pursuit of jogging. However, even in the latter he wears a blue singlet to help remind the audience of his working-class roots. Indeed, the Chesty Bond singlet reappears in *Dirty Deeds*, not only to reinforce the fact that the time is the 1960s but that criminal Barry Ryan has a working-class background. (On the other hand, to shed the grime of crime and corruption as well as to reveal the Brown torso, Cliff Hardy is without an undergarment in *The Empty Beach* (1985) when he changes his white shirt in his office.)

In terms of personal style and approach, Brown is direct, immediate and proactive. His instant response to any challenge is to meet it promptly and head on. There is nothing coy or studied about the figure. The performer's language is vivid, frequently vulgar and 'blue' but is particularly effective in communicating with others including police, criminals, politicians, high society and women. Few elements of vocabulary or behaviour are off limits. Meeting an old girlfriend Jo, now married, in *Far East*, he immediately offers to take her to bed. Except for early criminal roles in *The Money Movers* and *Palm Beach*, Brown is neither naive nor witless in his reaction to circumstances. Indeed, it is only in *Palm Beach* that he is seen to act without thinking, letting the situation get the better of him in robbing a store and killing a guard. Even in *The Money Movers*, the figure has developed sufficient nous to realize that his older brother is wasting valuable time during the robbery in picking up money that spilled on the floor in the security company. By the time of *Breaker Morant* (1980), this cunning has also extended to lechery, where he can briefly go awol to have afternoon sex with married Boer women. Challenged about this at the court martial, he frames his reply in terms of what sounds like a cynical street aphorism: 'They say that a slice off a cut loaf is never missed'.

In turn, this total lack of romanticism and sentimentality leads to other elements of the Brown *persona*. One part of this is the can-do fixer, con man and resolute user of others, as in *Rebel* (1985) and *Sweet Talker* (1991). In fact, the figure is seen to be at his strongest when he is being pragmatic and taking things as they come, and at his most vulnerable when he allows himself to be caught up in more idealized dreams and projects. In the early television series, *Against the Wind* (1978), Brown is least convincing as political romantic and far more persuasive as a violent rebel. Meanwhile in

85

Far East, recreating the role of Humphrey Bogart in *Casablanca,* Brown survives comfortably as the cynical owner of the Koala Klub who ignores the corruption all around him but is killed when he becomes involved on behalf of an old girlfriend. Hedonism is also a factor. Physical pleasure is always an element in dealing with the opposite sex, and Brown's characters frequently have a mistress as well as a wife. On the other hand, though, family is also important to him – he has a son in *Breaker Morant, Two Hands* and *Dirty Deeds* as well as a young masculinized daughter in the television mini-series *The Shiralee* (1987).

One other cluster of imagery associated with Bryan Brown should also be mentioned. This concerns the recurring connection with crime, physical action, guns and death. For the Brown *persona,* violence and guns can be seen as an obvious and logical extension of physical action. Hence, in *Dirty Deeds* he and his henchmen move into Sammy Lee's poker machine establishment and begin wrecking machines as well as beating up the owner when he learns that the latter has installed machines belonging to a rival; while in *Two Hands* he takes Jimmy to a deserted place to shoot him when the latter loses $10,000 belonging to him. Given all these involvements, Bryan Brown repeatedly meets a grizzly and untimely end in both television and films. Hence, as an Irish rebel he is killed in rebellion in *Against The Wind,* brought down by gunfire in *The Money Movers,* executed by firing squad in *Breaker Morant,* fatally cut down by military guns in *Far East,* shot by a young assassin in *Two Hands* and suicidally drives his sports car over a cliff in *On the Beach* (2000).

These remarks about Brown enable one to see further modulations and developments at work in his most recent crime film, *Risk,* which further extends both the domain of the Australian crime film and the Brown criminal *persona.* Kreisky (Brown) is a dishonest insurance assessor who deliberately recruits and corrupts a seemingly innocent newcomer Ben Madison (Tom Long) into ways of defrauding and cheating both the public and the insurance company for which he works. A latter-day Fagin or Svengali, Kreisky has already initiated a young woman lawyer, Louise (Claudia Karvan), who begins sleeping with the younger as well as the older man. Things come undone when she sets up a scam of her own and this results in Kreisky's death and her own imprisonment. However, the apprentice has learned well from the master and the end of the film finds him stepping into the latter's shoes with the same style and bravura of Kreisky himself. The rake's influence reaches back from the grave. Brown remains the Australian larrikin *par excellence,* a bodgie reminder of how deep crime and criminality may run in the Australian character.

7
The Detective Film

Types of Detective Story

As noted in Chapter 1, typologies of genre frequently omit the detective film. This is certainly the case with several taxonomies discussed there. Murray and Beilby (1980) and Pirie (1981), for example, only distinguish the thriller among genres having anything to do with crime. Grant (1977, 1986) and Gehring (1988) are a little more fulsome, recognizing two related types – crime and gangster films in the first instance, and gangster and *film noir* in the second. This underemphasis is, this book suggests, representative of a particular lack of investment in the elements of the genre both on the part of critical inquiry and also on the part of film makers themselves. For the moment, though, it is worth noting that this chapter follows both Derry (1988) and Neale (2000) in emphasizing the intimate connection between the crime film, the suspense thriller and the detective film. This chapter emulates the example of the previous one in being concerned with a double subject. More specifically, the film type to be looked at here involves both the investigation of a mystery or a crime, and the investigator conducting that operation, frequently but not inevitably a detective.

As Neale has pointed out, the usual point of departure for any discussion of this class is the hard-boiled tradition of detective fiction and the legacy of *film noir* (2000: 71–85). As colourful as the term is, the notion of the hard-boiled detective story is not especially helpful when it comes to deriving a firm sense of narrative pattern at work in this kind of fiction. Todorov has more usefully invoked the notion of the thriller and the suspense thriller in distinguishing this class of investigative story from an older more 'classical' type, frequently labelled as the whodunit (1977: 42–61). Drawing on remarks by author Michel Butor in his novel *Passing Time* (*L'Emploi du Temps*), Todorov invokes the notion of two stories at work in the whodunit. The first mostly takes place before the beginning of the plot in the whodunit and is the story of the crime. The second is the tale of the investigation and its intention is to recreate this first suppressed story. In the course of this investigation, the protagonist is 'never threatened by some danger, attacked, wounded, even killed' (Todorov 1977: 45).

Meanwhile, in a more recent type of detective fiction, these two stories are fused. The crime occurs not in the past but in the present and the narrative coincides with the action (Todorov 1977: 51). The emphasis falls not so much on what happened but what is happening and how will it end. If curiosity is a major motivation in the first kind of detective yarn, thrills and suspense constitute the engine of the second type. Noting structural elements including danger, pursuit and combat which are also found in the adventure story, Todorov emphasizes the significance of milieu and character behaviour as distinguishing features of the detective thriller (1977: 55). This discussion is significant for the concerns of this chapter not least in terms of suggesting a generic range of elements relating to the internal and external functioning of the detective story. However, as Neale has noted, much of the analysis of the detective genre has been developed in relation to literary fiction and not to the detective film as such (2000: 72–6). Hence, it is necessary to also draw upon a much smaller body of discussion that does take the cinematic story telling of detective tales into consideration.

Watching the Detectives

First, then, the classical film of investigation, the whodunit. Cowie, following Derry, has offered this useful designation of the type:

> . . . works which may or may not include a classical detective, but whose narrative is organized around the movement towards a final revelation which rationally attributes criminal culpability to at least one among a group of more or less equally treated characters. (Cowie 1988: 111)

Thompson appears to be the only author who has set out to examine the poetics of this type of film (1988: 49–85). Taking a Sherlock Holmes B film *Terror By Night* (1946), produced by Universal in Hollywood as an example, she is particularly interested in its 'staircase construction' and in the way that digression and delay function. Apparently a whodunit, the film appears to shift narrative gears, beginning as a murder mystery then draining the puzzle elements away to become a suspense film. In its second half, Thompson notes that the three investigations taken on by Holmes, Watson and Lestrade do in fact act to retard the denouement (1988: 50). As she writes:

... *Terror By Night* ... is basically a suspense film, but it disguises its delaying devices by motivating them as part of the investigation of a mystery. We are unlikely to notice that most of the investigatory action comes to little, that it has in fact primarily delayed, rather than promoted, a solution. The film begins with the convention of a murder committed in a sealed area which contains a small number of people, and at first most of them seem possible suspects ... But in between, Holmes, Lestrade, and Watson actually carry on three distinct lines of investigation, two of which will provide the delaying material for the third one which is, of course, Holmes's. (Thompson 1988: 63)

Put another way, Thompson's discussion, although focussing on a single film, nevertheless suggests that some generic distinctions obtained from literary fiction may not be as clearcut in film. Rather than labelling and fixing according to apparently irreconcilable types of detective fiction, it is necessary to be alive to the possibility of narrational shifts that might use some of the conventions of one type for quite other reasons in the service of another kind of film tale.

In this respect, it is relevant to attend to another Neo-Formalist film researcher, David Bordwell, and his remarks about the detective film (1985: 64–71). Concentrating on two Philip Marlowe detective films of the 1940s, *The Big Sleep* (1946) and *Murder My Sweet* (1944), Bordwell draws on the Russian Formalist distinction between story and plot to map elements of the 'two stories' at work in these films. The crime story involves cause of crime, commission of crime, concealment of crime, and discovery of crime; while the story of the investigation contains: the beginning of investigation, phases of investigation, elucidation of crime, identification of criminal, and consequences of identification (1985: 64–7). The genre of the detective film as it is located in these two films promotes curiosity, surprise and suspense. Part of the strategy of achieving these effects is to generally restrict the viewer's knowledge to that of the investigator or detective. In fact, Bordwell suggests that narration in the detective film is omniscient although it 'voluntarily' restricts itself for the most part to that of the detective in order to create its effects (1985: 67–70). What is at work is an alteration between omniscient and restricted narration, a constant zigzagging in a 'staircase construction'.

Returning to the matters of curiosity and surprise, Bordwell pinpoints other elements in the audience's relationship with the detective (1985: 70). Part of the pleasure of this particular film genre lies in the viewer being involved in the same puzzle besetting the investigator. However, on the big screen, this figure's thinking is usually closed until s/he elects to reveal it. Instead, the audience is forced to try to work out clues and their meaning

89

as well as what the investigator makes of these. Here, the voice-over found in some but by no means all detective films may be an aid or a hindrance to such a task. As Bordwell points out, the voice-over is there, in the first instance, to signal a flashback and may be more concerned with chronological recounting on the detective's part than with sharing the figure's ongoing thinking with the audience (1985: 70).

Finally, in this survey of authors relevant to the genre of the detective film, it is necessary to again draw on Derry and his work on the suspense thriller that was touched upon in the previous chapter. Although much of his study is devoted to victims of crime rather than either criminals or detectives, he has, all the same, several relevant things to say about this genre of cinema (1988: 50–8). These can be summarized in terms of two areas. First, the figure of the investigator. Following Cawelti (1976) and Kaminsky (1974), Derry notes that in the hard-boiled detective tale, matters arise concerning the figure's degree of altruism, commitment, honour, self-esteem and so on. Professionalism functions as the figure's ultimate motive. S/he is committed to seeing the job through. As the detective film proceeds, romance becomes another factor, thereby allowing an equivocation as to the commitment to professionalism and to romance (1988: 50–2).

Derry's other contribution to the vocabulary of the detective film lies in some remarks concerning the police procedural. As he points out, the latter involves a member of the law, whether police or plain clothes. Like the whodunit and the private eye thriller, there is a good deal of emphasis laid on particular routines and procedures of police work including the systematic questioning and interview with various suspects, the careful, detailed examination of objects and locations with the intention of discovering clues, the scientific scrutiny of dead bodies for telltale information, the amassing of necessary background data and the contribution of expert or specialised knowledge at laboratories, universities and other places. In other words, these three types – the whodunit, the private detective thriller and the police thriller – have a good deal in common so far as the mechanics of investigation are concerned. Equally, though, the last is characterized by more specific elements including problems with superiors, reliance and assistance from peers, and rule-bending by the protagonist to gain an end (1988: 55–7). And going with this emphasis on the larger workings of a bureaucracy, criminals may even be other members of the police force. In any case, like the private eye thriller, a police detective or uniform officer can commonly be involved in a personal way in the investigation taking place and their behaviour while on the case can very often compromise professional standing.

An Australian Tradition?

Altogether, then, the detective story is a rich genre capable of much variation and elaboration. When one turns to a consideration of its deployment in locally produced film, it is worth recalling some of the popular cultural context in which it finds itself situated. First, there is a home-grown tradition of detective prose fiction. Among earlier Australian detective writers are Arthur Upfield, Jon Cleary and 'Carter Brown' (Peter Yates) while more recent crime novelists include Peter Corris, Marele Day, Kerry Greenwood, Robert Gott, Derek Hansen, Gabrielle Lord, Barry Maitland, Shane Maloney, Tara Moss, Chris Nyst, Jennifer Rowe and Peter Temple. However, despite this presence as well as the continuing popularity of police detective series on Australian television, stretching from *Homicide* (1964–75) to *Murder Call* (1997–2000) and *Young Lions* (2001), detective films have been somewhat harder to come by. Derry has also noticed this development in cinema and has suggested that film makers are presently investing more time and attention in other areas of crime, notably to do with criminals and victims, than they are with investigators. This certainly turns out to be the case if one compares the number of films discussed below to those discussed in the previous chapter on crime and with Chapter 12 dealing with the suspense thriller.

Given that only a handful of detective films have been produced in the period since the Revival, it is no surprise to discover that none appear to conform to the classical whodunit pattern. As Neale notes about the division between cinema and television when it comes to the genre of the detective and investigation: 'While detectives of a relatively traditional kind have appeared with regularity on TV, they have, unlike investigative thrillers, been almost completely absent from the cinema' (2000: 73). The only screen version of this type seems to be the mini series *Grim Pickings* (1990) based on the crime novel by Jennifer Rowe. Briefly, the series concerns a murder mystery among the Allcott family at the family home in the Blue Mountains and the efforts of Verity Birdwood (Liddy Clark), a kind of Australian version of Agatha Christie's Miss Marple, to unmask the criminal. As an old woman herself, Miss Birdwood is never in physical danger and has no emotional or personal stake in the investigation. For her, solving the crime is an opportunity to match wits with the killer, to reveal the identity of the latter even while that figure seeks to remain undetected and anonymous. None of Rowe's other whodunits have been adapted to the big or small screen and indeed Rowe herself soon moved on to devising and writing for the

91

television series *Murder Call* (1997–2000), a broad shift from the first kind of detective tale to the third type of the police thriller.

In a nutshell, then, dealing with detective films produced in Australia over the past three decades, one is inevitably engaging with suspense thrillers of one kind or another. Some of these follow investigations conducted by law enforcement officials, although far more frequently the detective is a private eye. (As might be expected from the previous chapter, official police and plain clothes detectives frequently turn out to be incompetent if not corrupt themselves.) However, instead of using either narrative patterns or the public/private split as a means of ordering the discussion of subtypes, this chapter adopts an empirical division that identifies four Australian divisions of the genre. The remainder of this chapter is given over to four overlapping classes of the detective film – those concerning the male investigator, the woman detective, the comic variant, and the detective/art film.

Blokes

This type comprises a loose grouping of films concerning investigations conducted by males, whether police officers, private investigators, journalists or others. Some representative titles include *Scobie Malone* (1975), *Goodbye Paradise* (1983), *The Empty Beach* (1985), *The Big Hurt* (1986), *Backlash* (1986), *Grievous Bodily Harm* (1988), *Hurricane Smith* (1990) and *Deadly* (1993). Many are not easily available although judging from several unsympathetic discussions in print, this seems not to be any major loss (Pike and Cooper 1980: 293; Brown 1995a: 185; Quinn 1995: 336; Murray 1995b, 1995d). Even Mayer, in a highly sympathetic discussion of *Goodbye Paradise* and *The Empty Beach*, detects structural weaknesses in both – the military coup occurring at the climax of the former, and various liberties taken with the story source, including the reordering of episodes and the avoidance of voice-over in the latter (1993: 112–20).

It is hard to avoid the impression that many responses to this type of the detective film split along predictable gender lines. Hence, to those such as *Scobie Malone*, *Goodbye Paradise* and *The Empty Beach*, there attaches an obvious male romanticism in terms of the repeated references to Chandler, Hammett and the tradition of *film noir* and the blokey presence of such Australian stars as Jack Thompson, Ray Barrett and Bryan Brown. On the other hand, such films have occasioned somewhat less than visceral excitement and engagement on the part of many female viewers. Hence, using *The Big Hurt* as a means of offering comments on this cycle is useful because this film stands in the shadows of these more familiar films – not that it is any kind of masterpiece. Indeed, Suzanne Brown gives it a damning report in the *Cinema Papers* guide to Australian feature films:

> . . . the director opens this traditionally structured mystery film with a long winded attempt at artistic symbolism . . .

> . . . Lisa and the other female characters portrayed . . . are flat, one dimensional characters used to furnish this sub-standard script. The attention is focused on Price's dragging this crime story forward and surrounding him are a variety of unsatisfactory relationships. Uncreative camera work and stilted acting result in some extraordinarily still interchanges which make it difficult for viewers to lose themselves in the story. (Brown 1995a: 185)

Rather than engaging in judgements along these lines, what this chapter is interested in is the way the film works in terms of structure and imagery. As Bordwell notes, the detective film often imparts a good deal of screen information in opening segments and *The Big Hurt* is no exception. The viewer is introduced to the Walden Club, a sleazy sex club, which the protagonist will visit twice, once in the course of his investigation and also at the denouement of the film. Lisa Alexander (Lian Lunson) is an outside presence, observing its activities but without being seen. Hence, although the first segment will introduce the journalist-cum-investigator Price (David Bradshaw), *The Big Hurt* has already set in train a system of omniscient narration that will yet mostly appear to restrict audience knowledge to that which is encountered by Price. All the same, the film is clear as to how its narration functions in terms of audience curiosity, surprise and suspense. Without a voice-over that might have disclosed what the investigator is thinking, the film is careful to establish a pattern where 'field work' or snooping alternates with discussion and hypothesizing. In the first, Price speaks to various people, examines library records, checks out bodies at the morgue, people at the Walden Club and so on but never indicates the train of his thinking. Instead, it is in discussion with Harry the newspaper editor and, especially, with Lisa that he can articulate what he has found in the way of detail and information and can begin hypothesizing about what this might mean or suggest. A series of such scenes punctuates the film and serves as a means of signalling the attainment of particular steps in negotiating its staircase construction.

As suspense thriller, *The Big Hurt* frequently places the protagonist in situations of danger and threat. The most vivid of these is a chase and assault that begins with Price's car being stopped by another and the investigator pursued through tunnels, stairs and a disused factory. The segment is filmed in familiar *film noir* fashion so far as lighting, framing, montage and soundtrack are concerned and serves to remind the audience that the protagonist is as brave, resourceful, energetic and vulnerable as his more famous predecessors in the detective genre. However, that said, it must also be admitted that *The Big Hurt*, like most of the other lone-wolf male investigator films mentioned, now appears to represent something of a cul-de-sac so far as the detective film in Australia is concerned. Therefore, this chapter turns to some other variants that appear to have more contemporary resonance.

The Woman Investigator

As already noted, within the suspense thriller detective film, roles have mostly been allocated along conventional gender lines. The investigator is usually male while women can be suspects, bystanders, helpmates, victims and even criminals. More infrequently, women can also be the investigator. However, this regendering of the detective role raises issues relating to the 'independent' woman that are addressed by Cowie (1988). Examining the film *Coma* (1978), which stars Genevieve Bujold as Dr Susan Wheeler who is drawn to a medical mystery which becomes a murder investigation, the author deals with the issue of whether or not the film is 'progressive' (1988: 104–40). Rather than deciding one way or another whether the female's independence is reiterated by the film, Cowie insists on a process-driven understanding. As an independent woman, Susan runs up against an 'opposition of disbelief', which Cowie sees as a retarding device that operates in relation to this second investigation (1988: 124–36). Put another way, what is interesting in *Coma* is not any element of progressiveness nor its supposed reiteration of such an element, but the way in which the 'independence' of Susan Wheeler is constructed in order to fulfill a certain narrative strategy through which a different kind of suspense and tension (the holding off of the solution through a 'false' conspiracy) can be created in the detective film. With these comments of Cowie in mind, this chapter turns to two recent Australian films concerning female detectives.

The first of these is *Redball* (1999). The name refers to a particular homicide victim, a child that has suffered various sexual and other injuries leading to death. The film can be described as a police procedural and concerns Detective Jane Wilson (Belinda McClory) who, with partner Detective Robbie Walsh (John Brumpton), is working on a case involving multiple murders of this kind. Although the murders had halted for some time, they had resumed following the return of Detective Sergeant Brown (Frank Magee) to Melbourne where he is particularly known to Robbie, who is supporter and emotional anchor to Jane as she pursues the killer. Many in the force are corrupt, most especially those in the Drug Squad, but it is from one of these that Jane gets the tip that Mr Creep, as the killer has become known, may be close to the force. Jane cross-checks Brown with the crimes in Melbourne and in other cities and discovers a perfect match. Confronting Brown, she kills him but then has to deal with Robbie, who she discovers was himself deeply corrupt and Brown's henchman. The two finally face each other and Robbie goads Jane into shooting him dead.

As a film that follows the police investigation of a serial murderer of young girls, *Redball* is certainly a procedural detective film. By dint of standard rounds of police work including crime scene investigation, autopsy attendance, computer checking and the patient sifting of various bodies of evidence including the reviewing of a large amount of video surveillance footage, Jane succeeds in cracking the case when she gets a tip-off about Mr Creep's involvement with the police force. Also contributing to this element of factuality at work in *Redball* is the constant use of titles to introduce particular segments. Like the term 'redball' itself, these titles are invariably colloquial descriptions of the ensuing situation as they might be used by members of the police force itself. Meanwhile, a second narrative pattern overshadowing the investigative structure is the growing disenchantment and disillusionment of Jane with the police force. As she says at the beginning of the film in a scene that precedes the extended flashback, she joined the force because she believed that she could make a difference but has clearly lost that faith and hope. This trajectory is particularly linked to the discovery of Robbie Walsh's corruption. The latter appears different to the oafishness and petty corruption of other detectives. He seems thoughtful, supportive, sensitive and intelligent and treats Jane as a full partner. However, he is eventually discovered to be Brown's 'dog' and Jane's betrayer. So she finally nails the killer but is forced to kill Robbie and is subsequently burdened with the emotional cost involved in that decision.

Redball is structured in such a way that Jane's killing of Robbie has already taken place, so that the narrative can shuttle between the past when Jane was on the case to the present when her ability as a woman detective is in question. Cowie's remarks about *Coma* and the suspense thriller structure are relevant to this film in terms of the fact that Jane seems to be the only law enforcement agent who cares sufficiently to bring the killer to justice. In a force deeply ridden with corruption of one kind or another, Jane's gender falls under bureaucratic suspicion as the source of her difference. In *Coma*, gender is used as a retarding device in the investigation as it is in *Redball*. However, in the latter, this is further overlain with an additional irony that renders the ending more open. For although Jane has solved the chain of crime, this very success has made the woman detective's future in the police force highly problematic.

Gender and sexuality are also at the heart of the second film concerning a woman investigator. In *The Monkey's Mask* (2000) the protagonist is Jill Fitzpatrick (Susie Porter), a Sydney private detective who is also a lesbian. In the classic manner of the detective story, a case begins as the investigation of a disappearance which then becomes the hunt for a murderer. Jill is hired by North Shore parents to find their daughter Mickey Norris (Abbie Cornish). The latter is seen reading her poetry ('Victim poetry' according to her teacher) in a pub at the beginning of the film. Subsequently, her body is discovered and the case becomes one of homicide. Jill's investigation leads her into the world of Sydney poets and especially to Mickey's former teacher Diana Maitland (Kelly McGillis), with whom she has a romantic and physical affair. The liaison delays, retards the investigation as Jill reads Mickey's poetry and talks to various acquaintances in between sexual meetings with Diana. Indeed, the detective finds little in the way of clues and leads. As a very turned-on Diana outside a lesbian strip club says to her: 'You are a great fuck but very probably a very ordinary detective'.

Although Jill is reprimanded by a lesbian friend and even chides herself in voice-over for neglecting the investigation in favour of the affair, in order to comprehend first Mickey's disappearance and then her murder, Jill must come to understand her lover, Diana Maitland, and that woman's relationship with her husband Nick (Marton Csokas). The attempt to discover the truth of the first will bring about the exposure of the second. In *The Monkey's Mask*, the position of Jill as protagonist in possession of knowledge is clearly qualified. As the agent of the plot, she frequently appears to be the place of knowledge, and agent of the discovery of knowledge, although she is consistently displaced from this position by continued sexual encounters with Diana. As a private investigator, Jill is not in a position to bring Nick and Diana to justice. In fact she must put herself in the position of Mickey, the victim of the accidental killing, accepting heterosexual sex, in order to coax a confession from the husband. She is returned to the position of woman as victim in order to obtain this confession from the villain.

This brief discussion of the woman investigator should remind the reader of the physical presence of both Jane Wilson in *Redball* and Jill Fitzpatrick in *The Monkey's Mask*. Like their counterpart in *Coma*, the two women are of average height and small of build. Both, too, also exhibit some of that same androgyny displayed by Susan Wheeler in the earlier Hollywood film, a point that is emphasized in the first in relation to Jane's fellow male detectives and in the second in terms of Jill's short stature compared to that of Diana. As women investigators, Jane and Jill are far from being completely in command of events and situations. They don't really know but nevertheless act to move events forward towards resolution.

To date, however, they have not been joined by any other sisters in crime. Instead, as the last two variants of the Australian detective film suggest, it mostly remains as a male preserve.

Comic Sleuths

The third type of detective film considered here combines comedy with the investigation of crime. As noted in Chapter 5, film comedy is especially disposed to infuse other genres by way of parody and satire and also by the comic reworking of particular genre conventions. Such is the case with two recent Australian films that exemplify what happens when systems of ordering material in the two genres are combined. The first of these is *The Roly Poly Man* (1994), a parody of the male private detective film. Both a send-up and a homage to the *film noir* detective thriller, it features the seediest of private eyes, Dirk Trent (Paul Chubb), following a trail that begins with an apparently erring real estate agent in a motel room and follows a chain of murders to a deadly *femme fatale* (Susan Lyons) who has been masquerading as a medical scientist. As even these few details suggest, *The Roly Poly Man* is replete with intertextual references to other male investigator films, from *Murder My Sweet* (1944), *Trent's Last Case* (1952) and *Kiss Me Deadly* (1955) through to *Body Double* (1984). In the best tradition of the investigator thriller, narrative composition appears to be wedded to that of the protagonist so that the audience's knowledge is comically tied to that of Trent. Again, however, for the film to function as a thriller, even a comic one, the story telling must occasionally pass beyond this restriction, as occurs, for instance, when a hippie is beaten up and killed in a highly surreal segment early in the film.

If *The Roly Poly Man* does work with a staircase construction, it is one marked by many digressions, red herrings and other delaying strategies, as well as some unlikely narrative devices that move the investigation forward from one stage to the next. Here, particularly, the voice-over commentary by Trent helps mask the lack of narrative logic in what is happening. As voice-over, the commentary suggests that what is presented occurs in the past although the audience is soon humorously persuaded to forget this in terms of what seems to be a floridly 'poetic' stream of consciousness:

> I could feel it like a shadow on my heart, the unspeakable nameless truth of what had really happened, lying incubating like a succubus in a cold black dark behind a dead man's eyes . . . Someday, I must have my poetry published.

97

Meanwhile, *Bad Eggs* (2003) is a humorous reworking of the police procedural variant and concerns partner detectives Ben Kinnear (Mick Molloy) and Mike Paddock (Bob Franklin), who are demoted to uniform when they commit several blunders brought to public attention by cop-turned-reporter Julie Bail (Judith Lucy). Emphasizing its humour through such incidents as the runaway car in the opening credit sequence and Ben driving his car with a wheel lock in place, this is amplified by comic dialogue such as Ben and Julie's letter/number shorthand for many activities including sex and, most especially, the comic playing of the protagonists. Nevertheless, *Bad Eggs* also works as a police thriller. For although the pair function as an investigative duo who are the focus of the action, the narration is not restricted to their actions but on a number of occasions becomes more overtly omniscient in showing them being plotted against by the forces of corruption in the elite ZTU (Zero Tolerance Unit) squad. McFarlane has suggested that the film is part of a recent cycle of caper films (2004: 48–52), and certainly the segment in the middle of the film when the two break into the very heavily guarded tenth-floor ZTU computer system is a neat example of how this kind of film can combine comedy suspense with suspense thrills. On the other hand, *Bad Eggs* is also prepared to take its chances as a police thriller as is witnessed, for instance, in the construction of the final rendezvous segment when the corrupt Ben Pratt (Bill Hunter) arrives with a dozen police sharpshooters hidden in the back of his truck.

Art and Investigation

In Chapter 3 concerning the art film, it was noted that several such films have had recourse to the detective story structure in terms of organizing their narrative concerns. There, *Lantana* (2001) was offered as one example of an art film involving an investigation of a suspected murder. Not surprisingly for the genre of the detective film, *Lantana* opens this line of narration through a disappearance rather than a murder as such. What has happened to Dr Valerie Somers? Has she met with foul play and if so, who is responsible? Such is the investigative puzzle driving the second half of the film.

In turn, one can notice several other detective films that also veer in the direction of the art film. Three feature films might be noted. The trio are *The King of the Two Day Wonder* (1979), *Bootleg* (1985) and *With Time to Kill* (1987). Todorov (1977) mentions that the second story in a detective tale concerns a literary fact, the recital of the investigation. In turn, a philosophical reflection on such a process forms the basis for *The King of the Two Day Wonder*. In other words, the film moves away from the subject of crime

The detective art film: Lantana *(2001). Image courtesy of Palace Films.*

towards the matter of artistic puzzle. Made with a grant from the Creative Development Branch, the film has to do with a fiction within the fiction. It begins with Robert (or his name may be Damien) finishing writing a detective novel concerning a character called Blake that he has completed in two days. However, rather than submitting his manuscript to a publisher, he holds back to reexamine its relationship with his own life. As he sits at his typewriter, the audience sees parts of his past life intermingle with characters from the novel to the point where the audience loses all sense of the reality status of various scenes. Discussing this 'puzzle film', Clancy writes:

> The detective story provides opportunities enough for a film-maker to parody, pay homage to, or simply make references to other films, and the number and breadth of these references . . . indicates a love of cinema which is so often a feature of young film-makers' work, and a self-indulgent eclecticism which so frequently flaws it'. (Clancy 1995: 36)

Appearing almost a decade later, *With Time to Kill* (1987) was devised, directed and stars the painter and avant-garde dramatist James Clayton. The film's story (to the extent to which it has such a structure) concerns two policemen who are progressively corrupted by the underworld. Again, though, the emphasis is not on action, suspense and spectacle but rather on experimentation and a self-reflexive playing with elements of the thriller genre. Martin describes it as:

> ...a 'mutant' genre film, deliberately 'making strange' conventional elements and mixing them (with equally deliberate incongruity) with avant-garde elements. As in many a *nouvelle vague* film, brutish gangsters quote Dostoevsky, and violence is both treated playfully (as an obvious screen illusion) and fetishised as a dark, spellbinding, almost abstract spectacle. Clayton takes the modernist celebration of the near-impenetrability of classic thriller plots to a dizzy extreme indeed, many of the plot 'links' joining improvised scenes that appear to have been devised arbitrarily, at the post-production stage of voice-over narration. (Martin 1995d: 236)

Bootleg (1985) is yet another instance of the detective film encountering the art cinema out in some filmic wasteland. Although made on a very low budget that has clearly affected both structure and style, the film ends up as a kind of parody or caricature of the detective film, not so much in the interests of comedy or satire but rather in the service of 'art'. As in the hard-boiled *noir* detective film, both private detective Joe Hart (John Flaus) and audience scramble to comprehend just what is going on. Briefly, a synopsis would mention the presence of the Queensland Special Branch agents as well as a band, musicians, a prostitute and a fanatical demagogue, Dr Brown, whose daughter has disappeared to Brisbane. Joe is sent to hunt her down and discovers plots within plots that lead him to recognize Brown's fanaticism for what it is. The investigator deliberately fails to return the daughter, instead allowing her to escape her father in the company of her young partner.

Outlining the film in this way gives it more coherence and continuity than in fact it actually has. Indeed, in a kind of self-reflexive comment to the audience, Joe at one stage in the muddled proceedings remarks in voice-over: 'How all the pieces hang together, I'm not quite sure'. Clearly the victim of its budget, *Bootleg* jumps wildly from one scene to the next with a compositional pattern that is unintentionally Brechtian in terms of its jagged, incongruous stylistic effects. Here, digression and delay play touch football with the narrative and win hands down. Yet, *Bootleg* is unflinching in its determination to wring art from the popular culture of the detective film. How else to contemplate so many elements let loose under its umbrella including the summative words of the detective: 'Life's a bit like one of those all-night diners . . . pretty seedy and lousy decor . . . but it don't close on you'.

Post Mortem

This chapter has been the second of three having to do with the general matter of crime. Previously, the world of crime and criminals has been examined, whereas this chapter has been concerned with the detective and the investigation of crime. Where the previous chapter furnished an abundance of illustrations and instances, the present one has been more restricted in number. Even so, it has still been possible to argue for the presence of at least four distinct subtypes inside the detective film in Australia, two having to do with gender and the other two relating to other generic relations of the category. In each of these chapters, the term suspense thriller has been used several times, but only the most cursory of designations for this particular film type have been offered. Chapter 12 develops a more extended and systematic account of this particular class of the crime genre.

8
Horror

Introduction: The Fantastic

The fantastic is an overarching category that tenuously joins three genres: fantasy, science fiction and horror. The common thread that links the genres, which makes them all part of the fantastic, is hesitation. The Russian Formalist, Tzvetan Todorov, wrote about the fantastic as establishing 'that hesitation experienced by a person who knows only the laws of nature, confronting an apparently supernatural event' (1975: 25). Hesitation is the crux: 'either total faith or total incredulity would lead us beyond the fantastic: it is hesitation which sustains its life' (1975: 31). The viewer reaches a point where disbelief is almost suspended, but it is the 'almost', the pause, that marks this branch of the narrative film. The name of the Academy of Science Fiction, Fantasy and Horror Films in the United States bears testimony to the common foundation of the genres.

The genre of fantasy is not normally associated with Australian cinema except in some examples of animation, or as a secondary element of the narrative in certain art and period films and in some films that have Aboriginal themes and concerns. For example, *Picnic at Hanging Rock* (1975) is generally regarded as an art and period film, yet the denouement hinges around an unexplained fantastic event – the disappearance of the young women. Thus many films draw on fantasy in sections of the narrative, but it is not the organizing principle around which the film is created. Peter Weir's *The Last Wave* (1977) might be considered a fantasy film, as it draws on elements of fantasy, but is closer to the horror genre and is placed there in this discussion.

To delve more deeply into Australian films reveals a rich lode in the fantastic genres, ranging from horror at one end of the spectrum through to science fiction. The model of a spectrum explains the lack of clear boundaries between the two genres. Rather, a film might be predominantly science fiction with strong links to horror, such as *Thirst* (1979). Produced by the Samuel Z. Arkoff figure in the Australian industry, Anthony I. Ginnane, the

Horror in the period art film: Picnic at Hanging Rock *(1975). Image courtesy of Peter Weir.*

film has links with the popular vampire theme of the 1970s, which suggests a classification as a horror film. Yet the human farm that has been set up to harvest and then package blood in containers resembling milk containers in preparation for wide distribution to other vampirish consumers resembles the factory in *Soylent Green* (1973), where human beings are recycled as protein for other humans to eat, without their knowing the source. Obviously, that was before the appearance of mad-cow disease, with its warnings about eating the flesh of similar species. This global perspective suggests a science fiction classification, a discussion we will continue below. It is clear then, that while some films might be classified as either horror or science fiction, others, such as those thematically oriented to the destruction of the world – *War of the Worlds* (1953 and 2005), for example – cannot be classified as horror. One could turn to the arbiter of these matters, the local video hire shop. But here the problem is similar: the two genres are often conveniently blended into the 'science fiction and horror' category.

To help in the understanding of the two genres, it is useful to examine them juxtaposed with each other. Briefly discussing the science fiction genre at this point means that one is entering the territory of Chapter 10, but

103

this jigsawing is a fine method of examining the differences between the genres. Such differentiation has occupied critics since the 1950s, when 'the genre without a name' – from 1920 – became 'science fiction' (Willis 1985: 1–27). Before that, horror was the genre of the fantastic, leading back into mythology and Romantic literature such as Mary Shelley's *Frankenstein* and the gothic novel. One marker of the horror text – either print or film – declares itself in these texts: the concern with individuals and their quest for knowledge. This is an individual quest that is constructed as in some way opposed to the laws of nature, which themselves have been constructed by an impersonal and external deity (Vieth 2001: 23). The consequences of this interference in the implacable will of the deity are confined to the local, rather than the global. Thus, for example, *Amazing Colossal Man* (1957) concerns itself with scientists playing god and in this instance the 'victim', Colonel Manning, sees himself as being punished for unknown sins: 'What sin can man commit in a single lifetime to bring this on himself'. Yet the film is amenable to the 'science fiction' classification because it infers a global consequence of exposure to a nuclear explosion.

Given that science fiction can be seen as a manifestation of an emerging 'global consciousness', it follows that a film can be identified and classified as science fiction through the global significance of its narrative. The frame for horror is often a small village, such as the Transylvanian castle in the Frankenstein stories, the stone, gated residence in an unnamed village in the German Alraune (*Unnatural* 1952) or a similar gated residence in the West Indies in *I Walked with a Zombie* (1943). Science fiction operates on the global scale even though the frame might be the local. *The Thing*'s intellectual carrot landed near an Arctic military base, the blob (*The Blob* 1958) took over a small mid-western town in the United States, and the saucer men invaded another small US town (*Invasion of the Saucer Men* 1957). Nevertheless, the implications are always global (Vieth 2001: 26). Horror is the genre where chaos plays havoc with the moral order and thus threatens home and hearth, whereas in science fiction, chaos confuses the social order and is thus a threat to civilized society (Sobchack 1987: 30).

Many genre films nudge the envelope of acceptability and conformity – playfully at times – rarely challenging accepted conventions. The action-adventure film in Australia, with its early fascination with bushrangers and cattle rustlers and the derring-do of *The Man from Snowy River* – in a 1920s version and later, in 1982 – simply projected in large format the stuff of one Australian legend, the masculine, heroic bushman from the high country. Similarly, Australian crime films – such as *Two Hands* (1999), *The Bank* (2001), *Dirty Deeds* (2002) and *Gettin' Square* (2003) – focus on situations that emerge from conventional contexts of culture and the unquestioned place of crime within that context. The criminal usually gets his comeuppance, a finale that does not fundamentally question the grounding of Australian civilization. Some social realist films – such as *Jack and Jill: A Postscript* (1970), produced by Phillip Adams and Brian Robinson – do question the values and traditions underpinning Australian culture and the perhaps unintended consequences that adherence to those values and traditions brings. While such films are not a major element in Hollywood genres they constitute, for reasons that are elucidated in another chapter of this book, a significant Australian genre. But the genres of the fantastic do threaten civilized existence and question the boundaries of that existence. That questioning will form the subtext for the discussion of Australian horror and science fiction films.

The Horror Genre

The film maker's craft is to make the unbelievable credible and in one sense a well-made horror film is the best example of this craft. Why? Because horror films uncover elements of the human character that exist at the edge of the world of credibility and reason. For example, psyches that trouble and disturb through their nonconformity with known models, scientists whose minds have no connection with the normal world that we, the audience, exist in and believe is the reality. Yet the audience has some tenuous knowledge and can recognize these aberrant psyches as somewhat closer to them than it might like to readily admit.

Horror films uncover a world that is turbulent, where 'reality' is distorted, where elements of dis-ease are magnified and further rewoven in a narrative that holds up a mirror to parts of the culture and the common psyche to discover aberration mixed with, in recent instances, violence. To clarify the description of the horror genre it is necessary to look at its history and the threads that constitute the genre.

One thread within the horror genre derived from the European – especially German – Expressionist movement after World War I, producing films like *Dr Cyclops* (1940) and *Unnatural: The Fruit of Evil* (1952). This thread is a determining element in classifying horror film, and in differentiating it from science fiction. While science fiction films involve whole communities immediately, either within the plot or outside it, the primary concern of horror films belonging to this thread is the quest for knowledge on the part of an individual, generally a scientist. The quest is in defiance of the laws of nature, which are presented as being god-given, and therefore any examination of them with a view to assuming god-like responsibilities can lead only to the abyss for the person whose curiosity overrides 'common-sense'. The text judges such men – for in these films such curiosity seems a

105

characteristic of the male – as guilty, and even if the scientist comes to see the error of his ways and is reconciled, punishment is always meted out; the laws of nature can never be transgressed without serious consequences, no matter how abject the transgressor.

Another thread in this web of horror appears when any character in the film crosses over into areas which are generally taboo in mainstream society. Just as the scientist crosses the line in search of omniscience, so too did others cross the line for other reasons, or they simply emerged from the murky and less positive elements of our culture: insanity, alienation, sexual deviance, obsession, violence. The imagery, narrative and tension of horror films are drawn from the world of less acceptable stories and darker values that work to embarrass and subvert the traditional values of US and other Western cultures.

The science or art of psychology diverged from philosophy only well into the twentieth century – signified in academia by the establishment of separate departments of psychology at that time – and the darker aspects of culture became, once again, the subject of scientific investigation. 'Once again', because the idea of 'madness' is a constructed one (Foucault 2001). The popularization of psychology, psychiatry and contemporary concerns about the mind is evident in films like *Invaders from Mars* (1953 and 1986) and *Invasion of the Body Snatchers* (1956 and 1978), where one of the scientists is a psychiatrist. This public interest in deviance, in disturbances of the mind, is reflected in the growing numbers of horror films since the 1950s that drilled down into the world of deviance and abnormality.

Australian film makers only rarely delved into the world of the European or US scientist who wanted to explore natural laws with a view to transgression. There is nothing in the history of Australian film making to suggest that, in the pre-1970 period, such topics were of interest to audiences who, for whatever reason, were most often immigrants or immediate descendants of immigrants and who found themselves in a very different and sometimes hostile environment. Yet, since the Revival of the 1970s Australian film makers found deep seams of horror in the Australian psyche and a ready audience for films of this genre. This should not be surprising. Increasingly, Australian audiences are as diverse as those in other Western cultures and respond to the same kind of filmic stimuli in the same way that others do.

Funding the Genre

The other consideration in thinking about the genre of horror films in Australia is the support – or lack of it – given to such films by funding agencies. The emergence and viability of film genres is just as much a product of the Commonwealth and state government funding agencies as it is of the availability of screenplays and directors. As with science fiction films, the general lack of support that these funding agencies gave to horror films engendered a different set of priorities for film makers. Thus the production of films without government backing was often hamstrung in attracting other funding from, for example, private investors; films were made on low or limited budgets and blowouts in a budget were not acceptable; and, finally, the only return came from box-office receipts, meaning that each film had to attract an audience. In this situation film makers and investors backed both their own reading of audience desires and interests, as well as their ability to produce an attractive, coherent narrative. If not that, then something that would have some appeal to enough members of the public to allow the producer to report a net profit. Having said all that, it is important to note that funding for horror films seemed to be more readily available than for science fiction, although not to the extent that one might say that horror was a preferred genre in the eyes of the funding agencies.

The discussion of films and the lack of government support begins with the exceptions to the rule. Jim Sharman directed *Summer of Secrets* (1975) with a budget of $370,000, provided by government and private sources: in this case, the Australian Film Commission (AFC) and the Greater Union distribution sector, Greater Union Organisation Film Distributors. Peter Weir's horror film *The Last Wave* (1977) had a budget of $810,000 financed by the AFC, the South Australian Film Corporation (SAFC) and from an advance sale to United Artists. Solid returns were generated at the Australian box office with a 50% profit on the production budget; an even greater return came from a successful overseas campaign. The support of the funding agencies was not speculative: Weir had shown his credentials in *The Cars That Ate Paris* (1974) (known in the United States as *Cars That Eat People*) and more spectacularly in *Picnic at Hanging Rock* (1975). The confidence that the AFC and SAFC had in Weir was not misplaced from a high-cultural perspective: *The Last Wave* won two AFI awards (cinematography and sound) and was nominated for five others in 1978. It was nominated for two Saturn awards by the Academy of Science Fiction, Fantasy and Horror Films in 1980 for best fantasy film and best director.

The AFC co-produced Ian Coughlan's *Alison's Birthday* (1979), with the 7 television network as the other producer. (Note here the problem associated with attaching years to films. In this case, the film was made in 1979, and was copyrighted in 1979, but not released until 1981. Thus, some sources give the earlier date, others give the later.) In 1979, the New South Wales Film

Corporation (NSWFC) and the Victorian Film Corporation (VFC) were producers, with F. G. Film Productions, of Rod Hardy's *Thirst*, which had a budget of $750,000. On the basis of having made *Tail of a Tiger* (1984), the SAFC partly backed Rolf de Heer's *Incident at Raven's Gate* (1989), which had a budget of $2.5 million, a considerable sum given the funding provided for other films. This funding also makes an interesting comparison with the privately funded *Wolf Creek*, made some sixteen years later for $1.4 million, with far greater success both internationally and in Australia.

At this end of the scale as well, Russell Mulcahy's *Razorback* was funded totally by commercial backers to the tune of $4.3 million and was Mulcahy's attempt to break into the international market, having been emboldened by his success making music videos. However, only about US$150,000 was returned at the box office in the United States. Village Roadshow funded Alex Mills' *Bloodmoon* (1990) but in this case the support meant little as the film was not successful financially.

Few other films of the genre received any government or industry support, yet remarkably – in the light of the thesis that government funding alone was responsible for the renaissance in the Australian film industry in the 1970s – this did not stop many films being made in the next two decades. Terry Bourke made *Night of Fear* (1973), originally as a television film for the Australian Broadcasting Commission (ABC), but when the ABC rejected the proposal, Bourke transformed it into a feature film. Labelled as indecent, it was banned in 1972, which doubtless helped the box office when it was released on appeal. Before this domestic release though, the film had recouped its production costs in the overseas market. More recently, Greg McLean's *Wolf Creek* (2005) was made on a budget of $1 million and apparently actually cost $1.4 million. In the first three weeks after release, it made over £1.5 million in the United Kingdom alone, and was purchased by Miramax for US$8 million. Written by Australian director McLean with an Australian cast, *Wolf Creek* topped the Australian box office in its opening week, an accomplishment achieved by only a few films. Whether *Saw* (2004) and *Saw II* (2005) can claim Australian lineage is arguable, although both films had significant Australian creative input through James Wan and Leigh Wannell, who shared writing, directing and producing roles across both films. Certainly, no finance was forthcoming from state or federal agencies. The total budget for the first film was US$1.2 million and it returned US$18.3 million in its opening weekend, while *Saw II* cost US$4 million and returned US$31.7 million at the first weekend's box office. Suffice to say that recent Australian input into the horror genre has been creatively significant and economically successful.

History of Films and Film Makers

If Antony I. Ginnane was the Samuel Z. Arkoff figure for science fiction films, then David Hannay was the equivalent producer for horror films in Australia, although perhaps he was involved with fewer films. His second production was the biker film, *Stone* (1974), followed by *The Dragon Flies* (1975), the horror film *Alison's Birthday* and, nine years later, *The 13th Floor* and *Stones of Death* (also known as *Kadaicha*). He has been involved in making some twenty-nine films in Australia and the United States, usually as a member of the production team. Miranda Otto made her third film appearance as Rebecca in *The 13th Floor*, and she has gone on to significant roles in Australian films (Patsy in *Doing Time for Patsy Cline* (1997) and Alice in *Dead Letter Office* (1998), for example) as well as in Hollywood and international productions (Eowyn in *The Lord of the Rings: The Two Towers* (2002) and *The Lord of the Rings: The Return of the King* (2003), and the mother Mary Ann in *War of the Worlds* (2005)).

Summer of Secrets was Jim Sharman's third film. His second was the brilliantly successful *Rocky Horror Picture Show* (1975), which cost approximately $1.2 million, and grossed US$140 million in the United States alone. Earlier, he had made his directorial debut with *Shirley Thompson Versus the Aliens* (1972), a comedy which takes the conventions of the horror genre into the realm beyond which they are believable as real and thus becomes comically absurd. The willing suspension of disbelief is no longer so apparent. Yet this film was made on 16mm film, with a budget of $50,000. Ironically given the success of the subsequent *Rocky Horror*, the production company, Kolossal Piktures, was formed for 'the mass production of B-grade movies, serials or anything else away from the treacherous art, underground or worst of all commercial circuits' (Pike and Cooper: 263). His next film – *The Night, the Prowler* (1978) – was both panned and applauded, whereas *Shock Treatment* (1981) did not meet with critical or popular approval, even though or perhaps because it tried to mimic the earlier *Rocky Horror*. That was Sharman's last involvement with feature films.

Following on from *Night of Fear*, Bourke made *Inn of the Damned* (1975) but this film lacked a coherent narrative probably as a result of the open conflict between the producers and the principal backer, the Australian Film Development Corporation (AFDC). Of interest is the rapid change in community standards that the censorship agency seemed to have reflected. The first film was banned as indecent, but contained little that was offensive. Appearing two years later, the second was not banned but contains graphic violence in the form of axe murders, foul language, and lesbianism. Shortly after, John Lamond produced and directed *Nightmares* (known as *Stage Fright*) (1980), a horror film in the slasher mould, complete with violent murders, images of blood and psychosis. *Nightmares* did not attract the ire of the censors.

Russell Mulcahy's *Razorback* (1984) is one of the more successful attempts at the horror genre. Mulcahy learned his craft directing – very successfully – music videos for MTV before turning his attention to film, moving back to Australia and easily translating gothic images from the music video genre into those of the horror film. This film was nominated in five categories at the AFI awards in 1984 and won the award for editing. The Australian Cinematographers Society voted Dean Semler cinematographer of the year, adding to an impressive array of awards that he had won and would continue to win. Building further on his expertise in the genre, Mulcahy moved to Hollywood, where he made both *Highlander* films (1986 and 1991), *Tale of the Mummy* (1998) and *Resurrection* (1999), among others. His story of the Fingleton swimming family, *Swimming Upstream* (2003), was well received both in Australia and the United States returning a 100% profit at the US box office. (See Chapter 4 for more discussion of this film.)

Australian Philippe Mora is a horror genre director whose credits include *The Beast Within* (1982), *Howling II: Your Sister is a Werewolf* (1985) and the Australianized werewolf parody, *Howling III: The Marsupials* (1987). His feature film directorial career began with *Mad Dog Morgan* (1976) and has continued steadily, generally outside Australia. On the other hand, Greg McLean's *Wolf Creek* was only his second film after *ICQ* (2001), while John Jarratt, known previously as the amiable host of the TV series *Better Homes and Gardens*, has had a string of film appearances – generally in a supporting role. His role in *Wolf Creek* comprehensively destroyed any intertextual associations of goodness and clean, suburban living that may have been associated with his screen persona.

According to some definitions, *Wolf Creek* may not be an Australian film, although it meets the criteria of significant Australian creative input. Yet the globalizing of the film industry is apparent: films are products of people, places and financial backing that have no fixed national identity in these days of open borders and significant cross-fertilization of ideas and talent. It is important to balance such statements with a clear understanding that globalization, when applied to matters of the cinema, generally refers to Western countries. The horror genre lends itself to this globalization as the motifs and narratives are not linked to a particular country. Rather, the attraction of revulsion – or some other reaction – invoked by films of the genre is common to many people in Western cultures. Australians have had success in other examples of the genre such as *Saw* (2004) and *Saw II* (2005). Malaysian-born Australian James Wan was writer and director of the former and executive producer of the latter. Australian actor Leigh Wannell – whose television credits include *Blue Heelers* and *Neighbours* – wrote the screenplay and played the character Adam in *Saw* and was the writer and executive producer for *Saw II*. Using the criteria of significant creative input and control, these films can be classified as Australian.

Themes and Other Discussion

One-dimensional analytical frameworks and all-embracing theories, especially those associated with psychoanalysis and psychology, fail in their endeavour to explain and account for horror films (Neale 2000: 98). Rather, multi-dimensional theories involving audience, industry and culture are more valid and are detailed elsewhere (93–9).

Peter Weir's *The Last Wave* is classified as a horror film because, even though the theme of underground civilizations underpins the narrative, the subject is not globally significant. The film maps the geography of the unconscious, a kind of exploratory journey into the psychologically significant 'land of the dead' theorized by Jung (Kawin 1986: 241). At the same time the film is not a typical example of the horror genre since genre films often follow a particular model, with some variations on the theme. Given that this film was made at an exploratory and innovative period in Australia's film history, an attempt at strictly generic classification is not likely to be successful. The film's narrative links external, unusual events such as hailstorms in the desert and black rain to an internal premonition of disaster. Parallel to this narrative thread is the juxtaposition of Aboriginal lore as articulated in the Dreaming with that of Western lore and culture.

As with many horror films the monster(s) is the being that threatens normality. Apparently friendly relatives and strangers who turn out to be monsters capable of the most heinous evil feature in many horror films; a recent incarnation was Mick Taylor in *Wolf Creek*. Ian Coughlan's *Alison's Birthday* is an earlier film made without recourse to violence and graphic terror, instead slowly uncovering the core of horror layered underneath the trappings of civilization in a quiet, charming middle-class family. What is unstated in horror films is the source for the monster; what is suggested is that the monster is quite close to us, even within each of us. Thus the monster that terrorizes the suburban couple in Richard Wolstencroft's *The Intruder* (1994) forces them to look at their own fears.

Brain Films

The exploration of the function of the human brain and its association with life and individual identity has fascinated scientists as well as writers and film makers. As early as 1936, director Robert Stevenson explored the idea of swapping human brains, at least in terms of the memories and other data stored in them, in *The Man Who Changed His Mind*, starring Boris Karloff. These 'brain films' became a separate subgenre in the 1950s, and because they were often associated with aliens and/or other aspects of science, they more appropriately fit into the science fiction genre. The crucial difference is the sense of global significance. If a scientist wanted to explore the nature of human life, then that determines the film as horror, but if that exploration had significant global consequences, then the film moves into the science fiction genre.

Australia's own version of the brain film was Jim Sharman's *Summer of Secrets* (1976), and here the consequence was not globally significant. The plot mirrored that of Joseph Green's *The Brain That Wouldn't Die* (1962), where a man kept his wife's head alive in his laboratory after she died (to all intents and purposes) in a car crash. In *Summer*, the stereotypically hermit-like scientist, the ambiguously named Doctor Beverley Adams, discovers that the kernel of human life lies in the brain and in memory – a thread continued in Ridley Scott's *Blade Runner* (1982). Armed with this knowledge Adams restores his dead wife, Rachel, to life but the subsequent events are not as Adams may have considered.

The Ghostly (Un)Dead

The notion of some kind of existence beyond the corporeal human form that we all know has existed since time immemorial, and was reflected in conceptions of angels and, on the other hand, devils. Yet these were not transformations of the human existence but rather were a separate group of beings. It was the late eighteenth-century advent of modern gothic horror that introduced and reflected different attitudes towards death, the past and the mortality of a human existence (Neale 2000: 93). In Australian horror a manifestation of this is the unsuccessful, Chris Roache-directed *The 13th Floor* (1987). The plot hinges around the murder by electrocution of a young boy by a man some twelve years before the time of the filmic events, observed by the man's daughter. In the filmic present the boy's ghost returns to the adult girl and together they conspire to have revealed the sins of the father.

The notion of the living dead has been an element of the horror film genre since at least 1943, with *I Walked with a Zombie*. The interrogation of humanity implicit in the losing of that humanity is revisited in many films including those assigned to other genres, such as the science fiction masterpiece *Invasion of the Body Snatchers* (1956 and 1978). In other films the zombie(s) returns or is unleashed simply to extract revenge for some crime. In Barrie Pattison's *The Zombie Brigade* (1987) a Japanese developer wants to build a theme park on the site of a cemetery containing graves of and a monument to the local Vietnam War veterans. When the monument is blown up the undead veterans rise out of the graves as zombie vampires, intent on living on the blood of the town's citizens. It transpires that an Aboriginal elder, Uncle Charlie, has the power to raise dead soldiers from previous wars and they take on the vampire zombies to resolve the crisis. Vampires also play a role in Jon Hewitt and Richard Wolstencroft's *Bloodlust* (1992); however, this film owes much to the shlock splatter variation of the genre.

The Supernatural

The arrival of some kind of force that changes the skein of civilization in some way is another thread in the horror tapestry. For films like Rolf de Heer's *Incident at Raven's Gate*, the catalyst for change in the apparently civilized behaviour of a small, outback community is a visitation from some kind of alien consciousness, although this is never revealed but rather hinted at. Conformity is the result of such a visitation in *Invasion of the Body Snatchers* but in *Incident* the result is an exaggeration in aspects of human behaviour while the rules of the natural world twist into the 'unnatural': waterholes dry up, dead birds fall out of the sky, dogs turn into violent creatures. The narrative depends on the disturbance and distortion of the rules and traditions of civilized life to fix its claim to horror and the film does this without the violence and splatter that marks other examples of the genre.

Disturbed Murderers and Ordeal Horror

Marriage infelicities are the backdrop to John Lamond's *Nightmares*, when a small girl, Cathy, after seeing her father and mother in sexual encounters with others, unintentionally kills her mother after a road accident. The resulting trauma and nightmares so affect Cathy that she goes on a murder spree some sixteen years later, generally attacking when the victim is engaged in sexual activity. Mark Savage's *Marauders* (1986) was shot-to-video and is now little known. However, it draws on the narrative where murders are committed by sociopaths who are then in turn destroyed by unhappy friends or relatives of the murdered people.

The horror genre abounds with examples of narratives that are based on fact and where the horror that resonates in the audience is even stronger than that evoked by films that are unreal. Any fiction depends on the ability of the reader or viewer to suspend disbelief but in stories based on fact disbelief is not a factor in the equation. Yet in itself, a factual story is not horror. In the case of *Wolf Creek*, the horror lies in the discovery that a psychotic killer lurks inside the character of a lifesaving stranger. The story was loosely based on a number of stories that resonate in Australian history but the film's claim to authenticity is stretching the bounds of credibility. The apparently amiable bushman, Mick Taylor (a passing reference to the *Crocodile Dundee* character, Mick Dundee), emerges from the outback to provide assistance for young travellers whose car had broken down. As mentioned above, for Australian audiences the horror is more profound as Jarratt (Mick) was known as the affable host of a lifestyle television program. A relaxed holiday transmogrifies into a blood-curdling, extremely violent nightmare that approaches, if not surpasses, the standard set by previous splatter benchmarks like Alexandra Aja's *High Tension* (2003) and Tobe Hooper's *The Texas Chainsaw Massacre* (1974). The vast and implacable Australian outback once again assumes a brooding malevolence, apparent to a lesser extent in films like *Picnic at Hanging Rock* (1975). *Wolf Creek*, the location of a prehistoric meteorite strike, is the site for the manifestation of this malevolence.

Parody or Serious Horror?

Very often, parodies of any genre are seen to comprise a separate genre altogether. In parody, the rules of genre are broken; that is, one or more of the rules of character, of setting or of narrative are violated (Harries 2002: 281). Not only are they violated, but may be completely reversed. Some examples suffice: of the science fiction genre, *Mars Attacks!* (1996) and *Galaxy Quest* (1999), and of the horror genre, *Dracula: Dead and Loving It* (1995) and *Shaun of the Dead* (2004). Sometimes though, the sense of parody is lost on audiences, generally those of a different cultural background.

Like the *Mad Max* trilogy, Russell Mulcahy's *Razorback* is set in the Australian outback, complete with the detritus of civilization – such as rusting car chassis – overlaid with the rock video effects produced by synthesizers and smoke machines and with the sound of pigs as an additional effect. With Dean Semler behind the camera, the outback takes on an almost quasi-mystical character of burnt landscapes and vermilion sunsets. The plot is different from many horror films in that the forces for good are overwhelmed by the character of the big pig, a feral boar of rhinoceros proportions and bulk. For an Australian audience the film is difficult to take seriously, from the opening scenes where the razorback abducts a young boy (a send-up of *Evil Angels* (1988)) to the scenes of the razorback-eating Benny Baker, brother to Dicko (both are psychopaths in the vein of the hill people in *Deliverance* (1972)), among the gore of the abattoir that processes pet food. In summary, '[a]lthough at times gratuitously tacky, *Razorback* is a hilariously funny send-up . . .' drawing on an outrageous visual technique (Murray 1995a: 151).

Yet this sense of parody was lost on film critics in the United States who generally liked the film but saw it as being a contender in the serious horror genre. Parody, like other forms of comedy (and not all parodies are comic), relies on the violation of rules, and if the rules are in some way bound to culture then it is likely that those who do not recognize and resonate with the cultural mores will not read the film as comic. This is not to say that the film has no serious subjects: for example, rape is not about sex, rape is about power; introduced organisms are dangerous to Australian fauna and flora without being violent and huge; people die in the outback through their own ignorance and foolishness. *Razorback* was not as popular nor achieved anything like the success of the *Mad Max* trilogy.

Howling III (1987) was released under this title in the United States, as *Howling III: The Marsupials* in Australia, and as *The Marsupials: The Howling III* in the United Kingdom. Directors Joe Dante (*The Howling* (1981)) and Philippe Mora (*Howling II: Your Sister is a Werewolf* (1985)) had pushed the werewolf theme to its limits, so Mora wrote the Australianized version with human-like marsupials as werewolves. The horror effect lies in the inter-species copulation between humans and the marsupials as well as the disturbing killings. In the United States the film was panned by critics, although those critics did understand that the film was a parody, unlike their response to *Razorback*.

Conclusion

Why do horror films have such an attraction for so many people? Why is it that audiences can be convinced that they want to watch a film where they can become traumatized by the viewing experience? Are the critics right in saying that viewers like to watch aberrations of the human, monsters created who are totally outside the definition of a compassionate human being yet who are so seemingly 'normal'? The genre of horror explores the dark side of the human psyche, domains of the mind that are taboo and are, it seems, attractive in their revulsion. Monsters are created that arise like 'Monsters from the Id', as Dr Morbius opined in *Forbidden Planet* (1956). Yet these monsters are for the most part 'normal' with just a small misalignment of their neuron paths creating terrible consequences.

Many theories have been advanced in the search to explain the genre but none have been totally satisfactory. Psychological theories have been popular but have diminished in their expository power; for example, it is difficult to talk about horror films being a manifestation of repression when we live in a time marked by a lack of personal or cultural repression. Rather, the films might be seen as examples of our fascination with aberration but explaining either such attraction or such aberration might be difficult.

In Australia the genre has been popular with audiences since the Revival of the 1970s and its popularity has ensured that the genre has continued to appear in the oeuvre of Australian film makers. While some films have received some government support, this appears to have been based on the success or perceived potential success of the director rather than the generic nature of the film. The increasing trend to films that draw on human and financial resources and expertise without regard to national boundaries will mean that defining films as 'national' – 'Australian', for example – will become more difficult. Nevertheless, the horror genre will not be negatively affected by this; indeed, the genre might be further enhanced.

9
The Musical

Musicalizing Australia

At first glance, it might appear that local film shows little proclivity towards this genre. Indeed, what seems to have been the only early example of the type, *Showgirl's Luck* (1931), a backstage musical, was not known to have existed when Pike and Cooper published their historical canon of Australian feature films made between 1900 and 1978 (1980). Instead, the film was only discovered and restored in 1989 (Verhoeven 1999: 449). Otherwise, no musicals appear to have been made in the period between the coming of sound and the Revival. By contrast, in the US, there were as many as 200 musical films made each year with the development of the talkies until the mid to late 1930s. When the genre was at its peak so far as output was concerned, Hollywood made more than 1,000 musicals (Neale 2000: 106). Australia produced only one solitary feature of the type.

Such scarcity is not surprising. After all, through these decades, Australia lacked much in the way of a musical theatre legacy. Without a Broadway or a Tin Pan Alley, there was almost no institutional foundation for a film musical tradition. In the early 1930s, the country had undercapitalized music publishing, recording and radio industries. It is no wonder, then, that film producers would, by and large, look in other generic directions for film subjects.

On the other hand, the past twenty-five years shows an improvement in both achievement and prospects in the Australian film musical. Three films – *Star Struck* (1982), *Strictly Ballroom* (1992) and *The Adventures of Priscilla Queen of the Desert* (1993) – have enjoyed a good deal of popular and critical success, while others such as *Cosi* (1996), *Bootmen* (2000) and *Moulin Rouge* (2001) have gained a modicum of recognition and acclaim.

On reflection, there are grounds for this expansion of musical output. Since the 1950s, a vibrant popular musical underpinning has emerged, most especially around rock music. Government funding for arts and theatre has also played its part, as has television, in consolidating an institutional base for an Australian film musical tradition (Bennet and Carter 2002). Hence, since the early 1980s there have been approximately a dozen films produced that all answer to the name of film musicals. Of course, the same period has seen several hundred narrative features made so the musical output remains small. Regardless, given the almost complete dearth before the Revival, the genre is certainly now within the national film imagination.

Defining the Musical

Before examining this cycle in more detail, it is worth recalling just what the label 'film musical' designates. After all with music constituting a major element of the soundtrack of most feature films, it is necessary to ask just what marks off a film musical? The question of definition is important given the presence of song and music in the diegesis of many Australian feature films. Both *Palm Beach* (1979) and *Dust Off The Wings* (1997), for example, contain a series of rock music numbers on their soundtrack but do not qualify. Neither does *Monkey Grip* (1981), which features Chrissy Amphlett and the Divinyls working in a music recording studio; *Bad Boy Bubby* (1993), which includes a segment where Bubby briefly performs with a punk band; or *Lantana* (2001), where several of the leading characters take dance lessons at a studio. More than many of the other genres discussed in these pages, the musical is a mixed, hybrid form. As discussed in Chapter 1, the type is a complex rather than an elemental genre so that it is necessary both to understand the type as containing many particular variants and to seek a definition that allows for this possibility. Therefore, a base-level designation might be that it is a genre that contains music, song and dance to various degrees and in various patterns. As Neale puts it:

> The musical has always been a mongrel genre. In varying measures and com-
> binations, music, song and dance have been its only essential ingredients. In
> consequence its history, both on stage and on screen, has been marked by
> numerous traditions, forms and styles. (Neale 2000: 105)

Given this possibility of diversity, it is only to be expected that various sub-types of the musical exist. To canvass the range of possibilities, Collins under-takes a historical analysis of Hollywood's output, examining such types as Paramount musicals of the 1930s and Fox musicals in the 1940s (1988: 269–84). Obviously, this kind of historical inquiry is not possible in the Australian situation. Altman is altogether more ambitious in drawing up a structural typology of three exclusive types – the fairy tale musical, the show musi-cal and the folk musical (1987: 102–15). This breakdown is certainly more

118

potentially applicable to the Australian oeuvre. In fact, though, Altman's scheme assumes the invariable presence of story in musicals as well as a certain kind of relationship between narrative and number so that it is less useful than it first appears. Meanwhile, Neale suggests that it is more fruitful to define musical subtypes empirically (2000: 108–11). These variants include the review, the opera or operetta, the musical comedy, the musical drama and so on. Such a delineation is rudimentary but it offers the advantage of focussing incidental attention on types often ignored or forgotten. In Australia, where the total is as small as a dozen films, it is only to be expected that several musicals turn out to be the sole example of some of these subgenres. Some of these one-offs or orphans are interesting only in terms of reminding us of the variety of types in the genre as a whole. Others invite attention because of particular critical issues that they raise. This chapter now looks at these matters in turn.

Musicals on the Margin

Neale settles his empirical subtypes by drawing on an article in *Variety* in 1942 (2000: 108–9). The latter arrives at a range of types beginning with the musical revue and the film operetta. These two subgenres are frequently denied recognition yet both feature music, song and performance. What sometimes leads to their exclusion is the fact that they often render musical performance more or less intact, more or less as these might be said to occur 'in the world', on stage or in a performance space. The impulse behind both subtypes is a kind of documentary factualism even if the films are sometimes not immediately recognizable as operating in this mode.

The film revue like its stage counterpart is a miscellany of musical acts or numbers, which are not connected by narrative or diegesis. Instead, what these have in common is the fact of proximity and succession. The feature-length *Good Afternoon* (1971), a film record of rock and folk music at the 1971 Aquarius Festival held in Canberra, represents one of the few examples of this type found in Australian feature cinema. Originally deriving its impulse from the music hall and vaudeville, the musical revue exists only as a succession of numbers but without a framework or 'hook'. In *Good Afternoon*, the type takes the form of a multi-screen record of the many different 'happenings' that occurred during the eight days of the Festival, most especially the performance of various bands. Equally, another documentary musical, *Bran Nu Dae* (1991), concerns another pro-forma event, namely the Aboriginal stage musical *Bran Nu Dae*, itself the story of Jimmy Chu, with music performed by the band Kuckles. The musical is directed by Jimmy Chu, who also wrote the story. Thus, although the film is a documentary about

119

Jimmy and about the musical, it qualifies as a musical because it records a series of musical performances. As films of record, these two musicals are unified only by the facts of time, place, themes and subjects.

Another subgenre founded on the same principle of rendering musical performance is the film operetta, of which *The Pirate Movie* (1981) is a good example as well as being the only one to be produced in Australia to date. The type frequently relies on nineteenth-century stage operetta, uses a kind of fairy tale plot and setting, and depends on quasi 'high art' singing, especially the romantic duet. Its filmic precursor is the 1930 cycle at MGM of musicals starring Jeanette MacDonald and Nelson Eddy. Where the latter looked to European operetta for its inspiration, *The Pirate Movie* is an adaptation of Gilbert and Sullivan's late nineteenth-century popular classic, *The Pirates of Penzance*. In the latter, like both operetta and opera, music, song and dance occur in the course of a comic-romance narrative. By contrast, the film – instead of being confined to the area of the theatrical stage – 'opens up' its narrative so that it occurs in a series of outdoor and indoor settings. Deploying a framing story set in the modern world, *The Pirate Movie* renders its operetta as a dream, set in the past and marked by song and dance as well as romantic, melodramatic and sometimes comic story. In the world of the latter, the space of music and song and the space of the story are one and the same. And although the operetta has been 'opened out' to overcome its theatrical origins, the film's action and performance remain extremely 'stagey'. In this sense, *The Pirate Movie*, like *Good Afternoon* and *Bran Nu Dae*, does much to transmit a musical experience derivable elsewhere rather than originating in the cinema.

The uniqueness of the films based on the Aquarius Festival and the Aboriginal dance performance and, to a lesser extent, that based on the Gilbert and Sullivan operetta, underline the overall reliance on narrative in the film musical as a whole. For the most part, Australian film makers, like their counterparts elsewhere, have seen narrative as a necessary vehicle for supporting and anchoring the musical number. Indeed, a general hallmark of what can be called musical drama, one of the elements it derives from operetta and opera, is the importance of a storyline. The Broadway stage had a simple name for this element, referring to it as 'the book'. As Neale points out, this kind of general structure is mostly necessary in the musical, accommodating as it does 'pathos, dramatic conflict, and even on occasion, an unhappy ending . . . (attending) to situation and character, and the "sharply integrative" organization of its music, its singing and its dancing' (2000: 106).

To underline this point about narrative and music, two other musical hybrids should be mentioned. The first is the biographical musical, which has been and continues to be a staple in Hollywood output. Although produced for the small rather than the big screen, nonetheless *Shout: The Story of Johnny O'Keefe* (1986) is a dramatization of the career of Australia's home-grown 'King' of rock-and-roll from the 1950s to the early 1980s. O'Keefe was an important musical celebrity and the mini series is as fully a musical as it is a biopic. Over the four hours of screen time and twenty-five years in the life of the subject, the audience follows the latter's rise, fall and subsequent recovery and further triumph. Meanwhile, another subgenre that has also made a brief appearance is the comic musical or the musical comedy. Although this variant has been Hollywood's most recurrent type of musical over seventy-five years, nevertheless there has been a relative absence of this form in Australia. Only one instance can be marshalled although it is funnier and more tuneful than its critical reception at the time of its first release might have suggested. The film in question is *The Return of Captain Invincible* (1983). In the early 1980s, *Captain Invincible* was heavily criticized as it seemed to represent the kind of mid-Pacific commercial excesses encouraged by the 10 BA tax scheme (Dermody and Jacka 1987). In fact, the film is a witty satire of the action-adventure genre wherein hero, villain and others break into song as part of its parody of the superhero adventure genre.

The collective point made by the example of these one-off subgenres is the importance of storyline to song in the musical. Whether the type be operetta, biopic or comic parody (or any of the other forms to be considered below), most operate in terms of an integration of narrative and music, story and song, drama and dance. And as Solomon (1976), Collins (1988) and Neale (2000), among others, have pointed out, there is no inherent reason why there must be integration between music and a narrative vehicle. Even so, in the musical in general and in the Australian film musical in particular, a high degree of fit between music and story has generally existed. In the case of *The Pirate Movie* and *The Return of Captain Invincible*, musical numbers are extensions of the narrative action and are expressive registrations of situation, location and character. Song and dance appear to be natural, spontaneous expression and require no particular occasion or space for their delivery. This puts these films at odds with a rather different subgenre that has been more popular with Australian film makers. It is to this type that the chapter now turns.

The New Musical

Telotte coined the phrase, the 'new musical', defining the novelty of the type in terms of a different kind of integration of fiction and music (2002: 48–61). Whereas in many musical cycles and traditions, the ordinary world is seen as the wellspring and occasion of song and dance, here the musical space is noticeably restricted and contained. Films of this kind inhabit a world where, as Telotte puts it:

> ... prime expressive elements – song and dance – are clearly circumscribed. In these films, people no longer suddenly burst into song or go into a dance, for in this era the hills are obviously no longer 'alive with the sound of music'; and, whenever anyone does engage in overtly expressive activities, it is usually within a restricted arena, a limited space the boundaries of which weigh heavily on the moment of song or dance. (Telotte 2002: 55)

He sees this condition operating in a series of recent Hollywood musicals running from *Saturday Night Fever* (1978) to *Footloose* (1985), but his observation can also be applied to a cluster of Australian musicals over the past twenty-five years. What the new musical is concerned to do is to strictly limit and mark off the arena of performance from everyday life. Unlike other traditions, such as the Fred Astaire/Ginger Rogers RKO song and dance films of the 1930s and the Freed MGM musicals of the 1940s and 1950s, which insisted on the 'everywhereness' of music and song, the modern type suggests that while musical numbers have a place in life, they are circumscribed and limited. Tunes, melodies and dance belong, for the most part, in the lounge and on the stage in *Star Struck* (1982), in a Sydney wartime nightclub in *Rebel* (1985), in performance in *Heaven Tonight* (1990), *Cosi, Kick* (1999) and *Garage Days* (2003), in real and improvised cabaret on stage-like spaces in *The Adventures of Priscilla Queen of the Desert* (1993), at the ballroom in *Strictly Ballroom* (1992), and on the music hall stage in *Moulin Rouge* (2001). *Bootmen* varies this somewhat by having the final tap performance occur on a Newcastle steelworks workfloor. The steelworks has just been shut down so that this space is seen as a kind of makeshift, community theatre. Former workers and their families provide an audience for this show. And indeed the presence of public onlookers is an integral part of these occasions, further marking them as performance. Put another way, the musical tradition of cinematic song and dance is continued but only in the constrained circumstances of the show and the number.

If this kind of circumstriction has a precedent, it lies in the Warner 'backstage musicals' of the 1930s. The latter cycle was concerned to show music and song happening only in theatre and on the stage. The films orchestrated a dichotomy between the grim business of life outside for stage dancers, producers and musicians in Depression America and the entertainment and escapism provided by stage performance of music and dance (Bergman 1971; Roth 1981; Collins 1988). In films such as *Footlight Parade*

(1933) and *42nd Street* (1933), music and dance are confined to the stage performance. The backstage musical, like the new musical, insists on the same demarcation between a common, everyday world and the uniqueness of stage performance of song and dance. However, a marked difference between the two traditions is the fact that in the Warner backstage musical a transcendence of stage space in terms of a cinematic space is achieved in the finale of musical numbers, whereas this is mostly never attained in the new musical.

A second important difference with the new musical lies in the fact that central characters in the new musical are generally aspirants rather than professionals. The two exceptions are the singer Kathy, who is also the romantic lead in *Rebel*, and the trio of drag queens in *Priscilla*, who are professional cabaret artists. Otherwise, the final performances in *Star Struck*, *Heaven Tonight*, *Cosi*, *Strictly Ballroom*, *Kick*, *Bootmen* and *Garage Days* are by first-timers, debutantes. Picking up from such overseas musicals as *Saturday Night Fever* and *The Commitments* (1991), these films involve the breakthrough debut. Very often, too, to underline the grimness and reality of life in the world of the new musical, these climactic performances are frequently the single artist's or the group's last number. What they gain is not so much stardom as a brief time in the spotlight, a moment of fame, before mundanity and everyday life reclaim them again. Even in *Priscilla*, one of the queens elects to leave the group so that in their last performance back in Sydney, the threesome has been reduced to a duo.

The link with the Warner backstage musical is important in validating the credentials of these recent films in Australia and elsewhere in terms of being understood as musicals. As Telotte notes, the circumscribing of the conditions of song and dance together with the deployment of narrative conventions drawn from other genres can appear to overwhelm their recognition as musicals. Several of the Australian films ascribe music, song and dance to the teenpic. The result has been a cycle of films that link the vicissitudes of teenagehood, the restless years of first romance, Oedipal trauma, the drama of coming of age, and the abandonment of artistic aspirations, with melody and dance. Such is certainly the case with *Heaven Tonight*, *Strictly Ballroom*, *Kick*, *Bootmen* and *Garage Days* (and, more marginally, with *Star Struck* and *Cosi*).

Except for *Star Struck* and *Moulin Rouge*, which have female protagonists, all these films are concerned with young males who have to come to grips with their own energy and creativity as this leads them in the direction of music. Each is sufficiently idiosyncratic or rebellious to break away from other forms of musical performance orthodoxy, in favour of more instinctive and natural styles. Hence, for example, Matt in *Kick* has an irrepressible urge to dance. Early in the film, he slips away from school to visit a deserted hall at Luna Park and here, bare-footed and stripped to the waist, he unleashes pent-up forces driving him to movement and dance. His urge is not to perform but rather to give expression to, to release natural physical forces welling up inside his body. He decides to audition for a performance of *Romeo and Juliet* not because of any desire for public acclaim or recognition but rather to exorcize the physical demons inside himself that drive him towards dance.

Films in the new (Australian) musical are all, then, concerned with the business of putting on the show, staging the big number. If the latter provides the narrative climax, then the film's events concern the trials and tribulations that mark the pathway to the final successful performance. Although the show is the thing – and like all shows, must go on – these films are at pains to trace the human effort and cost involved in the novelty and intractability of performance, and also to show the apotheosis and vindication of effort achieved there. Hence, for instance, in *Cosi*, the ordeal over which Lewis must triumph in staging the Mozart opera using the inmates of a mental asylum are two-fold. On the one hand, there is the difficulty of working with some of the inmates, who are often highly erratic and unpredictable in their behaviour so that rehearsals and the final public performance are fraught with surprises and complications. But adding to this is a personal situation of suspected unfaithfulness, seduction and adultery, wherein – in an instance of life appearing to imitate art – Lewis' domestic relationship increasingly parallels the situation of *Cosi Fan Tutti*, the Mozart opera he is directing.

Mediating Tradition

In grouping a series of somewhat disparate films under the heading of the new musical, it is also necessary to be aware of individual variations and differences. *Heaven Tonight* focusses not on the young star performer Paul (Guy Pearce) but rather on his father, an ageing rocker who must finally realize that his days of glory will never come around again. More generally, though, the focus here is on variations to the general pattern of the new musical as these appear in one of the more popular musicals in Australia in recent years, *Strictly Ballroom*, emphasizing the degree to which it belongs with the more 'realistic' musicals outlined but also how it connects with other more utopian and transcendent elements of the musical. Hence, one can begin with the matter of genre.

While comic moments occur in several other musicals in the group, including *Star Struck* and *Garage Days*, nonetheless it is only *Strictly Ballroom* that warrants the label, applied to its video cover, of romantic comedy. Romance is certainly there in the figures of Scott (Paul Mercurio) and Fran (Tara Morice) and the outline of their coming together as the heterosexual couple. Their winning of the Pan Pacific Grand Prix for Latin dancing stands as a sign of the appropriateness of their union confirmed in a final kiss. Meanwhile, the film's comedy is principally found in the actions of many of the secondary characters, most especially the villainous Barry Fife (Bill Hunter). In this respect, the film is one of those which operates in that odd zone described by Adrian Martin as 'somewhere between naturalistic cinema and the "tall tale", a style that is a mutation of the "poetic realism" that surges and falls away throughout international cinema history' (Mayer 1999: 178). This matter is revisited below in Chapter 11 concerning social realism.

As a musical then, *Strictly Ballroom* varies the world of the everyday in three ways. First, while music is confined to occasions of dance, whether rehearsal or performance, the diegesis of the film eschews the world of mundane reality in favour of that of dance and the spaces that it owns or can appropriate. Hence, Scott and Fran dance not only in the rehearsal studio and at the Grand Prix ballroom but also on the roof of the building and, most especially, in the garden area of her grandmother and father's house. Secondly, the film affirms itself as a partial example of Altman's category of the folk musical already mentioned above. This type moves away from the backstage by using music and dances indigenous to a particular temporal and geographic setting. Usually, there are few formal performances or shows in such settings. Instead numbers seem to be a spontaneous and anthropologically correct outpouring of a specific culture (Altman 1987: 107). In the film, Fran is Spanish and is the first to draw Scott's attention to the rhythms and pleasures of Spanish dancing. In the small Spanish neighbourhood, her grandmother shows him how to connect his body rhythms with those of the dance while her father Rico teaches him the steps of the paso doble. *Strictly Ballroom*'s credentials as folk musical are reaffirmed in the finale of the Grand Prix when Scott wears the matador jacket given him by Rico.

Adding to this variation on the realist musical is the deliberate exaggeration and artifice – the 'tall tale' effect – at work in the film. Hence, for example, even everyday spaces such as the rooftop of the Kendall dance studio and the small courtyard of the grandmother and Rico's house become transformed into sites of dance, thereby tending to musicalize the world. In addition, there is also a recurring note of reflexivity in the film found, for instance, in the dropping of a stage curtain at the end of the film and the succession of highly surreal flashback cameos of Doug Hastings. Similarly, when the spectators at the dancing competition join Scott and Fran on the ballroom floor just before the curtain, the viewer registers the fact that this community of ballroom competitors and onlookers are celebrating dance and the musical itself and 'only the fluidity of the cinematic medium captures its all pervasive spontaneity' (Collins 1988: 275). What is at work is a Chinese boxes effect which dissolves distinctions and collapses the film into one megatext. Hence, where the presence of Altman's folk musical has been noted within this example of the new musical, here is registered another type that he has called the show musical. In other words, *Strictly Ballroom* works to diffuse realism in favour of entertainment, to show that ballroom dancing is part of show business, to affirm that transcendence and utopia can be glimpsed within its conventions and forms.

Musical Magic

In contrast to the realistic narrative of the new musical, and its transformation in a film such as *Strictly Ballroom*, stands another tradition of the genre wherein various codes of verisimilitude are deliberately ignored. Although it is the only instance produced in Australia up to the present, *Billy's Holiday* (1995) is a good example of this type. The film can be linked with a small handful of Hollywood musicals of the past twenty-five years including *Grease* (1978), *The Wiz* (1978) and *Xanadu* (1980) that stand in opposition to the new musical. *Billy's Holiday* came and went in cinemas and is not well known so it is worth offering a brief outline. One short synopsis goes like this:

> In the eyes of his teenage daughter, he is a 'loser' and his girlfriend can't seem to find the key to his heart. But when his pub jazz band takes off after Billy finds that he can sing like his idol, the legendary Billie Holiday, Fame, fortune and Faust turn Billy's world on its head until what emerges is the true romantic spirit of Billy Appleby – voice and all. (Verhoeven 1999: 232)

Actually, the film is an allegory that is for the most part uninterested in developing a realistic narrative. Instead, Billy begins singing with a different voice, finds stardom but loses lover, band and community only to then be caught up in a reversal wherein he ceases to be a celebrity and regains his loved ones. In its own way, the film conforms to Altman's first type of the 'fairy tale' musical, where the film ends with the restoration of the couple and the restoration of the kingdom (1987: 107). Instead of filling out this narrative chain with realistic events, settings and characters, *Billy's Holiday* has been composed as a parable with the fable operating at two levels. At the first, it concerns a magic, ineffable transfer whereby Billy comes to sing in a soft, feminine negro voice that is a gift from the ghost of Billie Holiday. The latter makes two appearances in *Billy's Holiday* both as the transfer is occurring and towards the end of the film when Billy has recovered his own voice.

The film recalls a Columbia B comedy of the early 1950s featuring the Bowery Boys, *Blues Busters* (1950), wherein one of the gang, Snatch (Huntz Hall), is suddenly discovered to have an attractive crooning voice after a tonsillectomy. However, the voice and stardom are lost when Snatch has another operation. In the Australian film, there is a series of visual signs to the audience that suggests that magic is causing the transformation. Allegory is also at work in terms of the liberties that the film takes with its narrative of Billy's rise and fall. For instead of tracing these reversals in detail in action, event and character, *Billy's Holiday* merely refers to them in a series of jazz numbers that trace this pattern in an abstract, schematic and shorthand kind of way.

Indeed, the film is highly intertextual, referring to several other musicals. It constantly passes beyond the confines of the here and the now very deliberately embraced in the new musical and suggests that song, music and dance have quite a different relationship to the world other than that proposed there. One of its many touchstones is a classic of the genre that is also organized around a narrative of the singing voice.

This is *Singin' in the Rain* (1952), a film to which *Billy's Holiday* returns again and again. Three examples of this kind of citation and adaptation can be mentioned here.

First, there is the referentiality of character, most especially that of Louise, Billy's ex-wife, and Lina Lamont in *Singin' in the Rain*. Like the latter, Louise is a creature of ego and can be ruthless in dealing with others. And just as Lina has a voice that is marked as inappropriate for the new medium of talking pictures, so Louise has an incongruously masculine voice that overwhelms other female voices in the chorus at Billy's concert. Second, there is the direct homage to the famous 'singing in the rain' segment performed by Gene Kelly in the 1952 Hollywood film. Although the homage segment in *Billy's Holiday* is shorter than the original, nevertheless Billy matches the steps of Don Lockwood in an inner-city street, although the film is modest enough to use other music on the soundtrack. All the same, the point is well taken. Music, song and even dance can happen not only in performance venues such as a pub, a recording studio and a concert hall stage but also in the world at large, the ordinary humdrum realm of everyday existence. In *Billy's Holiday*, music is there in the streets of Newtown. Song and dance have by no means retreated to only the performance spaces suggested in the new musical.

Even more importantly is the precedent created by various numbers in *Singin' in the Rain*, including those involving the coming of talkies and the 'beautiful girl' sequence. In these and in the numbers in *Billy's Holiday* when he is singing in the feminine Billie Holiday-type voice, theatrical space gives way completely to cinematic space. Graphically matching shots and soundtrack of song and music bind together segments of surrealistic montage. Colours are aggressively primary and the film also resorts to black and white in Billy's concert scene. Perspectives are frequently impossible, created specifically for the camera, with the positioning of characters and sets subservient to the overall visual pattern within the frame. Although the work of Hollywood dance directors such as Busby Berkeley and George Sidney had already been alluded to in *Star Struck*, the numbers there are as nothing compared to the dazzling panache on display in this film.

Billy's Holiday emphasizes nostalgia, sentimentality, referentiality. These are deployed in a narrative that eschews realism in favour of allegory. Not surprisingly, despite the highly stylized pleasures of its many numbers involving song, music and dance, the film seems not to have gathered much attention whether in the form of box office or critical analysis. For the most part, it is another one-off so far as the principal direction of the Australian musical in the past 25 years is concerned. Telotte notes that musicals that emphasize the 'everywhereness' of music including *Grease*, *The Wiz* and *Xanadu* have been in a minority in Hollywood in the recent present and the same is certainly true of Australia. Nevertheless, *Billy's Holiday* is a highly engaging film, marvellous on both the eye and the ear, recalling as it does some of the most acclaimed films of the genre in Hollywood in the classic studio period. Altogether, it is a worthy last example of the musical genre in Australia.

Encore

As this chapter has suggested, there is some point in discussing the Australian feature musical. The genre is alive and well even if it remains a minor one in the ongoing canon of films produced since the Revival. In particular, the Australian version of the genre has gained considerably from the vigour of the new musical that has been in evidence elsewhere since the mid 1970s. No longer based on stage musicals, the latter overseas has integrated dramatic plot with music, song and dance in a string of films from *Saturday Night Fever* to *The Commitments*. In these films, song and dance still have a part to play in the world even if that role is confined, restricted to the dance floor, the stage, the concert or the cabaret space. No doubt to suit more sombre and difficult times, the genre has lowered its musical ambition. For the most part, melody can no longer burst forth from the ordinary everyday world but is, instead, only to be found in the confines of a performance space. Despite this limitation, the new musical remains vigorous and imaginatively inventive in searching out different occasions and settings of song and dance.

Needless to say, these prototypes have not been lost on Australian film makers. Beginning in the early 1980s, there has been a small but steady stream of tuneful, melodic narrative features running from *Star Struck* to *Moulin Rouge*. Where comedy was a recurring generic element in many musicals in the past, and even had an ill-fated outing in the parody *The Return of Captain Invincible*, the recent crop of Australian musicals has turned towards more realistic types of film genres, most especially the youth film. Clearly, such films are designed to persuade one of the most important segments of the film-going public to buy tickets, rent or buy. At the same time, though, the new musical often does such a good job at disguising its domain that it is easy to miss recognition of the type in the steady output of the Australian cinema as a whole. Hence, musical films which do gain public and critical attention, such as *Star Struck* and *Strictly Ballroom*, are likely to be thought of as one-offs, orphans without cinematic family. This is far from being the case. Accordingly, this chapter has been at pains not only to delineate the important features of this generic subtype but has also examined *Strictly Ballroom* at some length to suggest its generic roots and allegiances.

As with many other formal types of cinema, it is always a mistake to forget that a genre is usually composed of many subtypes rather than being resident in one type alone. This is certainly the case in Australia so this chapter has also investigated several other variants of the genre. In particular, the chapter has called attention to the new or integrated musical as a significant variant although not especially current. However, there has been one interesting exercise in the subgenre of the fairy tale musical in the shape of the jazz-based *Billy's Holiday* and this has been examined at some length. Altogether, the musical is alive and well in Australia and will certainly repay further attention and investigation.

10
Science Fiction

Introduction

In Chapter 8 the point was made that the distinction between horror and science fiction was sometimes tenuous. Revisiting that rationale is a useful exercise. First, both horror and science fiction fall under the umbrella of a division of narrative called the fantastic, which is broadly described – rather than defined – as marked by a sense of hesitation in the viewer. This pause in credulity is the essence of the fantastic, but it is only a pause (Todorov 1975: 31). Hesitation is an initial response; beyond that the suspension of disbelief takes control in the best examples of the genres.

This book has made the claim that horror was more significant than science fiction in the first half of the twentieth century. Yet science fiction was one of the earliest film styles. (Because so few films had been made at that time, it is difficult to speak of film genres, which require tradition as a component of their definition.) In 1902, George Melies produced *Le Voyage dans la Lune* (*A Trip to the Moon*), which was the most significant – in the sense that it is the most remembered – in his oeuvre of over 300 short films. Yet it contains elements that are now strongly associated with the genre: special effects, space travel, non-terrestrial beings and the interaction between them and earthlings, scientists, science and adventurers, and characters who are curious about what may exist outside the normal, everyday world.

The literature of science fiction is rich in attempting to identify the elements and conventions of the genre (for example, Rickman 2004; Sobchack 1987; Todorov 1975; Vieth 2001). Few genres have had such difficulty in being classified and identified but there is a reason for this, as will be seen. Many definitions claim to describe and define the genre; it is important to realize that describing the genre is a far more profitable task than defining it. Author Kingsley Amis suggested that:

Science fiction is that class of prose narrative treating of a situation that could not arise in the world we know, but which is hypothesized on the basis of some innovation in science or technology, or pseudo-science or pseudo-technology, whether human or extra-terrestrial in origin. (Amis 1976: 11)

There is an important qualification to this description, though. Amis suggests that the situations could not exist in the world we know, yet it is the suggestion that they could exist which makes science fiction so powerful. Remember the sense of hesitation mentioned in the previous chapter? It is the hesitation here, the pause that is followed by a conviction that such events could occur, that makes and marks the genre. Science fiction is the popular discourse about science and humanity and many films throw into relief those conflicting sets of beliefs and practices. Science fiction films often debate the meaning of science and humanity, through making suggestions about what current trends may lead to – that is, through extrapolation. Examples abound. In the 1950s, *It Came from Beneath the Sea* (1955) highlighted the changes in the roles of women made possible through science (Vieth 2001: 137–60). At the other end of the time scale *Gattaca* (1998) explores the relationship between being human and genetic engineering.

Both examples above illustrate the difference between science fiction and horror. As was pointed out in Chapter 8 the frame of horror is generally the local. Events happen to and as a result of individuals. However, what makes a film a science fiction film is the global consequences of the events depicted in the film; that is, the frame is enlarged to the planet or the galaxy or the universe (Vieth 2001: 23–8). In part, this global consciousness is a product of science and the communication technologies that are turning the world into a global village – arguably.

Above it was mentioned that the genre is difficult to describe. The reason is quite simple. Science fiction is grounded in science in some respect and science is the paradigm of change. By virtue of its exploratory nature science can never be static because that would not be science. Hence the topics of science fiction constantly change in keeping with discoveries and shifts in science and its branches.

Science fiction films have not featured strongly in the total output of Australian films. Nevertheless, significant films have been made.

Australian Science Fiction Film

Funding the Genre

Australian science fiction is not the most significant genre either in absolute numbers or in the quality of the films. Outstanding examples temper the

131

generalization: *On the Beach* (1959), the *Mad Max* trilogy (1979–85), *Dark City* (1998) and the *Matrix* trilogy (1999–2003). If significant creative input is regarded as a criterion for classifying films as Australian – and the Film Funding Corporation has adopted that criterion – then these films are clearly Australian.

The first *Mad Max* film marked a watershed in the Australian industry. It was one of only two major successes of 1979, a year when twenty-one Australian films were released. The other was *My Brilliant Career*, one of the last of the art and period genre that was the favourite candidate for government funding. To understand the impact of the *Mad Max* films one needs to recall some elements of Australian film history. The production of films was to a large extent dependent on government funding through one or more of the Commonwealth and state funding bodies. These began with the Australian Film Development Corporation (AFDC) to fund script and film development, replaced by the Australian Film Commission (AFC) in 1975; and in 1998 the Film Finance Corporation (FFC) was established to provide equity investment in film production. Over the nine years from 1972, each state also set up a film development organization, beginning in South Australia with the South Australian Film Corporation (SAFC). Without these funding organizations, the film industry in Australia would not have developed to the extent that it has.

The funding agencies acted as the Australian equivalent to Hollywood studios. The agencies determined which scripts would be supported, which directors would be given approval and which genres would be most conducive to the aims of the agency. In this sense, they acted as de facto studios. In the early years of the Revival – that is, from the early 1970s – the funding agencies supported particular genres and did not support others. Thus, the agencies at first supported 'ocker' comedies such as *Alvin Purple* (1972), but these were seen to be exhibiting something less than the sophisticated mores that the arts bureaucrats and politicians wanted Australian films to project. The 'art and period' genre, beginning with *Picnic at Hanging Rock* (1975), was encouraged through government funding for such projects. Other types of narrative were also supported, while some, such as the biker film *Stone* (1974), were originally funded for production but not marketed after the change in attitudes occurred in the agencies.

The film Revival of the 1970s was not restricted to the genres that were, at any one time, favoured by the AFC's funding committee. Other genres also benefited from the general interest in watching and making Australian films (Blackford et al. 1999: 128–9). Science fiction films generally did not receive government assistance but there were exceptions. *City's Edge* (1983) received some funding from the NSW Film Corporation as did *Dead-End*

Drive-In (1986). The SAFC provided some finance to fledgling director Rolf de Heer to develop the horror film *Incident at Raven's Gate*, but by 1994 his developing reputation played a part in his obtaining funding from the FFC for *Epsilon* (1995). Alex Proyas received initial development funding for his self-produced *Spirit of the Air, Gremlins of the Clouds* (1989). One film that stands outside the general 'no funding' rule is notable for many reasons. New Zealand director Vincent Ward received funding from both the AFC and the Film Investment Corporation of New Zealand for *The Navigator: A Medieval Odyssey* (1988). Not only was the film a co-production, but its budget was a considerable \$4.3 million, eclipsed in this genre only by the privately funded *Mad Max 2* (1981) at \$4.5 million. *Navigator* returned \$1.3 million at the US box office. Certainly the faith the funding agencies had in Ward's ability was repaid, if not in box-office receipts, then in prizes and awards. The film received a five-minute standing ovation at Cannes in 1988, won six AFI awards in the same year and it won 11 prizes at the 1989 New Zealand Film and Television Awards. Few other significant science fiction films were supported by funding agencies.

The consequence was that science fiction films in Australia had to pay for themselves. Their only income with which to pay their supporters who had put up the funds in the first place came from box-office receipts. The success of the *Mad Max* trilogy paved the way for other films of the genre, by showing that science fiction films could be profitable, even if they were not supported by funding agencies and even if they were lambasted by critics. A consequence of this funding situation was the emergence of production companies and individuals who made films under the same financial constraints as some in the US. For example, Samuel Z. Arkoff set up American International Pictures to make films to set budgets with shooting schedules of a few days and little time for extra shoots (Vieth 2001: 122–5). The films were aimed at the youth market and AIP's most famous director, Roger Corman, worked on many of these films. In Australia, various companies copied the AIP model and those associated with Anthony I. Ginnane have been some of the most successful.

While the details of funding and its lack is one element of the context within which science fiction films emerged and to which they contributed, another element was the increasing ease with which special effects were created, through ever more powerful computers and the ready accessibility of specialist software. As is already clear, the iconography of science fiction has much to do with special effects and while every film is itself an exemplar of special effects, it is the iconography of space, aliens and other strange creatures, surreal lights, abnormal transportation devices (commonly vehicles that travel in space or devices that transport people and objects without reference to laws governing time and space) and strange weapons that define the genre and make it recognizable for an audience.

History of the Films and Film Makers

Few Australian examples of science fiction appeared before 1959, but this is not significant because science fiction films were produced in the United States in noticeable numbers only from 1950 onwards. After *On the Beach*, science fiction film making lay dormant until 1970 when *Part One: 806* (also known as *806: The Beginning*) was released. Cut from 76 minutes to its final release length of half that, the film lost its feature status in the attempt to splice a coherent text. *Thirst* was released in 1979, the same year that the first of the *Mad Max* films was released. The trilogy – *Mad Max* (1979), *Mad Max II* (1981) (also known as *Mad Max 2: The Road Warrior* in the United States) and *Mad Max III: Beyond Thunderdome* (1985) – changed perceptions about the production of science fiction and related films in Australia (Martin 2003). *Mad Max* was panned by some critics in Australia: one of the major personalities in the revival of the industry in the 1970s, Phillip Adams, lamented its violence and fascism and the possibility that it was 'doomed to make a great deal of money, both here and overseas' (Adams 1979: 38). The high-cultural critiques from the arts bureaucracy and others were not all so dismissive; many found that the commercial success of *Max* reflected a new kind of anti-hero (or heroine, in a new, gender-neutral world) modelled on Max, a 'nomadic warrior alone with himself or herself against the Beckett-like dead landscape in a nuclear, post-capitalist society' (Watson 1984: 69).

In 1985 – the year of *Thunderdome* – came the release of *Starship. Dead-End Drive-In* followed in the next year, whilst in 1987 came *The Time Guardian* (produced by Ginnane) and *Sons of Steel*. Turning his hand to the horror genre for his second film, Rolf de Heer directed *Incident at Raven's Gate*, which he co-wrote and for which Ginnane was executive producer. In 1989, Alex Proyas, the Australian who was later to direct the critically acclaimed *Dark City* and *I, Robot* (2004), directed *Spirits of the Air, Gremlins of the Clouds*, while David Peoples directed Rutger Hauer in *Salute of the Jugger* (exhibited as *Blood of Heroes* in the United States). After his earlier success with *Raven's Gate*, Rolf de Heer wrote and directed *Epsilon*, with financial assistance from the FFC. John Tatoulis directed *Zone 39* (1996), Terry Kyle directed *Terrain* (1997), and in 1998 *Freedom Deep* (Aaron Stevenson) was released.

In the 1990s, the genre continued to flourish and new agglomerations of expertise and finance cautiously heralded a globalized industry. In this new formation, some films were no longer so easily identified as the product of a particular country or of Hollywood, because the resources – finance, cast, crew, production personnel and so on – were not from one country, neither were individuals working only in one country. In addition, in these films the global narratives no longer are identifiable as emanating from a particular nation. Recent films fall into this category. Stuart Gordon's *Fortress* (1993) – partly funded by Village Roadshow – was nominated for several international awards. Shot at the Movieworld Studios in Queensland the film is an example of the Hollywood industry capitalizing on cheaper Australian production costs and such films did feed expertise into the Australian film industry. Yet the film did not live up to expectations, revealing the risks taken by those who provide funding. Costing an estimated $12 million, US returns were just over half of this at $6,739,141. In 1998, Alex Proyas' *Dark City* was released. Like Gordon's *Fortress, Dark City* is a product of a multinational and international film industry, with significant Australian creative input. The film was shot primarily at Fox Studios in Sydney, Proyas is Australian, and Australian actors Bruce Spence, Melissa George, David Wenham and Colin Friels played substantial roles. Village Roadshow was one of three production companies for *The Matrix* (1999), *The Matrix Reloaded* (2003) and *The Matrix Revolutions* (2003). For the first film, Sydney was the location for most scenes – either in Fox Studios, or on the streets of the city. Most shooting for the second and third films also occurred in Sydney with some scenes shot in California, USA. Australian special effects company Animal Logic – located in the Fox Studios, Sydney – played a considerable role in developing the special effects newly used in the trilogy. Australian actors Hugo Weaving (Agent Smith), Robert Taylor (Agent Jones), Bill Young (Lieutenant), Belinda McClory (Switch), Ada Nicodemou (Dujour) and Robyn Nevin (Councillor Dillard) were among the cast.

The Revival of the 1970s opened new opportunities for Australian film makers, as well as those from overseas who came to Australia to work on one or more films. Some were carving significant names for themselves in Hollywood and also in science fiction film making. Roger Christian, after winning an Academy Award for set decoration on *Star Wars* (1977), worked with George Lucas on *Return of the Jedi* (1983). Earlier, he had been nominated for an Academy Award for his art direction in Ridley Scott's *Alien* (1979). In Australia, he directed *Starship* (1985) (also known as *2084* and *Lorca and the Outlaws*), which was nominated for an International Film Award in 1987 at the specialist fantasy festival, Fantasporto. David Peoples, one of the writers for *Blade Runner* (1982), came to Australia to direct *Salute of the Jugger* after writing the screenplay. The film constructed a similar dystopian world to that of *Blade Runner*, but with closer links to *Mad Max III:*

Beyond Thunderdome (1985). Peoples went on to write the screenplay for the anti-western *Unforgiven* (1992) and the Terry Gilliam science fiction film *Twelve Monkeys* (1995), where civilization had once again found sanctuary below ground, as it had in *Jugger*.

Themes and Other Discussion

The genre of science fiction may have emerged from the literature and pulp magazines of the 1930s, marked by stories of technological wizardry and space travel, but the best examples of both print and film productions moved quickly beyond those superficial tales of adventure and posed more serious questions about the nature of life and human community. Thematically, the most interesting science fiction posed questions based on 'What if . . .?' For example, 'What if the world was changed through nuclear war?', 'What if we change one element of our culture?', 'What if other intelligences do exist in the universe?', 'What is the nature of human community?'.

From the late 1970s however, science fiction films have posed questions about the quality of 'humanness': 'What is the difference between machines and humans?', 'Where is the boundary between the two?', 'What is the essence of a human being?'. The science fiction genre, to some extent or other, extrapolates on the present and questions elements of human culture.

The End of the World

A significant narrative in science fiction concerns the end of the world, the apocalypse. It was no accident that such films began appearing in the early 1950s. In the United States, the first film was *Five* (1951), released just a few years after the atom had been split for the purposes of war. The world was astonished by the power of nuclear devices. Significant was the fact that the tools and machinery of science, which once promised progress and a happier life, were now in the absurd situation of being able to destroy all life on the planet. Absurd, because science was supposed to be about discovering how life and the universe worked, not how it could be snuffed out. Suddenly the sphere of influence of ordinary people shifted out beyond the nation to the planet, and global consciousness – as distinct from national consciousness – began to play a part in the discourse of nations, institutions and individuals. Arguably, the era of postmodernism began with this absurdity of science that was, on the one hand, dedicated to working for the benefit, progress and enlightenment of the human race, yet was also providing the theoretical and technological tools for the annihilation of human life on this planet (Milner 1994).

Science fiction films note the internationalizing influence of postwar culture, whether that be through an appreciation and consciousness of the planet Earth as a unified body in the solar system, or through the international catastrophe of a threatening nuclear war. That this apprehension of a global catastrophe affected other countries attests to this consciousness, which manifested in even more sophisticated technologies that could bring information quickly from other parts of the world into living rooms, via television and later communication technologies.

The Australian-US production *On the Beach* (1953) was made in Australia from a novel by Australian writer Nevil Shute and is therefore regarded as an Australian film. It portrayed a world dying from radiation from nuclear fallout, gradually enveloping the planet from the northern hemisphere, killing the inhabitants of Australia as it moved south, until Melbourne became the last significant place on Earth to be silenced by radiation poisoning. The film marks the mainstreaming of the debate about the possible effects of nuclear war, signified by director and producer Stanley Kramer and stars like Ava Gardner, Gregory Peck and Anthony Perkins. Success was indicated by box-office returns and in critical acclaim; the film was nominated for two Academy Awards and four Golden Globes and won a British Academy Film and Television Award (BAFTA) and a Golden Globe.

Quite clearly, science fiction films generally contain a message, a warning about an event, or simply an extrapolation on current trends, examining the possibilities inherent in them. The exposition is not always about the destruction of the world by nuclear weapons, but through other means as well. Such a didactic 'warning' is Rolf de Heer's *Epsilon*. We see the 'civilization' of the planet through the eyes of an alien who appears to a surveyor camping in the outback and explains to him the insanity of the actions that people take, in terms of destroying a beautiful world. De Heer removes specificity and particular identity from the characters, as in *The Tracker* (2002), generalizing the characters through not naming them ('She', 'The Man', 'Grandmother').

Dystopian Worlds

Nuclear destruction and the social apocalypse that might follow was the jumping-off point for the *Mad Max* trilogy, as it was for many films here. The breakdown in the social fabric, a breakdown in the consensus that is a fundamental element of most societies had disappeared; all that remained was a shell of a society where revenge had become the dominant driving force. The outback had transformed into an anarchy of lawlessness, in a parallel with the frontier as the iconic symbol of lawlessness in the American western film (Kitses 1969: 8). *Max* was not the first film that constructed the outback as the domain where law and civilized society break down.

Peter Weir made *The Cars That Ate Paris* in 1974, set in an isolated town in the Australian outback, where teenagers attack travellers in the area, not for their money, but for pieces from their vehicles, which the teenagers use to turn their own cars into battle machines, another icon that features in the second and third of the *Mad Max* trilogy. Even the name *Mad Max* has tenuous links to a character in the biker film *Stone*, Bad Max. Even some cast from that film – such as Hugh Keays-Byrne who was Toecutter in *Max* – were enlisted from *Stone*, as was the idea of outlaw bikers. Other films used the actors, iconography and settings of the *Mad Max* trilogy. *Salute of the Jugger* built on the theme of post-apocalyptic survival in the desert landscape, where wandering contestants played a version of football, but even more brutal.

Although shot in Australia, Stuart Gordon's *Fortress* has little else that would identify it as an Australian film, yet its science fiction credentials are impeccable. The narrative is set in the United States in 2018 and bleakly tells of the prison (The Fortress) to which a couple is sent for flouting the law that prohibits women from having more than one child. Most human activity is banned in the Fortress, even dreaming, and prison officer Poe – an impotent and asexual being – has the ability to lock on to the dreams of others, like a scanning radar.

The Cyborgnetic Dystopia

The cyborg is an oft-recurring motif in the decade of and after the 1980s (Melehy 2004). The cyborg is a cybernetic organism, part-robot and part-human. It is often but not always a transformed human being, a blend of the characteristics of the human and the machine with enhanced powers of one or the other or both, most often violent. Examples abound: the Terminator in the *Terminator* films, the *Robocop*, the brave and self-effacing Bishop and the alien creature in *Aliens* (1986). Similar trends appeared in Australian science fiction at the time.

Nuclear war ended global civilization in Brian Hannant's *The Time Guardian* (1987), but here one city escapes the holocaust by escaping into a different time. The narrative is difficult to unravel, as there are many red herrings. Hero Ballard (Tom Burlinson) is able to travel through time independently of the city. However, the evil Jen-Diki cyborgs want the city for themselves and the action of the film is basically a battle between these two groups. The costumes of the Jen-Diki are devil-like, complete with horns. Their speech is electronically distorted making comprehension difficult, and therefore the audience is prevented from gaining any insight into their character and actions. The characters of the 'normal people' are just as flawed. It's a wonder that the civilization lasted so long, as people shout and yell at each other continuously, except for Annie (Nikki Coghill) who smiles inanely for much of her screen time.

The importance of memory for personal and cultural identity was a significant theme in the dystopia created in and by *Blade Runner*. Proyas' *Dark City* further explores the nexus between memory, reality and identity, yet this film goes beyond that to explore the age-old question of the degree to which reality is a construct of the mind, or whether reality is objective and independent of the person perceiving it. The real question posed by the film is to ask about the essence of a human being; what it is that makes one human. Proyas constructs a compelling, dystopic world with a visual and aural texture that rivals *Blade Runner* and Proyas' earlier film, *The Crow* (1994). Alien visitation and attempted domination is a parallel narrative which differentiates this film from *Blade Runner*. In the *Matrix* trilogy, reality is an illusion, the Hindu-derived Maya which must be seen through in order for one to comprehend the true reality. With links back to William Gibson's novel *Neuromancer*, reality is a cybernetic construct and it is possible that human beings simply exist within that constructed cybernetic space. Humanity, then, is open to question and interpretation; here the aliens are from Earth.

Underground Civilizations

Linking both the idea of a dystopian future with an underground civilization (a worker's city) was *Metropolis* (1927), undoubtedly the first film to examine the possibility of a dystopia predicated on science and technology. In literary science fiction, a recurring theme is that a more advanced civilization exists, or existed, below the Earth's surface. Richard Shaver initiated the theme in a series of stories beginning with 'I remember Lemurius' in 1945. Films that draw on this narrative model include *Forbidden Planet* (1956), *Time Machine* (1960), *The Abyss* (1989); and in Australia, *Salute of the Jugger*, which links the theme of dystopian futures with that of advanced underground civilizations. Perhaps hoping to draw an audience through establishing a link with *Blade Runner*, the production team for *Jugger* cast Rutger Hauer (the Nexus 6 replicant from *Blade Runner*) in a starring role, with Hugh Keays-Byrne in a minor part as Lord Vile – continuing from roles in both *Mad Max* and *Stone*. The desolation of parts of the Australian

139

outback played a starring role in the narrative, as it did in the *Mad Max* trilogy. The outback is the vast expanse of nothingness, the land beyond the sedate culture of a compassionate and nurturing civilization, replaced by the parched mental and emotional landscape of outlaw gangs. In *Jugger*, the underground civilization replicates that of Bartertown in *Mad Max: Beyond Thunderdome* as do the gothic themes, the medieval costuming and the gladiatorial sphere.

The Road and the Punk Gothic

As is already clear, the road, vehicles and those who drive them are a significant element of Australian science fiction cinema, underscoring the narrative and iconography in *The Cars That Ate Paris*, the *Mad Max* trilogy, and *Salute of the Jugger*. These elements appear again in *Dead-End Drive-In* (1986), based on a story by Peter Carey, but with the significant difference that the battles between the road warriors are fought in urban Australia. In common with those films that have already been examined, the dystopic future has been brought about by a cataclysm, not of nuclear warfare but from race wars in South Africa, a second crash on Wall Street and the associated economic anarchy. The result is violent riots resulting in state declarations of emergencies, which allow for almost unlimited police powers. In this scenario, the streets are owned by the 'Karboys', marauding gangs of youths who compete for dominance. Here, the ultimate symbol of fifties and sixties car culture, the drive-in, becomes the prison where young people are held by an anonymous government.

Alex Proyas' *Spirits of the Air, Gremlins of the Clouds* has similarities with the *Mad Max* trilogy, *Jugger* and *The Cars That Ate Paris*. First, the film establishes a world after the apocalypse and second, the plot is precipitated by the location of the outback, immediately setting up resonances of alienation, solitariness and a dearth of emotional experience. Third, the lead character, Norm, wears the armour of post-punk fashion – black coat, black boots and black gloves. Whilst the film is narratively weak, it has an 'extraordinary visual and aural texture' (Murray 1995a: 286), yet it remains a window into the talent of Proyas and was a training ground for further achievements in the genre.

Conclusion

The science fiction genre, as represented in Australian cinema, mirrors many characteristics found in science fiction films from Hollywood or from other national cinemas. The general lack of government support for the genre meant that some films had to be made to tight budgets with specific distribution and exhibition planning in order to return a profit. In this sense, many films resemble the B movies that came out of studios like American International in the 1950s and 1960s, with low production and narrative values. For some directors and other crew, these films were a training ground for their development as competent and talented practitioners, whilst for cast members, roles in such films provided both training and a meal ticket between other films or television appearances. Nevertheless, strong characters and powerful films arose out of that production baseline, as has been suggested. When significant funds were provided, either by government agencies or by public companies like Village Roadshow, the result was generally a film of high production values and coherent narrative, yet few of these were box-office successes.

While science fiction films suffered initially because of the high cost of special effects, resulting in the familiar and cheap explosions and transformations that mark some films, digital manipulation makes it easier for professional special effects to be mastered without the high costs of filming actual events. Paradoxically, the low cost and innovation of Australian special effects companies, in comparison with the somewhat factory-like production tradition of US companies like Industrial Light and Magic, have meant that film making has been less expensive in Australia than it would have been in Hollywood.

In very general terms, science fiction has something to do with science and it is clear that science is not limited by national or ethnic boundaries. Science is, in its unsullied guise, an international endeavour. Thus science fiction narratives are often global narratives, without specific reference to a particular country. When a setting is in a particular country, the narrative extends beyond that. The Australian industry reflects that generalizing, yet its landscapes fit in well with themes of desolation, alienation and lawlessness, and with consequent reconstructing of the hero, or anti-hero. Given the vagaries and variables involved in film production, it is unclear to what extent Australian film production will blossom, if at all. Yet it is clear that the science fiction genre is one that is likely to survive in Australia – if not clearly marked 'Made in Australia', then at least with significant Australian input into global story telling.

11
Social Realism

The Label

Film genres such as romance, comedy and action are easily found on the shelves of video and DVD stores. On the other hand, try finding a section having to do with social realism. This is not to say that plenty of examples of the genre cannot be found, usually mixed up with others in other generic groupings. (One shop owner jokingly suggested that a handy label for the type might be 'misery'.) Yet beyond this kind of popular check, the category of social realism appears to offer no problem in the classification of Australian feature film. After all, many films are contemporary in setting, deal with particular social milieus and groups and attempt to be honest and straightforward in approach. Murray and Beilby's 1980 designation of the field includes this type of film, and a string of examples cited there include *Between Wars* (1974), *Sunday Too Far Away* (1975), *Stone* (1974) and *Dawn!* (1979).

Others might object that this kind of designation appears to be loosely sociological rather than filmic. The claim is that – as exemplified in Murray and Beilby (1980) – social realism is thematic and subject-oriented and not a genre of the cinema. This is the position taken by Malard (1988: 305–30) even though his discussion of the American social problem film is included in Gehring's anthology concerning different Hollywood film genres (1988). On the other hand, one of the few books that has treated social realism as a genre – Roffman and Purdy's book (1981) on social problem films in Hollywood – includes so many different films that it inadvertently weakens its generic case. In fact, the book tends to treat the type as one bound together by theme and subject matter rather than by stronger generic ties. The authors' analysis neglects matters of form, style and imagery in favour of subject matter and thematic approach. The same is true of Neale who does identify the social problem film as a major genre of Hollywood. However, his discussion turns out to be a reading of Roffman and Purdy and of Maltby (1983) rather than a full-blown analysis in its own right. All the same, his outline is useful in pointing out several features of social problem films. Indeed, it is worth noting that this kind of label (as well as this book's preferred term 'social realism') are critical inventions for film types, whereas the industry uses terms such as 'sociological' and 'message' films. More important and limiting is the fact that, as Neale points out, the Roffman and Purdy account is tied to a cycle of mostly left-liberal films that appeared in the period from the early 1930s up to the 1950s. Maltby analyses some of the same films in terms of populism and disputes the point of seeing this as a totally separate genre. In any case, one must tread carefully in terms of extrapolating from this period to the recent present. Hence, while this previous work on Hollywood social problem films seems initially relevant to the particular concerns of this chapter, it turns out to be less so.

Two other writers are more pertinent and helpful. The first is McKee (2001), who in a discussion of the TV drama series *A Country Practice* (1981–94) suggests that:

> The term 'social issues', or 'social problems' (the terms are often brought together), is one which, as well as circulating commonly in popular culture . . . also has [been] in academic existence. It is used in sociological disciplines to describe 'some aspect of society about which large numbers of people are concerned [which] lends itself to change as a result of people's effort' . . . If a situation is seen as undesirable, if it is caused by social organisation (rather than, for example, natural forces . . .), and if it is solvable by means of changes in social organisation, then it is a 'social issue' or 'social problem' . . . In contradistinction to 'personal' problems of the individual . . . these are problematic issues about the way in which 'society' is organised. (McKee 2001: 205)

The second useful point of departure is Lay's recent book on social realism in British cinema (2002). This author is sensitive to the charge that the label 'social realism' describes a recurring kind of film content rather than a genre. It is sometimes said that the name fails to conjure up a specific sense of form, iconography, imagery, character types, narrative, and ideological discourse, elements that are seen as some of the characteristic registers of genre. However, by treating aesthetic matters in a much more consistent way, Lay's study advances the case for considering 'social realism' as a genre. Although this investigation is British in its focus and historical in its analysis, nevertheless it is extremely pertinent and suggestive, and this chapter will return to some of its main points below.

Definition

First, though, one must begin with a delineation of what is meant by asserting that social realism is a genre of Australian feature film. As Lay has pointed out: 'Realism is the attitude that man is a social animal and that she is inseparable from her position in society' (2002: 4). In other words, social realism as genre starts with the ideological universe in which its characters are located. This is the world of the ordinary, the everyday, the mundane, the here and now. Above all, it is the world of the social, the milieu of a community, a setting of ordinariness in which social issues are precipitated and explored, social concerns raised and social themes probed. While such a class of film is not a category often used in popular classifications of Australian film, it is important to insist in the present context that social realism is more than a mode or a style of treatment, although it is also certainly these. Rather the class is a genre that deals with ordinary people in the here and now and the social problems and issues that beset their lives. 'Realism' seems generally to be concerned with life as it is lived, such that when one also adds a prefix such as 'social' it causes the reader to think of the who, where, when and why of such realism (Lay 2002: 4–9).

This genre is of pivotal and continuing significance in Australian feature cinema since the Revival. Through different decades of this cinema, through the comings and goings of different film agencies and government policies, through the incidental success of specific films and through a constantly changing agenda of social issues particularly important to the Australian social fabric, the social realist film has had a permanent place in the local film making imagination. Not surprisingly, the genre has shown the most prolific of outputs. An indicative roll call of some of its many filmic instances includes *Mike and Stefani* (1952), *You Can't See Round Corners* (1969), *Three To Go* (1971), *27A* (1974), *Backroads* (1977), *Mouth to Mouth* (1978), *The Devil's Playground* (1978), *The FJ Holden* (1978), *Cathy's Child* (1979), *Hard Knocks* (1980), *Monkey Grip* (1982), *Freedom* (1982), *Moving Out* (1982), *Fighting Back* (1982), *Fast Talking* (1984), *Annie's Coming Out* (1987), *Return Home* (1990), *Angel Baby* (1994), *Bad Boy Bubby* (1994), *Metal Skin* (1994), *Life* (1996), *Blackrock* (1997), *The Boys* (1998), *Australian Rules* (2002), *Rabbit Proof Fence* (2003) and *Somersault* (2004).

What is impressive about such a listing is the steadiness and persistence of output in this genre. In terms of numbers of titles, social realism is far more significant than some of the other genres dealt with in this book, such as the biopic and the musical. The latter are much more occasional in their appearance and more marginal in their importance, whereas this kind of film has been well suited to institutional pressures at work in the system of Australian film making, not to mention the imaginative engagement of writers and directors with matters besetting Australia and Australians. A large number of feature films have come about because of the financial and distributive interaction of a corporate and a public sector. The involvement of the latter has, one can suggest, made 'significance' an important ingredient in the textual system of many films. A historical art cinema was one generic solution to such a need. However, following the Australian art cinema cycle of films that appeared between 1975 and 1983 and their increasingly indifferent performance at the box office, there has been a more general recognition that social realism is a more amenable genre so far as 'significance' and 'worthiness' are concerned.

Many such films have gained recognition at the annual Australian Film Institute (AFI) awards, thereby attesting to the industry's recognition of their merit. In fact, historically, it would seem that this particular type of film is more flexible than the art film in accommodating conflicting demands for consequence and relevance, budgetary considerations and dramatic expectations, critical success and box-office popularity. This is not, of course, to suggest that all Australian feature films in this genre have been universally successful at the box office. Cinematic misery does not add up to a nice night's entertainment. Rather, the point is that films in this genre often gather prestige in Australian cinema circles, in the AFI awards, in school study, and in other places even if they are not usually financial bonanzas. In fact, within the larger field of the film industry and film culture, 'worthiness' has often served as a useful excuse for indifferent revenue returns.

Social realism is, then, everywhere recognized but usually left undefined. The genre creates a narrative for and dramatizes social issues and problems, the intention being – to jumble a phrase of John Reith, the first director-general of the BBC – to inform and educate as well as to entertain. Such films aim to be representative, so that over and above their particular dramatization they are also concerned with a larger social issue or problem whose pervasiveness and representativeness is implied. In practice, the project of a modernist social realism in Australian cinema can be seen to have been initiated in 1952 with the feature-length film, *Mike and Stefani*, produced by the Film Division of the Australian National Film Board, the predecessor to Film Australia. A careful consideration of the film's form and style does much to introduce the viewer to the matter of just how social realism as genre can operate.

Mike and Stefani

This dramatised documentary feature film is concerned with the plight of European refugees in the period immediately after 1945. Taking the two actual figures of the title as its focus of narrative interest, *Mike and Stefani* aims at exploring not only their particular story and situation but, by extension, that of many other refugees displaced by war. Filmed on location, using non-professional figures in all the story's roles, the film draws on both conventions of documentary as well as those of narrative cinema, the latter filtered through the spare, restrained, even detached, style of Italian Neo-Realism. Like other films in the genre, it is contemporary in terms of time and place and gravitates towards a *mise en scène* of the familiar, the everyday, even the seedy and the down-at-heel.

Mike and Stefani tells of the wartime and postwar displaced people of Europe and in particular of the Ukrainian couple, Mike (Mycola) and Stefani. It was filmed by producer Ron Maslyn Williams and photographer Reg Pearce in Europe in 1948–49. Williams had journeyed there to make a film about the work of the International Refugee Organisation. At one camp at Leipheim in Germany, he met Mike and Stefani, who were about to be interviewed by an Australian immigration officer for permission to come to Australia. Williams filmed their interview and, while they waited to hear whether they had been accepted, he reconstructed the filmic details of their life from the late 1930s, often with thousands of other refugees acting as extras in crowd scenes. Williams had little in the way of film equipment, in fact only what he and Pearce could carry between them: a 35mm camera, a half-dozen or so lights and a wire recorder. Williams was away for over a year. On his return, the footage was edited. Dialogue was post-synched, commentary inserted. A musical soundtrack of voice and sound added. The result was *Mike and Stefani*.

Pike and Cooper have described the film as Neo-Realist and the description is an apt one (1980: 214–6). It is loose and episodic in structure without the tight cause-effect chain of Hollywood narrative. Like several Neo-Realist films, for example Vittorio de Sica's *Ladri di biciclette/ Bicycle Thieves* (1948), its conclusion is open-ended: Mike and Stefani are on their way to Australia but have been warned that, because of the shortage of housing, they may have to separate again. Stefani's brother Lazlo has not come with them. The sympathetic camp director, Valerie Paling, has also been left behind in Europe. The narrative chain of the film is loose too because the characters are caught up in large public events beyond their control: thus they are unexpectedly separated, Mike's return is surprising and is given little explanation,

146

the refugee camps are closed with little warning. Like the Neo-Realist films of Rossellini, de Sica, Visconti and the other Italian film makers, the causes of character actions in *Mike and Stefani* are seen as concretely economic, political and historical, most especially to do with the Second World War and its aftermath.

The film too has much of the same *mise en scène* and iconography of Neo-Realism. The characters depicted are in no way extraordinary or heroic; rather they are common, banal, everyday people, much of the film has been shot on location and the film depicts a set of contemporary events. *Mike and Stefani* has a raw, rough feeling to its images. The black and white photography here seeks neither the chiaroscuro beauty of Hollywood *film noir* nor the elegant pictorialism looked for by some other directors at the unit at that time.

(A slight qualification should be made that highlights the way that a more poetic tendency is compatible with social realism. After Mike and Stefani and their child are ordered to the labour camps in Germany, there are several shots of masses of people being loaded onto goods trains for the journey. A train door, almost filling the film frame, with strong horizontal lines on its wooden surface, slides shut on the people, right to left in the frame. In a fine example of graphic matching, the shot fades into a beautiful long shot of the train on the horizon starting a slow journey left to right across the frame, the left-hand side and top left half of the screen bordered by the gaunt shape of a barren tree, the brightness of the sky counterpointed by the darkness of the land and the silhouette of the tree.)

Clearly too, knowing something of the circumstances of *Mike and Stefani* as well as the evidence of the images on the screen, one can make further connections with social realist forms, especially as it is incarnated in Neo-Realism. The film was mostly shot in available light. And apart from the close-up of Mike's face, against a black background when he becomes a German prisoner, it avoids the 'three-point' lighting system of Hollywood. In other words, the film's tendency is not to dramatise the central figures but rather work in a more detached, observational manner. And further, just as de Sica chose a real factory hand to play the central worker character in *Bicycle Thieves*, so Williams chose Mike, Stefani, her brother Lazlo and Valerie Paling, the Australian official, to all play themselves.

Finally, mention should be made of the use of voice-over narration by an omniscient unidentified commentator, who constantly works to link the story of Mike and Stefani to the larger arena of events: 'Peace came back to Europe/peace came back/and the cracked monuments stand like gravestones over a dead dream of conquest . . . those who neither won nor lost . . . eight million people and among them Mike and Stefani and their

147

baby'. This voice, like the titles at the head of different segments of the film, has parallels in other Neo-Realist films such as Rossellini's *Paisa* (1949). The tendency running through these practices of the spoken and written word is to elide the narrative, to de-dramatize the story of the central characters in favour of pointing to the more general, public and historical events in which they found themselves.

Types and Cycles

Mike and Stefani is, then, both a historical sociological object and an aesthetic one. For while social realism speaks very much to the here and now, it marks itself as a genre of the cinema in terms of the artistic attention and choice that govern how these social concerns find articulation. In what follows, one pays attention to the often distinctive handling of human character and location, the recurring imagery and iconography and the playing out of ideological themes in social realism. In terms of the genre's aesthetic operation, it is also necessary to consider the deployment of particular narrative strategies as well as the ideological discourse pervading the genre.

Some preliminary distinctions are in order concerning different subtypes. For again, in keeping with the repeated emphasis of many of the chapters in this book, one should think of this genre not in terms of a single, homogeneous, stand-alone model or type, but rather as housing many films whose connections are outward to a host of other types, cycles and genres. There are several ways in which these relationships can be encapsulated. In terms of social groupings and themes, there are at least four major subtypes of the genre of social realism, which can be summarized as follows.

Troubled Guys

One very large, recurring subject found in Australian social realist films has to do with young men trapped in milieus and circumstances for which there is no escape. Under the impact of adverse social conditions having to do with both dysfunctional families and relationships and also due to unemployment, these men find themselves caught in a meaningless cycle of boredom, alienation, frustration, aggression and violence. Set in outer working-class suburbs, these films follow tough, hard-edged stories that concern males with no way out from nihilistic futures. The protagonists are caught in the dislocations of lack of paid work, alienation, violence, racism and psychological breakdown. These are victims but they are also capable of victimizing others. In films as different as *Backroads, The Boys, Romper*

148

Stomper (1992), *Blackrock, Metal Skin* and *Idiot Box* (1996), male groups or even gangs become substitutes for family wherein the weak are both protected and bullied by others in the group. In turn, as also discussed in Chapter 13, this male-oriented social realism also finds itself coupling with the teenpic in several others in which 'boy meets car' stories are pursued. This cycle began as early as 1977 with *The FJ Holden* and characteristic examples include *Freedom* (1982), *Running on Empty* (1982) and *Metal Skin*. The realism of *Running on Empty* is only incidental to its concern with teen culture and helps point up the overlap with the teenpic that is resumed below.

Women's Troubles

In contrast to this cycle of male social realism, it is worth noting a cycle of women's films inside the genre. In films such as *A City's Child* (1971), *Cathy's Child, Hard Knocks* (1980), *Monkey Grip* (1982), *Fran* (1985), *High Tide* (1985), and *The Fringe Dwellers* (1987), women are at the centre of the narratives even if they are often incapable of controlling or influencing the direction of their own lives. This cycle seems in part to be animated by a latter-day heterosexual feminism so that some of the women in these films are portrayed as attempting to build lasting relationships with inadequate males. However, romantic sexual relationships are not always paramount. Frequently, other familial and social connections are more important so that relationships with both mothers and with daughters finally turn out to be just as important, if not more so, than those with men.

Indigenous Issues

Mention of feminism also sensitizes the reader to the fact that Australian social realist cinema is a creature of the 1970s onwards, an era in which society was discovered to be more heterogeneous than was once seen to be the case. In the spirit of this plurality, attention becomes focussed on those who previously were socially invisible. Marginal groups are frequently the object of attention in many films in the genre. This is literally the case in *The Fringe Dwellers*, a film wherein an Aboriginal family moves from the shanty edge of a country town into a new house that is closer into town, including in the society of the town. *The Fringe Dwellers* is itself part of a cycle of social realist films concerning Aborigines that includes *Come Out Fighting* (1973), *Backroads, Tudawali* (1983), *Wrong Side of the Road* (1985), *Blackfellas* (1992) and *Rabbit Proof Fence*.

Ill and Disturbed

Several other situations and concerns recur. A number of these can be brack-eted together in terms of others who are marginalized from society through illness and disability. Hence, one can mention the alcoholic Bill in *27A*, the disabled boy Tom in *Fighting Back* (1982), the disabled mute Annie in *Annie's Coming Out*, the mentally disturbed and schizophrenic couple, Kate and Harry, in *Angel Baby*, the retarded incarcerated man in *Bad Boy Bubby* (1993), the mentally broken David Helfgott in *Shine* (1996), and the pris-oners dying of AIDS in *Life*. This last film is a reminder that prisoners have also been an object of concern in society so that several of these films deal with either life in a prison or in a prison-like situation. Hence, other films that should be added to this group include *Stir* (1980) and *Ghosts of the Civil Dead* (1988), although in these there is an overlap with action-adventure that stresses survival in confined spaces.

Artistic Categories and Tendencies

Overall, though, this kind of social grouping into four subtypes is only one way to conceive of difference within the genre. Another, more aesthetic line of approach is in terms of some of the formal properties of some of these films. Various artistic categories have already been mentioned in passing and a handful of these are pinpointed to further outline particular tendencies within the genre of social realism. One such term is that of 'documentary' and it is useful to remind oneself of the powerful institutional support that bodies such as Film Australia and the Australian Broadcasting Corporation (ABC) have given to the documentary type of stories involving social issues and problems. To the extent that both these bodies were historically important training organizations for Australian feature film makers, then they have helped set up a powerful impetus in the direction of the social realist genre.

None of the films mentioned in this chapter are documentaries yet many trade in some of the formal features of this type of film. *Mike and Stefani* has already been mentioned. Meanwhile, *Wrong Side of the Road* is a drama-tized documentary featuring an actual Aboriginal rock-and-roll band that was subjected to the racism represented in the film. Similarly, three quite different films – *27A*, *Bad Boy Bubby* and *Life* – are loose and detached in their narratives in a manner worthy of observational documentary. And indeed, even with films such as *Mouth to Mouth* and *Angel Baby*, which are more emphatically involved with central figures and have a high degree of dramatization, there is still a detachment and a distance between film and subject so that the audience is both empathetic but also critical and thoughtful.

Another mode that should be mentioned concerns magical realism. On the surface at least, this mode would seem to be completely absent in the Australian social realist film. Yet this turns out not to be quite the case – consider for example the fantasy segments in *Freedom*, *Australian Dream* (1986) and *Bad Boy Bubby*. In these and many other Australian films ostensibly concerned with social realism there is a frequent shift in and out of a more surreal, fantastic mode. Martin has suggested that this register lies somewhere between naturalistic drama and the tradition of the 'tall tale' (Martin quoted in Mayer 1999: 180). Meanwhile, *Romper Stomper* makes consistent use of rock video-style editing, wobblecam and jump cuts in various set pieces, most especially the fight between the skinheads and the Vietnamese, which also serves to detach audience involvement from the more lurid details of the story. All in all, then, social realism as a genre is constituted not by a single set of concerns or approaches but instead by a range of constitutive elements, a point already emphasized, so this chapter turns to another set of considerations.

Character and Location

Given these different structures at work within the genre as a whole, how can the operation of other elements of social realism be understood? In particular, how does one gain a bearing on the human figures and the environments that they inhabit in this kind of film? The answer seems to lie in the realization that, above all, social realism stresses an inevitable and constraining environmentalism at work between its characters and its locations. Where some other genres emphasize a lack of contingency between figure and background, where the latter can be changed at the desire and whim of the leading figure, this genre underlines the bounded, constrained nature of such a relationship. In social realism, characters are discovered in these milieus at the beginning or early in a film and they are usually still there at the end of the film. At most they move on, simply changing one setting for another but they are unable to shed their life circumstances. This boundedness is literally the case with *Monkey Grip*. The latter begins with Norah and Alice at a local swimming pool and ends with them there a year later. In *27A*, the alcoholic Bill is taken to a prison-like hospital where he tells another inmate that he will be out after a week but fails to live up to his promise. In *Queensland* (1976) the ultimate destination of the characters is signalled in the film's title but proves unattainable. The ironically titled

Freedom discloses that its male hero is totally unable to escape his circumstances despite his fantasies of power and movement associated with a high-speed sports car. With *Life*, the title is both literal and ironic. That is the duration of sentence yet these particular prisoners are dying of AIDS.

In fact, despite many fantasies of independence and sovereignty, characters in this genre are marked by being common and ordinary. Frequently, they have no particular attributes, visual features and so on that make them stand out from others. They are not especially gifted, handsome, clever, physically strong, agile, resourceful and so on. The social realist hero or heroine is, for the most part, little able to influence or direct the chain of circumstance and situation in which they find themselves. Usually, these figures are presented as social types rather than psychologically complex characters. The frequent impulse is to deliberately de-dramatize such figures. There is, for the most part, little desire to psychologize character, to suggest a complex emotional interiority. Instead, the clues about their being are meant to be environmental. Their identity is social rather than personal or inward. Hence, for example, in *Mouth to Mouth*, one of the two girls, Carrie (Kim Krijus), is drifting into prostitution but the film deliberately eschews opportunities to have the figure explain to the other characters just why this is happening.

(It is worth noting, in passing, that this kind of deliberate surface engagement is not completely and unfailingly the case with Australian cinema's social realism. Dramatization does occur from time to time – witness such films as *Monkey Grip*, *Fran* and *High Tide* for instance. And, indeed, in *Angel Baby*, the two leading figures of Kate and Harry are invested with considerable psychology, in being mentally disturbed figures. Nevertheless, even here, in having them ultimately motivated by the arbitrary sequence of numbers on a TV game show, the film reinforces the extent to which, like other social realist figures, they are bound by fate.)

Altogether, then, film makers in this mode are not concerned with posing the question in dramatic terms of what motivates or drives a particular character, what makes them tick. Instead, they are usually presented as a given. What is important is not the names, personal history and psychological presence of such figures but rather their situation, the identity conferred upon them by the milieu in which they are placed, the social type that they constitute. Hence, the principal characters in this genre include wartime refugees Mike and Stefani, Bill the alcoholic in *27A*, who has been forcibly incarcerated, young car mechanic Kevin living an aimless existence in Sydney's western suburbs in *The FJ Holden*, girl remand school escapees living with two country boys among the homeless (*Mouth to Mouth*), an ex-prisoner who draws his brothers into the same circle of angry hopelessness, where rules are to be broken (*The Boys*), a single mother in a web of casual relationships including one with a junkie actor (*Monkey Grip*), and a man, possibly retarded, who has been incarcerated and abused, and is subsequently let loose on the world (*Bad Boy Bubby*).

It should be added here that going along with this impulse in social realism is the desire to feature hitherto unrepresented character types. This is especially evident in Australian social realism of the 1970s and 1980s, where a social pluralist impulse resulted in the increasing cinematic presence of such marginalized figures as urban Aborigines, the disabled, the mentally disturbed and prisoners. In such films as *27A*, *Mouth to Mouth*, *Annie's Coming Out* and *Bad Boy Bubby*, the desire is to strip away the invisibility of various social groupings, to put them and the particular community problem or issue with which they are associated on the social agenda, to bring them to cinematic attention.

In turn, this outline concerning the depiction of character suggests how the iconography of setting operates in the genre. For the emphasis on ordinariness of figure extends to an apparent ordinariness of surroundings. While some social realist films such as *Backroads* and *Freedom* have their central figures flee their lives, as well as the police, in more rural parts, the more usual environment of the genre is that of the everyday, the commonplace, even the down-at-heel, the seedy, the sordid, the broken, the neglected. Frequently set in the suburbs of Australia's big cities, most especially in the outer parts of Sydney and Melbourne, these films locate themselves in areas that are marked by repetitive and cheap housing styles and anonymous and seemingly unending roads and highways. Sometimes this gives way to even more derelict buildings and scenery, as in *Mouth to Mouth* or to the factories and container areas of *Metal Skin*. This same landscape also frequently features garages, factories, suburban shopping centres, fast food outlets, malls, indistinguishable streets, highways, concrete bridges and flyovers. Almost always, too, there is the ubiquitous, high-turbine car, whether an expensive, new sports status symbol in more marginal fantasy teen films such as *The Big Steal* (1990) or an older vehicle reconditioned by its young owner as in *The FJ Holden* and *Metal Skin*. And, of course, even if the presence of the car suggests flight and escape, in point of fact it cannot offer deliverance and transcendence. However, to touch on these last concerns is to realize the necessity of examining how these films deploy narrative and discourse.

Narrative Structures

There is, of course, no single or multiple story pattern that is unique to social realism. Instead, the genre frequently criss-crosses other types, not least when it comes to the deployment of various story telling strategies. Hence, in *Shame* (1988), social realist concerns are mapped onto an action-adventure structure: the heroine rides into town at the beginning and, having helped the town to stand up against evil, rides out at the end of the film. Similarly, *Freedom* resolves itself into a tale of flight, a chase pattern, with the two central figures of Ron and Anna being pursued by the police across country roads.

Yet despite these immediate patterns, there are more recurring structures that link with the overall concerns of many of these films. Consider, for example, the endings of *Mike and Stefani, 27A, Mouth to Mouth* and *Freedom*. In the first and the last two, endings are fairly open-ended in that the ultimate fate of the characters is not disclosed. In fact, with *Freedom*, when all signs point towards the car death of Ron, the fact that he pushes the car over the side of the road and is picked up by a passing car adorned with the sign 'Jesus saves' makes the climax seem both erratic and whimsical. Meanwhile, in *27A*, the character is suddenly and unexpectedly released from the clinic. In other words, the narrative ending is arbitrary, a point of let up rather than a point of resolution. Bill has already made three unsuccessful attempts to escape, thereby underscoring a cyclical pattern of a certain hopelessness at work. The same structure has already been noted with the beginning and ending of *Monkey Grip*. Similarly, the pattern of murder, suicide, imminent murder and death at the end of such films as *Backroads, Angel Baby, Metal Skin* and *The Boys* also points up this same narrative pattern of a nihilistic, no way out, environmental hopelessness.

Again, though, it is important to qualify such a claim. Not all films follow this particular pattern. Behind at least some is a social reformist impulse so that films such as *Fighting Back, Annie's Coming Out, Bad Boy Bubby* and *Australian Rules* end on rather a different note. Roffman and Purdy (1981) define the social problem film in terms of a dramatic struggle of good and institutional evil, the latter personified in a particular figure, with such films ending in the triumph of good.

In the Australian cycle, the conflict is never as sharp, dramatic or polarized. Nevertheless, in these more reformist films, the socially marginal figure has overcome adversity and triumphed. By implication at least, the more gross abuses of power will be curtailed. The plight of the victim has drawn attention to a social ill which will now be corrected. In other words, an impulse towards reform, social improvement, a revaluation of the marginal is occurring so that hopelessness and despair are not the only options.

Themes

The ideological discourse at work in Australian social realism has been touched on repeatedly in this chapter. The emphasis is on a world in which characters have little autonomy but are, instead, largely determined and constrained by their social environment. Although some triumph over adversity – whether related to class, gender, ethnicity, disability or whatever – the emphasis is more usually to do with a kind of social determinism that limits and curtails the lives of these inhabitants. The socially marginal are the underdogs, the victims of social power, and even though they pursue impulses towards flight, escape, utopia and freedom, these attempts are mostly doomed to failure. In the physically mundane, frequently blighted, ugly, nondescript environments in which so many of these figures operate, life itself is often nasty, brutish and short. Nor is there any particular romanticism operating within this kind of determinism. The fault lies not with fate or chance but rather with the society. The setting thus becomes the stage on which the drama of futility is played out even as it becomes the embodiment of the powers acting upon the protagonists.

This chapter ends by briefly considering the extent to which there is a distinctive Australian cinema genre of social realism. As already noted, there is certainly an unbroken tradition of output going back to the Revival, but also even earlier to the 1950s. Here, the institutional presence of two major screen bodies is particularly important as background elements in stimulating and sustaining this output. The first of these is Film Australia, the government film information production body. As shown elsewhere, this organization has historically been highly significant in the output of films having to do with the nature of Australian society (Moran 1991). Meanwhile, the ABC has also been highly influential in setting the parameters of a cinematic social realism. For although the ABC does not produce feature films for cinema release, it has nonetheless produced many programs not only in drama but also in documentary that have sustained a thoroughgoing social realism (Moran 1991; Jacka 1991). Both these bodies have set benchmarks that have impacted on feature film making in the industry generally.

One other broad factor helping to sustain the climate for this output has been the changing nature of Australian society. Beginning in the mid 1970s and accelerating from the early 1980s, economic forces and social impulses have frequently been at variance. Over these years, deterioration in social conditions has turned the perception of Australia into that of the Unlucky Country. This, together with the increasing diversity of the social fabric, has proved to be fertile ground for film makers with an inclination towards social realism. This has helped create and sustain the space for an Australian cinema of social realism.

Finally, it is also relevant to mention a suggestion by Turner that the tradition of social realism has in part to do with a reaction against the historical art film, so much in favour with film policy officials and critics alike in the second half of the 1970s and early 1980s (Turner 1993: 102–11). There is certainly some truth in this suggestion. However, it underplays the role adopted by earlier films in sustaining and building such a cycle. Among relevant films that appeared before *Picnic at Hanging Rock* (1975) are *Mike and Stefani, You Can't See Round Corners, Three To Go* (1971), *A City's Child, Gentle Strangers* (1972), *Moving On* (1974), *27A* and *Promised Woman* (1975). Likewise, by only pointing to *The FJ Holden* and *Mouth to Mouth* during the era of the period art film's dominance, Turner underemphasises the continuing vitality of this tradition even during those years. Surely the appearance of such films as *The Removalists* (1976), *Queensland, The FJ Holden, Out of It* (1977), *Listen to the Lion* (1978), *Cathy's Child, Mouth to Mouth, Just Out of Reach* (1980), *Hard Knocks* and *Stir* make it impossible to see social realism only coming to the fore with the cessation of the period art film after 1983.

Put another way, the tradition of Australian social realism has a longer pedigree than might seem to be the case if one only assumes it to originate in the 1980s as a reaction against the quality period film. Rather, the two genres exist side by side, as do other genres. And while the cycle of quality period films was at an end by the mid 1980s, the social realist film has continued down to the present. In 2005, for instance, several such features played in Australian cinemas, including *Peaches, Three Dollars, The Oyster Farmer, Look Both Ways* and *Little Fish*. The situations and settings of these were all ostensibly different – a country town in South Australia whose local factory is dying and a young woman who aims at breaking away; a young Sydney man who loses his job; a man who ends up among a small community on the Hawkesbury River; a Melbourne journalist who learns that he has testicular cancer even as he encounters a lonely young woman; a young woman trying to stay off drugs even while her stepfather, brother and former boyfriend are all heavily involved in Sydney's drug culture. In all cases, the endings are open and indeterminate. However, what is not uncertain is that the tradition of Australian social realism is more deep-rooted and has greater longevity than might initially seem to be the case.

12
Suspense Thriller

Neither Detective nor Gangster

Yet a third subset of the meta genre having to do with crime generally – intrigue, conspiracy, tension, anxiety – is that going under the name of the suspense thriller. Such a name conjures up no particular sense of narrative or iconography as do the labels of some other genres. Rather, the suspense thriller is a class of film distinguished primarily by audience effect. This is no barrier to definition. After all, other genres such as comedy, adventure, horror and, in the case of television, light entertainment, are all designated in terms of affective qualities involving audience response to what is happening on screen. Having said this, one is still left with the difficulty of where to begin. After all, suspense and thrills seem as indeterminate in fixing particular generic boundaries as does the presence of other emotional qualities and responses such as alarm, horror, screams, anxiety, sobs, cheers and chuckles. And yet such terms as 'suspense' and 'thriller' are regularly and unhesitatingly used in reviews of films as generically different as adventure, crime, science fiction and horror.

Given this anomaly, it is no surprise to realize that serious authors have attempted to use these terms as a means of generic designation. Early in the international publishing boom in books relating to the cinema that began in the late 1960s came three studies concerned with suspense and with the thriller (Gow 1968; Davies 1973; Hammond 1974). However, as both Derry (1988) and Neale (2000) have noted, all three share a common weakness of equating the two terms of 'suspense' and 'thriller' so that they become interchangeable and less meaningful than they might be otherwise. These authors also define the genre (or the genres) so widely that it also includes horror, science fiction, mystery, and adventure films as well as others involving crime and spies. And, indeed, as I discussed in Chapter 2 concerning Ian Cameron on adventure in the cinema, Gow ends up implying that suspense is so common across so many different genres that it makes little sense to imagine that the term may be more specific in its reference. Fortunately, others have taken the trouble to be more precise.

Surprise, Suspense and Thriller

The first of those using the terms more carefully and exactly was the film maker Alfred Hitchcock, himself popularly known as 'the master of suspense'. Throughout his career, Hitchcock was emphatic that he did not make mystery films or whodunits. Instead, in a famous interview with French film critic and film maker François Truffaut, the director explained how he understood the concept of suspense by distinguishing between it and surprise (Truffaut 1967: 50–1, 76). In Hitchcock's example, a film shows two men come into a room, sit at a table, and carry on a long conversation. At the end of the conversation, a bomb suddenly explodes and kills both of them. The sequence would provide an audience with a surprise and may have also generated curiosity. Why, the audience might have wondered, was the sequence being shown – what was its point? Hitchcock then suggests to Truffaut that the sequence might be staged differently. Suppose it was preceded by a scene in which a third man comes into the room, unseen by the other men, and hides the bomb underneath the table. Because the audience has knowledge not disclosed to the two men in the room, the scene is now transformed. Instead of wondering about what will happen during and after the conversation, the audience now wants to know if the bomb will go off and whether the men will get out of the room in time. Pauses in the conversation would seem like moments when the bomb might explode and the talk itself would become irrelevant to what is really happening. Time itself could appear to have been stretched, elongated, as part of a torturing of the audience which might sit wondering whether its anticipation will be fulfilled or deflected. This is what Hitchcock meant by suspense.

In turn, the most useful and interesting analysis of the genre of the suspense thriller is that by Derry (1988). Significantly, his book acknowledges in its title – *The Suspense Thriller: Films in the Shadow of Alfred Hitchcock* – the seminal influence of the British-American film director on both the genre and on the author's thinking about this kind of film. Not surprisingly, Derry starts with an early explanation of suspense that directly echoes Hitchcock. It is, he notes:

> . . . a narrative construction whereby the spectator is made aware of certain facts of the plot before the work's protagonists are, thus allowing the spectator to anticipate plot developments (especially of the threatening variety) before the protagonists themselves. (Derry 1988: 9)

Implicit in this outline is a particular character figure that has already been mentioned in Chapters 6 and 7, namely the victim of crime. There, drawing on Poe's Triangle, the book also mentioned two other figures that have a mutual interdependence with the figure of the victim in the meta genre of crime, namely the detective and the criminal. Derry (1988) and Neale (2000) suggest that while the other two genres of crime and detective concentrate on the latter two figures, the suspense thriller focusses particularly on the victim and her or his involvement with the criminal and with crime. One can see that scenes of suspense in this genre of the suspense thriller have in part to do with extended situations of victimhood wherein a protagonist is under threat and is relatively powerless against criminal forces. Equally, though, as will be suggested below, there are other kinds of suspense thrillers that vary this pattern considerably.

But before examining subtypes, it is necessary to consider the other part of the genre's title. What, then, of the thriller component of the genre? The term 'thrill' refers to a particular state of feelings, very often with a physical, bodily component. Relevant synonyms include excitement, stimulation, palpitation, tingle and tremor. Derry considers the matter of the thriller part of the suspense thriller film by drawing on the work of psychoanalyst Michael Baliant in his book *Thrills and Regressions* (Derry 1988: 31–54). Thrills can arise from a situation of danger, of being at risk whether in a physical or an emotional sense. Thrilling occasions include those to do with height, speed, exposed situations or new sensations. Most relevant to the suspense thriller is the structure of feeling entailed in the constructed thrill, whether it be encountered in an amusement park or in the cinema. According to Derry's reading of Baliant, there would appear to be three phases to such an encounter. First, the recognition of an external fear or danger, followed by exposure to such a threat and, finally, a confidence that such a danger will be tolerated or mastered, will reach an end with a return to safety (Derry 1988: 39). In other words, the thriller component of the suspense thriller has to do with the deliberate manipulation of displeasure and pleasure that repeatedly operates across such a genre and finds typical extended expression in such narrative segments as attempted murders, escapes and chases.

Derry's Typology

With these considerations in mind, Derry then proceeds to undertake a content analysis of a large number of films that had been identified as either suspense films or thrillers or both (1988: 72–320). The result of this inquiry is a typology of six major types of the genre. In addition, in his conclusion he describes a further four subtypes (1988: 321–2). These variants can be summarised as follows:

1 The Thriller of Murderous Passions
2 The Political Thriller
3 The Thriller of Acquired Identity
4 The Psychotraumatic Thriller
5 The Thriller of Moral Confrontation
6 The Innocent-on-the-Run Thriller
7 The Thriller of Time
8 The Thriller of Place
9 The Kidnapping Thriller
10 The Thriller of Cultural Anxiety.

This is a very extensive inventory but Derry has taken the trouble to be both precise and comprehensive in his discussion of these, most especially the first six types (1988: 72–320). The last four are dealt with more cursorily although he does cite a number of films in support of each class. Hence, in what follows in this chapter, a particular Australian feature film is used as a means of exploring the majority of these types in more detail.

Sex and Murder

Derry's first category is that of the murderous triangle, a suspense thriller that involves a small group of characters, most typically a husband, wife and another male (1988: 72–102). Sex and murder are the principal stations visited by this kind of narrative. Frequently, the climactic segment of such a film involves the murder of one character by the other two and, subsequently, the two turning on each other. The cycle of this type in Hollywood is very extended and runs from at least *Double Indemnity* (1944) to *The Man Who Wasn't There* (2001).

In Australia, there would appear to be several films that qualify for inclusion in the type although these turn out finally to not quite fit the category. What they have in common is their concentration on a small group, a handful of protagonists, although the Australian features do not incorporate the adultery, sexual intrigue and passion of their Hollywood counterparts. Among some early, post-Revival candidates for the type are *End Game* (1975), *Final Cut* (1979), *The Dark Room* (1982) and (more marginally) *Double Deal* (1981). Meanwhile, a film with perhaps a stronger claim for inclusion is *Dead Calm* (1989). Lucas in particular has developed a psychoanalytical understanding of this film that would support its incorporation in this category (1993: 121–9). Nevertheless, because sexual intrigue is absent from the film, even despite the fact that Rae (Nicole Kidman) has to submit to the sexual advances of Hughie (Billy Zane), it is more useful to discuss *Dead Calm* below as a suspense thriller of moral confrontation.

Political Intrigue and Danger

Like the thriller of murderous passion, that involving political intrigue and danger is also uncommon in Australian film output. For the most part, local film makers have not been concerned with paranoid political thrillers evident in Hollywood in such films as *Suddenly* (1959), *The Manchurian Candidate* (1962, 2002), *Seven Days in May* (1964), *The Parallax View* (1974), *All The President's Men* (1976), *The Day of the Jackal* (1973) and *Absolute Power* (1997). However, even in Hollywood, this particular subtype is not found in great abundance (Derry 1988: 170–5). Australian films in the general class of the suspense thriller have usually avoided stories of political conspiracy and high-level intrigues, paranoid thrillers about the machinations of government, party leaders, bureaucrats, military and police, scenarios of political assassination and *coup d'état*, and corruption at very high levels of the state. As suggested in Chapter 7, a detective film such as *Goodbye Paradise* (1983) can very often invoke elements of political corruption. Similarly, *Far East* (1982) sets its love story among the military and political corruption of an unidentified South-East Asian country but hardly qualifies for extended consideration as a political thriller. In fact, almost nothing in Australian film output is comparable to the paranoid view embedded in the Hollywood films cited.

One of the very few exceptions is *The Year of Living Dangerously* (1982) which is, arguably, an American-Australian film (Lawrence 1995: 117). More importantly for this book's purpose, the film does not concern Australian government, public servants or military but is instead set in Indonesia, thereby indirectly confirming the point regarding the general absence of this kind of suspense thriller. All the same, the film adheres to specific conventions of the type by basing itself on fact and following the trail of a journalist who is conducting an investigation of what, in both a political and a military sense, is happening. Set in Java in 1968 against a real political situation, the film involves an Australian journalist Guy Hamilton (Mel Gibson) who gradually becomes aware of how dangerous the country has become even while he pursues an affair with Jill Bryant (Sigourney Weaver) who works at the British Embassy and may or may not be a spy.

While *The Year of Living Dangerously* is without the paranoid overtones of its Hollywood siblings, nevertheless there is plenty of intrigue, danger, tension and suspicion as the eruption of civil war seems very close. Pitted against each other are the Communist PKI workers' party and the Indonesian army. President Sukarno is nominally in charge as his posters are everywhere. While some of his supporters believe that he still has an agenda of reform, others such as Billy (Linda Hunt), Guy's native photographer, think that he has sold out. Guy is caught up in the PKI's stoning of the US Embassy early in the film and this segment is the prelude for a narrative twist with a PKI arms shipment and finally a coup by the army. Guy puts himself and Jill, his source for the arms story, in considerable danger. After Billy's death and Guy's bashing by a military official, Guy finally manages to scramble on board one of the last planes leaving the strife-torn country.

As this synopsis suggests, there is enough in *The Year of Living Dangerously* to support its claim to be an example of the political suspense thriller. The background story of the squashing of the popular uprising in Indonesia in 1968 that would end in Sukarno's overthrow is repeatedly touched upon and the intrigue and danger of the embassy attack and the intimations of the coup are highly graphic and involving. Equally, Guy's investigation of the arms shipment further heightens the sense of conspiracy and peril as does his relationship with Jill. However, unlike the other film examples cited, *The Year of Living Dangerously* never puts the protagonist in a situation where great political consequences are contingent on his actions. Danger there may be but, except perhaps for the attempt to board the plane at the end of the film, this rarely condenses into sustained suspense. Put another way, the film is at best only a marginal example of the type, suggesting that Australian film makers have yet to wholeheartedly embrace the political suspense thriller.

Dangerous Masquerade

If the first two of Derry's subtypes of the genre are borderline so far as having a presence in the Australian cinema is concerned, this is not the case with the next type, the thriller of disguise and changed persona. The narrative drive of such a type is clear. By posing as another, a protagonist very often isolates herself in a new environment wherein there may be danger, threat, violence and death. In any case, to sustain the new identity, to maintain the fictional self, to carry through the project or quest also generates thrills and suspense so that such films are doubly involving for audiences. In defining the type, Derry also lays emphasis on the protagonist's behaviour in meeting the physical and moral demands of the role especially in relation to a particular scheme or machination (1988: 175–93).

The Bank (2001) is an enthralling example of the suspense story of deception, and although it also answers to the label of the heist/caper crime film, it is treated here under the first heading. In brief, the film's story concerns Centrebank, whose ruthless CEO Simon O'Reilly (Anthony La Paglia) yearns to pull off a big financial coup on the global commodity markets. A young mathematical wizard, Jim Doyle (David Wenham), appears to have the software program to do just that so Simon decides to risk all in this endeavour. Meanwhile, a couple given deliberately misleading advice by the bank have been unsuccessful in a legal case. On the night when Jim's plan is put into action, various events come together. Michelle (Sibylla Budd), a young woman in love with Jim, discovers his real identity and the fact that his father also was ruined by a bank. At the same time, one of O'Reilly's lieutenants realises that Jim's scheme will in fact ruin the bank but Jim foils his attempt to shut down the computer program. Wayne Davis (Steve Rogers), the husband taking the legal action, confronts Simon in his home and inadvertently causes crucial and fatal delay in halting the transactions. The bank is destroyed financially, all its assets scattered and lost, O'Reilly ruined. Jim is leaving the country and explains to Michelle that he could not reveal his real identity as he could not be sure if she was one of O'Reilly's spies.

As such an outline indicates, *The Bank* is centrally a thriller revolving around an acquired identity. However, the film deliberately withholds the fact that Jim is under cover and setting an elaborate financial trap for Simon and Centrebank. Instead, early in the film, the financial trading desk computer is the location of thrilling action as it graphs various behaviours, real and projected, of the market. Later, of course, there is the extended suspense of whether Jim's scheme will be shut down or whether it can run for a sufficient length of time to allow it to reach its goal. Here, too, the suspense is further compounded by having Davis, the tragic parent, breaking into Simon's home and causing crucial delays to the latter's response to the engulfing crisis. Up to this point, this second story appeared to be in the film only to highlight the nefariousness of the bank and to introduce a social realist dimension to the film.

Finally, two other points are worth making about the plight of the protagonist in this kind of masquerade. Both have to do with the matter of identity. The first concerns the physical fact of vomiting that overtakes Jim after he has been forced to lie as a witness in the court case involving the parents' action against the bank over their son's death. His disguised identity has not yet been brought to the audience's attention, yet the scene is a useful means of indicating a moral gap between what Jim might be and what he is forced

163

to do. The second has to do with his leaving the country at the end of the film. Jim has already told Michelle to call him by his fictitious name; now he is about to disappear somewhere overseas where he will be without an Australian passport. The thematic suggestion is that he is now completely lost to his old self and that the new fictional self has taken over. Such may be the ultimate price of the masquerade in this type of suspense thriller.

The Living Nightmare

Although it sometimes overlaps the triangular situation identified as the first type, nevertheless this fourth class of thriller is more concerned with a victim who is shocked or traumatized, discovering that s/he is involved in a monstrous situation. Not surprisingly, women are frequently the psychotraumatized victims at the centre of this kind of narrative situation. A representative example of this general type in Australia is to be found in *Hostage: The Christine Maresch Story* (1983). As its title suggests, the film is also a biopic, based as it is on an account of an actual relationship between a young Australian woman and a German man. However, although there is a brief romance between these two young people, who find themselves working together in a carnival, the film soon reveals itself to be a nightmare thriller. Based on a real string of tense, dangerous incidents, *Hostage*'s narrative shuttles backwards and forwards between Australia and Germany. Generically, the film might be seen to be part of a cycle concerned with the fairy tale marriage that turns to nightmare wherein, like *Sleeping with the Enemy* (1991) and *Double Jeopardy* (1999), a new wife finds that a seemingly adoring husband is anything but that. Adrian Martin has also usefully compared the film to another paranoic nightmare based on a real-life case, Paul Schrader's 1988 *Patty Hearst* (1995c: 129). Like this cycle of films what is important in this type is not the fact of marriage but rather the transforming shock and trauma suffered by the protagonist when she realises what she is up against. In the best tradition of the suspense thriller, *Hostage* uses its 'furiously sudden opening, intercutting the wheels of a truck barrelling down the highway and quick flashes of Christine Maresch suffering domestic violence' (Martin 1995c: 129) as a means of tutoring its audience as to what lies ahead.

The action and narrative drive of *Hostage* are fast, tough and to the point. Physically attracted to Walter at the carnival, Christine is happy to have sex but uninterested in having a relationship with him. However, she is emotionally blackmailed into marrying. Discovering herself to be pregnant, Christine is persuaded to go to Germany for an abortion. Meanwhile,

Walter slowly discloses himself to be deranged. In a foreign country to her, Germany, he tricks her and she is forced to have the child, a girl. The young man now proceeds to reveal his Nazi affiliations, the screen filling with inserted footage of Nazi war rallies. By now drugged and disoriented, Christine is forced by Walter to rob banks and the two flee Germany, go to Turkey, move back to Germany, travel on to Australia. A further bank robbery and the family set sail again for Germany. However, the relationship between the two is a shifting elemental one and Christine finally calls Walter's bluff and breaks his hold on her. Thematically, the film also touches upon a couplet that is returned to in the next section. This concerns the fact that the two are less 'maid and monster' than they first appear, with more subtle areas of grey in-between. Overall, then, the film constantly and convincingly shifts gear between exploitation, melodrama and thriller making *Hostage: The Christine Maresch Story* one of the most arresting examples of the psychotraumatic suspense thriller to appear in Australia.

Maid versus Monster

This subtype concerns a moral confrontation, a clash between good and evil (Derry 1988: 194–216). In this kind of suspense thriller there is little in the way of ethical subtleties or motivational complexities. Instead, the struggle is an elemental and a physical one, a fight to the death, which also determines whether the force of good will overcome that of evil. The type has to do with the contest between a hero and that which is monstrous, evil. In fact, the clash is often enhanced by making the protagonist a woman rather than a man, as is the case in *Wait Until Dark* (1972), one of the most vivid embodiments of the thriller of moral confrontation wherein the protagonist, as played by Audrey Hepburn, is also blind and alone.

Although above it is noted that there is a temptation to offer *Dead Calm* (1989) as an example of the deadly triangle thriller, it is more usefully considered as an example of this variant. A partial synopsis runs as follows:

> After the death of their son in an automobile accident, veteran sailor John Ingram (Sam Neill) and his young wife, Rae (Nicole Kidman), escape to the seclusion of the Pacific Ocean on board their luxury yacht, 'Saracen'. But when they notice a man rowing towards them across the dead flat ocean, they have no idea of the terror that will ensue. The supposed survivor of a food poisoning epidemic on board his ship, the young American, Hughie Warriner (Billy Zane), is welcomed on board 'Saracen'. He sleeps while John more than

a tad suspicious goes to inspect 'Orpheus', leaving his wife alone with Hughie. When John finds the occupants murdered, he peers back towards 'Saracen' with a knowing glance, then jumps back into his dinghy and rows frenetically, heart pounding with every stroke. But he is too late: 'Saracen' pulls away just before he reaches it, a wry chuckle emanating from Hughie's demonic face. While Rae has the chance to kill Hughie on a number of occasions, she is inhibited by her recent brush with death and by an incredibly obedient dog, which foils several of her plans. Eventually she is forced to submit to Hughie's sexual advances in order to seize control. (Barlow 1995: 272)

Militating against the film being considered as a thriller of murderous passion is the fact that there has not been any previous relationship between the couple and Hughie. Although there is the familiar threesome of husband, wife and other male present, for much of the film John is stranded on the other boat leaving Rae to confront and deal with the deranged and murderous Hughie. Rae is not a *femme fatale* and there is no previous relationship between her and Billy. On the other hand, what links *Dead Calm* with some in the murderous triangle thriller, such as *Blood Simple* (1984) and *Red Rock West* (1992), is that the action occurs in a bounded situation. The Australian film is exemplary in this regard with its three characters limited to the two boats. But the situation is also constrained in terms of the fact that they are beyond contact with others and wife and husband must rely on their own courage and cunning in dealing with the psychopath.

This is not, however, to suggest that *Dead Calm* is without structural weakness in terms of its composition as a suspense thriller. Two segments in particular seem somewhat arbitrary and therefore narratively untidy. The first involves the opening scenes wherein Rae is in a car accident that kills the couple's only child and traumatizes her. Although the 'psychotraumatic' pattern is another plot in the suspense thriller identified by Derry (1988: 194–216), this accident and its aftermath prove to have little bearing on what follows. As played by a very young Nicole Kidman, Rae is remarkably uncomplicated aboard the boat and proves immediately and fully resourceful and ingenious in dealing with Billy. The second ineffective segment has to do with the last appearance of the psychopath. This occurs after he has apparently disappeared wounded into the water while Rae has taken a swim and John prepares breakfast. Like the final appearance of the monstrous threat in the horror film, Hughie's hands appear on Rae's hair before she and the audience realise that he is there. In terms of the classic distinction between surprise and suspense, this is a moment of surprise which, while startling, would, perhaps, have had more impact had Billy's existence been conveyed to the audience beforehand.

Be that as it may, *Dead Calm* works well as a thriller of moral confrontation. The death of the child in the accident at the beginning certainly increases audience sympathy and involvement with Rae and she is a sufficient, even if somewhat abstract, embodiment of goodness and virtue. Billy is also sufficiently distinct as the deranged killer and the film usefully has this dawn on John by what he finds aboard the other boat, rather than through any psychological complexity discovered in the young man.

Innocents on the Run

A further variant has to do with the innocent caught up in circumstances not of her making so that she is forced to flee for her life. However, not all suspense thrillers of this type inevitably gravitate towards putting the viewer through a kind of torture associated with anxiety and helplessness. Instead, the type can lean more in the direction of adventure and thrills, associated with chases, physical danger and vertiginous action. Such is the case with an Australian variant of the innocents-on-the-run suspense thriller, *Running from the Guns* (1987). The inspiration in this film is not from such masters of the genre as Hitchcock, Lang, Frankenheimer, Chabrol and de Palma, but rather derives from the teen or youth film whose antecedents go back to the 1950s. To that end, the film offers three protagonists, in the shape of two attractive and energetic males, Dave (Jon Blake) and Pete (Mark Hembrow), and a brave and equally handsome, ingenious crime commissioner staffer, Jill (Nikki Coghill). Murray summarises the plot as follows:

> On the lookout for a good deal, Davie and Peter purchase some toys from a bankrupt firm in Taiwan, but at the docks their container is switched for another, by Bangles, and they end up with a load of koalas . . . When Bangles tries to have his hoons take possession of the container, they lose out in a spectacular car crash. Negotiation with the container's real owner proves even more difficult and Bangles find himself out of his league (ending up a charred corpse). Davie and Peter manage to escape many close shaves (one by having Peter drive a diesel engine into a warehouse hideout of some crims where blowtorch is the preferred method of torture), and there are many car chases. They are joined in their adventures by Jill, who works for a federal crime commission, and seems to be the one honest person there. (Murray 1995c: 228)

As this outline suggests, *Running from the Guns* is short on suspense but long on thrills and occasional comedy with plenty of movement and action, 167 particularly that associated with cars, including chases, crashes, and ingenious action stunts. Nonetheless, the initial premise of the film, that Dave and Pete are inadvertent victims of the machinations of others, and that this immediately draws them into perilous situations from which they must flee, does conform to Derry's subtype of the genre (1988: 270–320). The guns of the title are everywhere in evidence as the two, often with Jill, are being pursued and are in danger, whether in the night scenes at the docks at the beginning, the chase along the ocean road that ends with the death of Bangles, or the final shootout with the thugs employed by the sinister commercial operation, Auspac, meeting their match in a group of armed dock workers who come to the boys' aid. However, *Running from the Guns* is finally more of a teenpic than a suspense thriller. There is little in the way of moral ambiguity or conflict in play. The three protagonists are bright, confident and upbeat. For them, there is no necessity to learn to trust others as they have never lost this optimism. Derry notes that the protagonists in this variant of the genre usually reach a new moral position as a result of their adventures. However, the innocents in *Running from the Guns* are as pristine and as faultless at the end of the film as they are at its beginning.

Desperate Hours

A well-known narrative device in Hollywood as well as in much other film and fiction is the storyline that pits characters in a race against time. Films with titles such as *Seven Days in May* (1964), *48 Hours* (1982) and *Thirteen Days* (2000) suggest the timeline against which characters in a thriller are striving. In his brief discussion of this type, Derry notes that the protagonist acquires a task she must undertake or a journey she must make as well as accomplishing this within a given time (1988: 321). The struggle is as much to do with days, hours and minutes as it is with enemies and other human agencies. As examples of the time-based thriller, he cites *Fourteen Hours* (1950), *Time Lock* (1957) and *Pursuit* (1970) although he reserves particular praise for *D.O.A.* (1949) which he characterises as a seminal film (1988: 321). *D.O.A.* (Dead On Arrival) was remade in Hollywood in 1994. However, less well known although worth extended consideration is *Colour Me Dead* (1969), an Australian remake of the Hollywood predecessor by visiting American producer Eddie Davis (Verevis 2004). Told in an extended flashback, the film begins with a man, a lawyer, staggering into a police station to announce a murder. Questioned further, he reveals that he is the victim. A week earlier, he was slipped a slow-acting poison in a drink in a bar by an apparent stranger without his knowledge. In the intervening time, he has discovered that he is dying, has found his connection with the stranger and the reason why the latter has sought to kill him. He has also finally confronted his murderer who now also lies dead himself.

A classic of *film noir*, *D.O.A./Colour Me Dead* is obviously a film marked by tension, thrills and suspense in a narrative that does not let up in its emotion and in its pathos. Altogether the film has a drive and an intensity that make it one of the most dramatic examples of this type of suspense thriller, with a cracking pace and narrative movement. Even in the Australian remake, although subject to negative comments at the time of its first release, *Colour Me Dead* remains, as Verevis has shown, a worthy reworking of a fine original.

In a Dangerous Place

If the suspense thriller can be oriented around time, then it can also be confined to a particular setting. An isolated region well away from civilization is an obvious setting for this kind of narrative. At least two films, *The Long Weekend* (1977) and *Lost Things* (2004), have chosen the lonely Australian beach as the site of suspense thrillers that border on the edge of the fantastic and the horror film. The outback is an even more obvious setting. Hence, for instance, the film *Fair Game* (1985) concerns a woman Jessica (Cassandra Delaney) who finds herself in an isolated wildlife sanctuary in the outback. She reports three males who are shooting and skinning protected kangaroos to the police but is treated in a patronising manner. The three then proceed to focus their attention on her and she becomes the hunted (Brown 1995b: 194).

In fact, in its use of general location, the presence of the shooters and the vulnerability of the woman visitor to the area, *Fair Game* is an interesting anticipation of the savagery of *Wolf Creek* (2005). Again, this is a suspense thriller of the Australian outback in the fictional place of its title. Formerly a mining encampment, it is now a ghost town set in the remote outback, one of many such spots that have, according to the film's villainous Mick Taylor (John Jarratt), simply disappeared, been lost. Visiting the area to see a crater, the film's young tourist trio – Lizzie (Kestie Morassi), Kristy (Cassandra McGrath) and Ben (Nathan Phillips) – are lured to the place by this outback shooter who appears to care little whether the 'vermin' that he destroys are wild animals or people. In its early scenes, *Wolf Creek* establishes that all three of the protagonists are of equal importance, thereby setting up the pattern for the nightmare action of the second half. Drugging them with tainted rainwater, Mick separates them so that the film then follows the individual plight of each – Lizzie, followed by Kristy and finally Ben – as they attempt to escape the certain death that they face at Mick's hands.

In between, there is opportunity for various intertextual references, most especially to another figure from the Northern Territory from the film *Crocodile Dundee* (1986). And indeed, Mick Taylor even gets a chance to utter what is destined to become another famous line, in remarking to the blissfully unaware young people at his camp site, 'Nothing tastes as good as rainwater from the Top End'. Similarly, recalling the mugger joke in the latter film ('That's not a knife – this is a knife') helps prepare the viewer for the horrific moment when one of the protagonists lunges at Mick with a pocketknife only to have him slash away a row of fingers with his hunting knife.

The surprise for both the protagonists and the audience occurs when Lizzie wakes to discover her hands and feet tied and hears the screams of Kristy. There follows an escalating series of nightmare incidents that generates a good deal of thrills as well as suspense. The latter particularly have to do with finding car keys, trying to get vehicles started, looking for weapons and, especially, attempting to outdo or outrun the savage force that is Mick Taylor. Equally, *Wolf Creek* also interposes moments of emotional release very much centred on the characters, as they appear to gain some ascendancy over the threat against them. Consider, for instance, the surge of classical music after Lizzie shoots and appears to have killed Mick and the moment on the bitumen highway when Kristy successfully flags down a passing motorist. However, such moments of release turn out to be the first step towards the next bout of heightened suspense and violence. Further compounding this pattern of suspense, thrills and horror is the fact that Mick Taylor is completely familiar and at home in his surroundings and has done this kind of killing many times before. At the end of *Wolf Creek*, the monster has not been vanquished. Instead, he walks nonchalantly off into the landscape, recalling his apparently friendly words to the trio around the campfire that he can just 'pop up anywhere'.

Post Mortem

As this chapter and that on crime have demonstrated, there is a great deal of generic variety in the area of suspense and crime currently being undertaken in Australian cinema. Whatever the case was in the past, both before the Revival and in its early years in the 1970s and early 1980s, the crime thriller is now one of the most popular generic forms so far as Australian film makers and audiences are concerned. Nor should this come as any great surprise. At the beginning of the first chapter of the three devoted to aspects of crime, the burgeoning of fictional writing in this genre in Australia is mentioned. Nor is this nation the only one interested in this type of story as the crime thriller is the most popular international genre of the present time.

Equally, another social tendency should not be ignored. This is the urge to mix the crime thriller with the youth or teen film. The latter type is dealt with at length in the next chapter. Here, though, the genre's immense popularity with youth is noted, as it is the most desirable demographic in the marketplace. Hence, it is worth ending this chapter by noting the recurrence of teenage or youthful protagonists in many of the different subtypes of crime film that have been encountered in Chapter 6 and in this chapter. On the other hand, in Chapter 7 on the detective film, a tendency was noted for that particular genre to stagnate, perhaps because there seems to be no obvious way to fully incorporate this other youthful demographic within its boundaries.

13
The Teenpic

Youth in the Cinema

Unlike some of the other generic classes adopted in this book, there is nothing obscure about the category of the young person/youth/teen film to be explored in this chapter. Even if terms such as 'youth' or 'teenpic' are not in popular use so far as labelling films is concerned, the presence and problems of young people in particular films are regularly registered in synopsis and review. Even so, there is by no means a complete unanimity about this generic category. Pirie (1981), Grant (1977, 1986) and Gehring (1988) do not include films concerning teenagers as a genre. In dealing with Australian film, Murray and Beilby (1980) and Stratton (1990) also omit the teenpic as a class. It is only Neale in a more recent study who recognizes the increasing importance of this type of film (Neale 2000: 118–25). His more recent anthology concerning genre in contemporary Hollywood also pays attention to the genre (Bailey and Hay 2002: 186–204).

However, the general disregard prompts two questions. First, what is one talking about in ascribing this type as a genre? Second, why is the type more important now than it appears to have been in the past? Obviously, a designation if not a definition is necessary to get an inquiry underway. Therefore, Schary will be followed in marking out the social group in question as that of youth aged between twelve and twenty years of age (2002: 1–15). Various names attach to this cohort, including young people, youth and teenagers and these terms are used interchangeably in this chapter. It is one thing, though, to indicate a social category but quite another to define a film genre. To do so, one must consider, no matter how briefly, the economic, social and cultural development of the category of youth over recent years. In turn, this permits a more nuanced consideration of the teenpic.

Teen culture is so much a part of life in the present that it is hard to realize that it has a history and a past. Yet, once upon a time, young people in the years between childhood and adulthood were neither heard nor seen. The teenager, as such, was not a category. Which is not to imply that young people did not exist. Rather, it is their perception that has changed considerably over time, itself an index of complex economic, social and cultural forces at work. In fact, it was soon after World War II that the teenager was constructed as an economic, social and cultural classification. Where once these in-between years had been undifferentiated, amorphous and unfocussed, the term 'teenager' gradually facilitated definition, government, study, celebration and, especially, elongation (Schary 2002: 1–52). The teenpic, which made its first appearance in the early 1950s, most especially in the shape of *Rebel Without a Cause* (1955), was part and parcel of this process of differentiation: at one level a reflection of the interest that financial institutions, social agencies, cultural entrepreneurs and others were showing in the teenager and on another level an active intervention in the debates that were underway.

Since the 1950s and the impact of television on the family audience, Hollywood has been relying on people under thirty years of age to keep attending films, thereby constituting the mainstay and the majority of its audience (Gomery 1992; Bailey and Hay 2002; Schary 2002). Yet the movie industry has been highly ambivalent towards the teenager. Interest in youth subjects has flowed and ebbed so that after an initial burst of engagement in the 1950s, Hollywood interest fell away in the next two decades only to revive again in the 1980s (Dixon 2000: 1–19). By and large, that commitment has been there ever since. Several factors help explain this renewal. For one thing, in the early 1970s television had moved away from programming for mass audiences (typically seen as entailing the family audience) in favour of catering for more specific demographically defined segments (the eighteen-to thirty-nine-year-old grouping was seen as the group with most appeal to advertisers). This reconfiguration had a particular and enduring impact on the look of television with a distinct 'juvenating' occurring in such areas as situation comedy, crime series and teenage drama serials (Saenz 1997; Rogers, Epstein and Reeves 2002).

Meanwhile, hard-top cinemas themselves were also undergoing transformation. The drive-in had already alerted the exhibition industry to the box-office significance of teenagers. With the advent of the multiplex, cinemas became smaller in size and more differentiated in terms of audience even as the overall number of screens across the country increased (Bailey and Hay 2002). A major development here was a new-found relationship between teenagers and public space in the form of the shopping mall (Schary 2002). Replacing older forms, including the milk bar and the pool hall, this new type of retail centre with its arcades and food courts became the locale for teenage congregation and independence. Since the 1970s, Hollywood had been closing many of its hard-top cinemas in older shopping precincts.

Instead, it entered into associations with the new shopping centres whereby blocks of multiple, smaller cinemas were built in the malls. Teenagers in the shopping centres became an obvious target as cinema patrons. To attract this young audience to the multiplex cinema, the teenpic had to be revised and updated.

Over the last twenty-five years, then, the genre has been consolidated as a central and sustaining part of Hollywood's output. And, as suggested below, Australian film makers have also responded to this viewing challenge. Here, though, it is worth noting three related features of the teenpic. First, that despite the ongoing need for the genre so far as this kind of venue and other subsidiary outlets are concerned, there has still been a tendency over the years for output to vary considerably in quantity and quality. A second anomaly that does not operate in relation to other classes of features is the obvious age difference between those who script, direct and produce these films and those who pay to watch them. There is, too, the fact that for those actors filling youthful roles in such films, their tenure in the type generally is likely to prove short-lived indeed.

Critical Perspectives

Given the historical currency of the genre of youth or teenage film, it comes as no surprise to learn of the paucity of critical writing about the type. As both Neale (2000: 118–25) and Schary (2002: 17–25) note, there has been relatively little written about the subject. One of the more notable of this handful is Considine (1985) but his discussion of the representation of adolescence on the big screen only runs up to the early 1980s. More generally, this early work also fails to draw a sharp division between adolescent and teenager, so that even in Considine one finds later cycles accorded no different an emphasis than earlier ones dealing with Andy Hardy, Henry Arliss, Corliss Archer, the Dead End Kids and the Bowery Boys. Accordingly, this chapter's account of the teenpic in Australia is mostly guided by a later author such as Schary, who sees the teenage film really taking off in the late 1970s (2002: 15–25).

Four Types

Unlike other genres that are based on subject matter, the youth genre has to do with the ages of the films' characters. Put another way, the film of adolescence is potentially capable of paralleling and mimicking all the current film genres that involve and concern adults. In practice, though, particular genres, such as subtypes of crime and science fiction, are left alone and not brought within the general domain of youth. Other genres have, though, proved to be more open to cross-fertilization with the teenpic. In any case, what is at work in such hybridization is not so much the simple replacement of adults by adolescents in specific (adult) genres but rather a particular cultural patterning that has to do with notions of different youth behaviours and styles. The teenpic does not develop any new ways of telling stories. One finds such narrative structures as those of the adventure, comedy, horror and thriller genres being deployed. Instead, what is different and distinct is the particular style and themes at work in the teenpic. Based on the analysis of subject matter in over 500 films produced since around 1980, Schary has suggested the existence of six particular subtypes of the Hollywood youth film. These are the horror film, the science/technology film, the sex comedy, the romantic melodrama, the juvenile delinquent drama and the school film (2002: 22–5).

As already suggested in previous chapters, the Australian cinema is by no means a direct imitator or slavish adherent of developments in Hollywood. This again turns out to be the case so far as teen film subtypes are concerned. Although he accords it separate status, Schary admits that there are few films that conform to his category of teen science, which begins with the film *War Games* (1983) and has to do with adolescent use of such technologies as electronic games and computers. There is nothing equivalent in Australian film output so that this category is omitted. On the other hand, as Chapter 11 has argued, social realism is an important class in local cinema so that one might expect this to prove fertile ground for the teenpic. Varying Schary's typology, the remainder of this chapter deals with four major classes of the film of adolescence to be found in Australian cinema.

School and Schoolies

Schary has written at some length about the school film, defining it as a central subgenre of the teen film (2002: 26–79). Although earlier films such as *Rebel Without a Cause* (1955) helped inaugurate the connection between the teenager and the school, this focus was not resumed until *The Breakfast Club* (1985), which actually inaugurates the contemporary phase of the school teenpic cycle. In this genre, the educational building becomes not only a location of the action but also a symbolic site for the development of social evolution on the part of teenagers who learn from and also chafe against both their elders in the form of teachers and others and from their peers (Schary 2002: 26–8). Matters of class, gender, ethnicity and popularity are negotiated. In addition, individual growth in physical and emotional terms also takes place both in the school and in the surrounding society. Various character types can be identified in such a setting: these include teachers, nerds, rebels and athletes. Overall, the school drama has had a good deal of currency in Hollywood and this is more than duplicated, albeit in miniature, in Australian popular culture.

Indeed, if television was anything to go by, then there was already a nascent Australian tradition with plenty of precedents and parallels for the Australian school-based teenpics that began to appear in local cinema from the late 1970s onwards. The first of the TV predecessors was *Class of 74/75* (1974–75) which was soon followed by *Glenview High* (1977–78), *Starting Out* (1983), *Neighbours* (1985–), *Home and Away* (1987–) and *Heartbreak High* (1994–95). Several of these dramas were open-ended serials and their multiple narratives were more than equipped to incidentally include many stories that concerned school, teachers and students. Hence, when Australian film makers decided in the early 1980s to concentrate on some of the same topics and stories, a rich background of narrative and iconography was already in place on the small screen. In fact, one of the many functions that this body of school-based television drama would render was to provide a repertory of performers who would take up roles in teenpics on the big screen. This unofficial repertory company of actors would, over the years, include Noah Taylor, Kylie Minogue, Jason Donovan, Russell Crowe, Guy Pearce, Vince Colosimo, Nicole Kidman, Heath Ledger and many others.

Arguably, the trend towards school-based youth dramas began in the mid 1970s but was not specifically recognized because of the subtype's insertion within the historical period film. Thus, the first phase of the film of school-based adolescence in Australia ran a short three years from 1975 to 1977 with relevant films including *Picnic at Hanging Rock* (1975), *The Devil's Playground* (1976), *The Getting of Wisdom* (1977), *The Mango Tree* (1977) and, belatedly, *Emma's War* (1985). However, modern-day school-based adolescent dramas kicked in from the early 1980s and have continued down to the present. A representative roll call would include *Puberty Blues* (1981), *Fighting Back* (1982), *Street Hero* (1984), *Fast Talking* (1985), *Bloodmoon* (1989), *Flirting* (1991), *The Heartbreak Kid* (1993), *Kick* (1999), *Looking for Alibrandi* (2000) and *Hating Alison Ashley* (2005). Many of these films are interesting, rich and frequently compelling representations of boys and girls negotiating the hazards of adolescence in a school-based or school-related setting. Nor are they confined to this locale or community and frequently extend their web of relations to include such elders as teachers, parents, grandparents and siblings.

It is beyond the scope of this chapter to trace the web of imagery, themes, characters and narratives operating in this group of films in any detail. Instead, this chapter takes one of these films, *The Heartbreak Kid*, as a means of pinpointing some of these patterns in more detail. The film is certainly worth such attention. It did good business at the box office at the time of its release and, subsequently, spun off into an equally popular television series, *Heartbreak High*. However, despite its title, *The Heartbreak Kid* does in fact divide its narrational attention between two protagonists, teacher Christina (Claudia Karvan) and student Nick Polides (Alex Dimitriades) who become romantically and sexually entangled. Set in a state high school in inner-suburban Melbourne, it follows the relationship of the two brought together by dint of the classroom and the sports field. Both are members of the local Greek-Australian community but find themselves occupying very different positions there. Christina is the daughter of a wealthy local figure and is engaged to Dimitri (Steve Bastoni), a businessman with ambitions to become a councillor and an identity in the community. Alex, on the other hand, comes from a poor Greek-Australian family, with only a younger sister and a father after the death some time earlier of his mother. His father, George Polides, although once a remarkable soccer player, having been part of the Greek national team, now works at a car assembly plant and has just been laid off work.

The film is very clear about the social and economic forces at work in the school and in the lives of Christina and Nick. Power runs along ethnic, gender, age and sporting lines. Hence, Christina struggles to persuade Nick and several of her other students of the value and necessity of school work and accomplishment even as other teachers, most especially Brian Southgate (William McInnes), believe that all that lies before them are menial unskilled jobs such as that in the car assembly plant. Soccer is dubbed a 'wog game' and Brian is determined not to share the school's sports field, instead preserving it as the domain of a more Anglo-Celtic form of football in the shape of Australian Rules. The affair between Christina and Nick is part of a displacement of this struggle in terms of highlighting other issues.

Unlike some other films in the Australian school film cycle, such as *The Mango Tree* and *Fast Talking*, there is no suggestion here that for the woman teacher and the younger male student this is the first time they have had sexual intercourse. Rather the reverse. Christina has had sex with her fiancé Dimitri. In addition, her Greek girlfriend, who lends Christina her flat for the affair, positively encourages her to take lovers as this will enhance her sexual attractiveness for her husband-to-be. *The Heartbreak Kid* is silent as to whether or not Nick is a virgin when they first make love. In fact, it does subtly suggest otherwise. There is at least a hint that

Nick is relatively experienced when some girls in his class invite him to a party at a house vacated by parents for the weekend. Neither Nick nor Christina confesses inexperience when they are first together. In fact, when the affair becomes public, Christina is not accused of seducing him but instead of violating both her own engagement and her professional standing as a schoolteacher.

Despite the age difference between Christina and Nick, *The Heartbreak Kid* suggests that the two are in fact at a similar stage of life so far as outlook and emotional needs are concerned. In fact, the film's style carries this same sense of the liberating effect that the relationship has for the two. As Conomos has written:

> ... the multiple camera and vivid visual style of the film, with its apt handheld camera scenes, gives *The Heartbreak Kid* the right kind of kinetic edge. It accentuates the dynamic character of Nick's world and personality and, at the same time, suggests the imminent consummation of the relationship between the teacher and her student. (Conomos 1995: 360)

At the end of the film, the promise is that the two will reunite although they will pursue study over the two years of deliberate separation. Christina has been a subject of Greek-Australian patriarchy in her own home and risks again falling under its sway when she marries Dimitri. Nick is seen as liberating, offering her some of the joys of adolescence hitherto denied her. At the same time, the film is ambiguous about elements of this relationship in terms of the extent to which she is inadvertently swapping one form of patriarchy for another. After all, it is Nick who has pursued Christina. A cutaway shot to her legs from his point of view as she hands out assignments in the classroom clearly suggests the sexual nature of his attraction although he later claims that she is 'coming on' to him. While she is attracted to him, the fact that he sees the development in these patriarchal terms causes the viewer to take a somewhat more detached view of the relationship.

Teen Horror

Meanwhile, a second subtype of the teenpic turns its back on those conventions of the ordinary and the everyday in favour of a class that is more deliberately dramatic and rhetorical. Schary traces the type back to the film *Carrie* (1980), with the hybrid at its height in Hollywood in the early 1980s. In cycles of films, most especially those to do with *Halloween* (1978, 1981, 1982, 1988, 1989, 1995, 1998, 2002), *Friday the 13th* (1980, 1981, 1982, 1984,

1985, 1986, 1988, 1993, 2001, 2003) and *A Nightmare on Elm Street* (1984, 1985, 1987, 1988, 1989, 1991, 1994, 2003), the new variant laid more emphasis on graphic violence than on horror (Schary 2002: 137–79). According to Clover (1992), the teen horror subgenre depended on traditional ideas of misfortune befalling transgressors of purity, only now such sins as premarital sex and adolescent indulgence brought about punishment not so much by social branding and outcry by bodies such as parents, school and the law but rather retribution at the hands of more sinister and overwhelming forces.

The horror film has been dealt with in Chapter 8. Here, the concern is with a recent tendency in Australian film making, following its earlier appearance in Hollywood, to combine the youth film with the tale of terror. Local films exploring this vein are all recent and include *Bloodmoon* (1990), *Cut* (2000), *Moloch* (2000) and *Lost Things* (2004). In addition, it should be noted that *Wolf Creek* (2005), while hovering in a hinterland between horror and the suspense thriller, also features three young people becoming victims of a homicidal madman. Although the trio are young adults rather than teenagers, the film has excellent credentials to be included in the category under consideration. However, rather than enumerating Australian examples of the type, it is more pertinent to identify classes. Two particular kinds of teen horror films can be pinpointed.

The first is the slasher, the graphically violent horror film and it can be represented here by *Cut*. The plot concerns a fictional slasher film, *Hot Blood*, that was in production in 1985 when the director was murdered and the film stopped. Some fourteen years later, a group of students decide to complete the film. Cast and crew return to the country house where the original filming took place. However, murder is soon unleashed again as a masked figure runs amok using sharpened garden shears to deadly effect. In a Grand Guignol of blood, slashed throats and bodies, in the usual tradition of the horror film, the monster is destroyed although the ending also suggests the figure's imminent return. Altogether, *Cut* is a latter-day exercise in the slasher tradition, with the film student teenagers quoting such precedents as *Friday the 13th* and *The Texas Chainsaw Massacre* (1974) in relation to *Hot Blood*, which also self-reflexively applies to *Cut*. In other words, this Australian venture into teen slasher horror is long on thrills and suspense even if only routine so far as horror is concerned.

A second subtype of the teen horror film has to do with the supernatural. *Lost Things* is an interesting instance, bordering as it does on the uncanny and the extraordinary rather than being located within the more melodramatic excesses of the horror genre. Indeed, the film even has strong claims to being a modern teen ghost story. Like *Moloch*, the film concerns four young people who leave the safety of the city for a lonely isolated place. Where the latter film takes its foursome to a mining site that is clearly haunted and where things start to go wrong, the former film follows its schoolkid protagonists – Emily (Lenka Kripac), Brad (Charlie Garber), Tracy (Alex Vaughan) and Garry (Leon Ford) – as they drive to a lonely beach to camp, surf and, the boys hope, have sex. Even before they arrive there, there are intimations of things out of joint – schoolgirl Emily is seen in the credits spending time with an older man in army khaki although she claims to her parents that she has not been seeing anyone behind boyfriend Brad's back; a wreath of faded flowers is seen on the sand; Brad has an arresting feeling of déjà vu when they interrupt their journey to check directions; the combie drives in five circles before pulling onto the highway.

Lost Things is highly cinematic in terms of creating a story that appears to blend past and a recurring present into an uncanny timelessness. The four meet a beachcomber Zippo (Steve Le Marquand), who warns them to leave the place because three people disappeared there and one was found dead. Meanwhile, the chain of strange events continues with deft use of cinematography, editing, *mise en scène* and soundtrack to loosen and disconnect time and causality. Motifs recur, elements of scenes are repeated, the sense of ominous brooding continues. It is only when Emily sees her grief-stricken mother place the wreath of flowers on the sand and realizes that she cannot see or hear the teenagers standing nearby that the audience grasps the fact that the remaining trio are indeed 'lost', caught in some weird situation between life and death. As the reprise shot of the combie circling before turning back to the highway at the end of the film suggests, the teenagers are now locked in a perpetual circularity that merges past, present and future.

Lost Things is clearly a film in the wake of *The Blair Witch Project* (1999). Displaying interesting continuities with an earlier Australian excursion into the uncanny, *The Long Weekend* (1976), it substitutes teenagers for an older, married couple. In truth, the fact that the foursome are adolescents is part of what makes *Lost Things* so painful and poignant. The four, most especially Emily and Brad, stand on the edge of sexual maturity, a stage of life that attracts but also confounds them. As Brad, confessing his virginity to his cousin Garry, agonises: 'Next year I'm going to be an adult. I don't even know what an adult is'. And in a more diffused and less explicit way, Emily's sexuality may in fact have played an important role in the chain of circumstances that has led the teenagers to the place in the first instance although she is not the kind of sexual transgressor that has frequently been identified in Hollywood horror films of the 1970s and 1980s (Clover 1992). In any case, whatever the particular chain of events, these young people must forever remain at the threshold between adolescence and adulthood, perpetually paralysed between the two states. This note forms an obvious prelude to yet another subtype of the youth film.

Coming of Age

Although any of the years between twelve and twenty might be the ages of the protagonists in the youth film, there is a clear tendency to concentrate on the later years as those marking the passage from adolescence to adulthood. Clearly, with the well-documented fact of the age of youths' first experience of sexual intercourse dropping across Western countries, it is no surprise to find the teenpic invading yet another genre of adult cinema in terms of the representation of love and sex. Schary principally deals with the cinematic rite of passage in the genre of adolescence through themes of romantic and sexual passion (2002: 209–54). Caputo has also adopted the same terms in examining three Australian films in this subtype of the teenpic (1993: 12–16). The fact is that various other elements come into play in relation to the process of initiation. Elsewhere, it has been suggested that relationships in Australian television soap opera occur, for the most part, outside the work situation and can be divided into three types – those to do with family, those to do with friendship and those to do with romance (Moran 1985: 190–205). This schema also constitutes a useful starting point in relation to the coming-of-age film, especially when one realises the inevitable overlaps and necessary synergies between the three types.

Love and sex acquire special significance and attraction during the teenage years. The restless years of adolescence, especially involving the struggle to negotiate the physical and emotional changes occurring – teenagers fall in love, get crushes, wonder about their sexuality, learn to flirt, renegotiate a sense of their changing bodies, puzzle about romance and sex and how these fit together – provide plenty of scope and subject matter for the teen film of amorous and bodily desire. Love and sex between a couple can occur with partners of different ages, as is the case with *The Heartbreak Kid*. Other films involving a younger male and an older female include *The Mango Tree*, *Devil in the Flesh* (1993) and, more tangentially, *Hammers over the Anvil* (1993). On the other hand, romantic and carnal passion also occur among young people more equal in years as part of the process of a coming of age. Some of the films that variously fall under this heading include *Street Hero* (1984), *Windsurfer* (1986), *The Year My Voice Broke* (1987), *Flirting* (1991), *The Nostradamus Kid* (1993), *All Men Are Liars* (1995), *Kick* (1999), *Bootmen* (2000), *Garage Days* (2002), and *One Perfect Day* (2004).

181

Flirting is especially interesting in this context in that it elides a difference in age between the female and the male in favour of a difference in ethnicity, class, politics and social background between the boy and girl lovers, a formula that would be taken up again in the television mini series *Marking Time* (2003). Danny Embling (Noah Taylor) is a nerd, a boarding student at St Albans, a boys' boarding college, but very much a reader and a loner. His restricted attempt at rebellion against the school's sporting ethos attracts the attention of Thandiwe Adjewa (Thandie Newton), a student at a sister school who is neglected by the girl students because of her Ugandan background and black skin. The two develop a relationship of friendship, love and eventually sex even as political events in Uganda are moving them apart. What is so appealing about *Flirting* is the deepening relationship between the two. Neither is classically glamorous or attractive, yet when they call each other beautiful, they are talking about their grace and charm as young human beings reaching out to further extend their sense of themselves and that of the world. The film ends *in medias res* – boy has met girl, got girl, lost girl but may get her back again. Whether or not *Flirting* was the second part of an intended trilogy on the part of John Duigan, the film's director, is not clear (*The Year My Voice Broke* was set three years earlier in 1962 and featured the same male protagonist). Instead, what is clear is that the film is able to take advantage of the fact that it is a teenpic by mapping the possible future of the relationship onto the emotional and physical future of the young man making the transition from adolescence to manhood.

However, as already suggested, the path of love and sex is only one route to the attainment of adulthood witnessed to in the Australian teenpic. Another shorter cycle concerning friendship is also part of the cinema of Australian youth. What is being considered here is not only *Puberty Blues* and *Muriel's Wedding*, where it is the filial love of two people for one another that helps them both to make the transition from adolescence to adulthood. Nor is it the fact that in both films the main characters are both female that is crucial. As the more recent *Australian Rules* (2002) shows, what is important in these films concerning the getting of wisdom is the fact that each of the two people finds solace and support in the other in the face of a social environment that is indifferent, if not hostile. In all three films, the rites of passage also involve a spatial transcendence of place with the couples in the two latter films actually moving elsewhere.

One further pattern in the Australian teenage film relating to rites of passage from adolescent to young adult concerns a different form of relationship on the part of the youthful protagonist. This has to do with an offspring-parent connection, very frequently to do with a father rather than a mother. Such a connection appears to be a highly charged relationship,

The social realist teenpic: Australian Rules *(2002). Image courtesy of Palace Films.*

whether the adolescent is a boy or girl. Indeed, Adrian Martin draws attention to Routt's passing remarks about the film *Jenny Kissed Me* (1986) in the context of noticing the frequently intense, ambiguous and perverse relations between fathers and daughters in Australian cinema (1995e: 199). In fact, the father figure in this film is not the biological father to the teenager, thus extending the range and emotional currents possible in relation to this subtype. Again, an inventory of some of the relevant Australian examples confirms the insight of Routt and Martin. Appropriate films include *The Coolangatta Gold* (1984), *Street Hero* (1984), *The Still Point* (1985), *Watch the Shadows (1986), Jenny Kissed Me* (1986), *Love in Limbo* (1993), *Initiation*

183

(1997), *Two Hands* (1999), *Looking for Alibrandi* (2000), *Dirty Deeds* (2002), and *Swimming Upstream* (2002).

Various of these offspring-father links have been noticed elsewhere in this book, so here only *Looking for Alibrandi* is mentioned. Unlike several representations of the male-male connection which end with the young man finally abandoning or disavowing the tie, this film includes Josie Alibrandi's growing relationship with her recently discovered father, Michael Andretti (Anthony La Paglia). For Josie (Pia Miranda) this linking occurs in her turbulent senior year at the exclusive Sydney girls' college, St Martha's. The film is based on a very popular teenage novel by Melina Marchetta, who had a major hand in the screenplay for the film. *Looking for Alibrandi* is intimately concerned with rites of passage for the teenager as she struggles to get a real sense of herself and those around her, including her mother Nora (Greta Scacchi) and grandmother, as well as two boys from other schools and, most especially, her newly acquired father who himself has just discovered that he had a daughter after a teenage romance with Nora. In a film that crackles with pace, vitality and engaging wit, Josie comes to realize that nothing is safe or fixed. One of the boys, John Barton (Matthew Newton), who seems enormously secure in his world actually feels under great pressure about the future and commits suicide; while the other boy Jason Coke (Kick Gurry), who is more underprivileged, turns out to have lost his mother when he was younger. As Josie stands on the threshold of adult life, she finally realises what she does have, especially the love not only of two very strong women in the shape of her mother and grandmother but also that of her newly acquired father.

Rebels and Delinquents

A final subtype of the youth film has to do with those films that trace the actions of young people caught in the throes of rebellion against elements of the social system. Again, there are obvious overlaps with some of the categories already discussed in different chapters but, nevertheless, this class allows for further groupings of the youth film. In such films, nonconformity may be directed against family and parents, against school, the law, other social institutions or, more generally, against the world at large. It may be inadvertent, a means of having fun, or deliberate, a more systematic attempt to transgress social limits and boundaries. Like the 'rites-of-passage' film, this subtype also concerns an adolescent gaining of identity and a sense of independence, although in this case those involved are on their way to becoming outsiders, outlaws, even criminals. Some of the various

184

avenues leading towards this transgression include motor bikes and cars, music, drugs, sex, prostitution and guns. Rebellious and delinquent style and action are important both as a sign of defiance and as the acting out of an empowerment. Films frequently celebrate rebellion, finding their spectacle and thrills in situations of danger and daring. As Schary notes about the type, the audience is often in the company of youth involved in thrill-seeking and the pursuit of pleasure (2002: 80–136).

Again, this subtype yields a significant number of Australian examples, whose roots date back to at least *The FJ Holden* (1977) and continue down to the recent present with titles such as *Ned Kelly* (2003) and *One Perfect Day* (2004). Two brief discussions must do service for the type. The films in question are *Metal Skin* (1994), one of the last of the boy-meets-car cycle already noted, and *The Delinquents* (1989), which is oriented towards music and the female. Although *Metal Skin* initially focusses on Joe (Aden Young), a youth of Romanian origin living with his father in desolate circumstances, who yearns for a girlfriend and to attain winning prowess with a hotted-up car, the film soon broadens its concerns, interweaving three other lives, those of Savina (Tara Morice), Ros (Nadine Garner) and Dazey (Ben Mendelsohn). Although all of them invest emotionally in Dazey, the latter repeatedly proves incapable of loyalty or love, resulting in the eventual deaths of both Savina and Joe. The latter is killed in a car crash after a suicidal race between Joe and Dazey in the railway yards that had earlier featured as the site of dangerous car racing, scenes whose great forebear is of course *Rebel Without a Cause* (1955). However, mention of the seminal forerunner serves to underline the despair and desolation underlining the Australian film as against the optimism of its predecessor. Although a little too prone towards the use of surrealism and conscious symbolism, the narrative of *Metal Skin* and, especially, its ending – with Ros and Dazey wandering dazed and wounded along alley after alley of large containers as Dazey mindlessly repeats 'I won, I won' and while the dead Joe slumps at the wheel of his car – offers a nihilistic conclusion to the acts of delinquency and rebellion of the young people.

As its name suggests, *The Delinquents* also attempts to address adolescence and rebellion. However, despite the plurality of the title, the film does in fact concentrate on Lola (Kylie Minogue) and especially the efforts of society in the shape of mother, foster carer, courts and remand school to police her sexuality. Set initially in rural Australia in the 1950s, it links the rebellion of young lovers Lola and Brownie (Charlie Slather) with the emergent sounds of rock-and-roll. The young teenager falls in love and shortly she is pregnant. After an enforced abortion, the two are separated and Brownie follows his dream to roam the world by becoming a merchant seaman. Lola meanwhile drifts close to prostitution and, being under age, is again separated when sent to remand school. After a suitable burst of delinquency in the shape of a colourful riot by all the girls, Lola serves out her time, decides to adopt the baby child of a dead friend and finally has Brownie renounce his vision of freedom and settle with her in marriage back in their home town.

As this outline suggests, *The Delinquents* deals with teenage rebellion and lawlessness only in the most cursory manner. Indeed, Lola's irrepressible sexuality is more evident in dialogue than on the screen. As Martin suggests, the film is far more a melodramatic morality tale than it is a teenpic of youthful misbehaviour (1995f: 274). Based on her own experiences, Lola appears to come to appreciate some of the norms of conventional morality even if she brings more joy and pleasure to such a regime than those around her. Brownie, too, abandons his youthful dreams and accepts marriage and an immediate nuclear family. (Although the film also tries to assert that the two will carry fun and joy into married life by having them dance with the baby to 'Lucille' as the final credits roll.) Martin sees this narrative trajectory finally moving the film into another category entirely – the women's melodrama:

> Like many of Hollywood's melodramatic heroines, Lola is presented as a woman imprisoned within a strict gender role. Her dreams of escape are no less socially conditioned – she is a sucker for the grand romantic fantasies . . . Completing this knot of patriarchal oppression, Brownie is, for much of the story, off on his own gender trip, sailing the high seas with his symbolic father figure. (Martin 1995f: 274)

Put another way, *The Delinquents* promises to be a contemporary film concerning adolescence. Yet in its confusions surrounding the matter of sexuality and love, it soon loses any semblance of social grounding or interest. Instead, chance, coincidence and ellipses come to the fore as the melodramatic trajectory moves its heroine back to where she came from, a so-called wiser and sadder figure after the moral vicissitudes to which she has been subjected.

Roll Call

As the various discussions contained in this chapter have indicated, the Australian teenpic has been a form much used over the past quarter century. In this respect, it forms a significant extension, parallel and alternative to the various fictional drama series and serials of youth in evidence on Australian television since the mid 1970s. The other obvious antecedents and examples lie in the Hollywood films of adolescence that began appearing in the late

1970s, which have been a part of the industry's output since that time. In particular, the discussion here has focussed on four specific types of the genre – those concerning the institution of the school including schooling, teachers and students; the mongrel breed of the youth film and the horror film; the onset of adult identity and the place therein of love, friendship and sex; and the attraction of social defiance, rebellion, delinquency and lawlessness. Not surprisingly, the ever-burgeoning body of films forming the genre displays a great deal of variety and significance in matters of narrative, imagery and ideological themes and there is certainly now the need for more substantial studies that go beyond the confines of a single chapter.

As is the case with other film classes discussed in this book, generic hybridity is also very much in evidence. Conventions of adventure, comedy, romance and horror have all been adapted by the Australian teenpic as a means of ordering and structuring materials. As mentioned in the last section, the film of adolescence is also not above adopting some of the conventions of yet another, more amorphous genre, that of the melodrama or women's film. It is to this category that the last chapter of this study turns.

14
Women's Film

Melodrama – The Standard Account

A good deal of uncertainty surrounds the category of the women's film. Among the authors on Hollywood genres examined in Chapter 1, Pirie comes closest to this type under the heading of the romance and, perhaps, drama (1981). Grant prefers to discuss the type under the generic name of the erotic (1977, 1986), while Gehring does not include this class of film in his collection, opting instead to deal with it under the category of the melodrama (1988). Neale also brackets the genre with melodrama, treating the type as a highly problematic class alongside *film noir* which he sees as equally perplexing in terms of definition, example, subtypes and history (2000: 179–204). Both of these types – the women's film/melodrama and *film noir* – have received a great deal of critical attention from film scholars over almost four decades, yet the research shows a surprising lack of critical unanimity or resolution about several aspects of their particular subjects. Critical matters still on the table include – what are the important films in the specific oeuvre; whether the type in question is a genre, a mode, a cycle or something else; how to develop a reliable definition; and, what are the important subtypes of each.

Putting aside some of the other terms mentioned, one must – in returning to the point of this chapter – ask which is the more critically useful term, 'melodrama' or 'women's film'? To answer such a question, Neale proceeds by breaking this down into a series of mini discussions dealing with these two types and issues separately. He begins with the matter of melodrama. The latter notion, he suggests, found critical validation at an apposite time in the development of academic film studies. In 1972, Thomas Elsaesser published his article, 'Tales of Sound and Fury', in the journal *Monogram* (1972: 2–15). Elsaesser's essay was a sustained argument in favour of taking the notion of melodrama seriously, as a means of understanding what he saw as key Hollywood films from the 1950s directed by Douglas Sirk, Vincente Minnelli and Nicholas Ray. Where the epithet had previously been a term in popular

188

vocabulary describing either a visual form of action and thrills in cinema or a pejorative label for failed or non-credible drama, Elsaesser revalorised the term. In his essay, melodrama was a critical expression that could sum up a type of film making that was highly expressive and even excessive in form and style to the point of critically distancing and disengaging an audience from what was happening on screen.

In turn, this articulation of new terms for the discussion of the family melodrama proved to be highly attractive and intoxicating to film researchers. As Neale observes, the label of melodrama was deployed in what he calls the standard account by such writers as Mulvey, Nowell-Smith, Gledhill, Johnson, Cook, Modleski, Kaplan, Klinger and others, where it drew on a wide range of cultural theory having to do with psychoanalysis, feminism, ideology, hegemony and literary modernism, to name but a few areas of knowledge (2000: 181–8). As Bordwell has suggested, the elaboration of this kind of conceptual machinery was part of larger intellectual struggles of the time including the quest to have film studies gain a central place within humanities curricula in universities, an undertaking that was entirely successful (1989: 1–18).

Yet there are various problems associated with this critical paradigm. First is the fact that this orthodoxy fails to be clear about the scope and nature of the term melodrama (Neale 2000; Mercer and Shingler 2004). Is one talking about a mode, a cycle or a genre? The designation of the family melodrama also raises the problem of whether there are other kinds of filmic melodrama and, if so, then what is their status? A further worry related to this is that various authors, starting with Elsaesser himself, are highly non-specific when it comes to explaining just what are the poetics of film melodrama. Instead, as instanced by Cook, matters of theory are pursued at the expense of considerations of pattern, style and theme in the films under consideration (2002). A fourth problem is one pointed out by Neale (2000: 184) and has to do with the fact that many writers on film melodrama betray a good deal of historical ignorance about the deployment of the term in earlier periods of Hollywood cinema. As he shows, melodrama was a label in common use in both the industry and in popular reviewing. The designation was used without any gender disposition and suggested a mode of film marked by spectacle and action, so that one synonym for melodrama might be 'thriller'.

Other Accounts

This last objection is especially interesting in implying that there is at least a popular alternative to the sense of film melodrama that has come down

189

as the standard account of the category. In fact, two other approaches are worth sketching.

The first has the advantage of taking into consideration the earlier use of the term melodrama, a blind spot so far as the standard account is concerned. It also has the virtue of organising the melodrama in relation to a series of other genres, another area mostly untouched by the standard approach. Meanwhile, the second account, offered by David Bordwell in his discussion of narration in the fiction film, has the advantage of specifying how melodrama functions as a form of narration.

In contrast to the theoreticist account, Michael Walker in an article in the magazine *Movie* in 1982 drew attention to a different way of regarding film melodrama (1982: 2–38) and Neale has recently drawn attention to this model (2000). According to Walker (who is echoed and endorsed by Neale), it is necessary to differentiate between two broad types of film melodrama. The first he labels as 'action melodrama', a type that includes the various subgenres of the adventure story already discussed including the jungle, combat and war film, the swashbuckler film, the western, the epic and the disaster film as well as crime thrillers, horror and science fiction. All of these deploy coincidence and chance in moving forward their narrative concerns. Hence, a descriptive term such as 'melodrama' is appropriate as is another label, 'thriller'. This kind of film usually involves a struggle between the hero and an adversary or enemy although in some cases the contest may be with the physical world and surroundings. Adventure heroines also turn up in this type although such a variation is the exception rather than the rule. For the most part, women characters are peripheral to such action although usually a series of subsidiary positions is available.

On the other hand, Walker draws attention to a second type of melodrama that he calls the 'melodrama of passion'. In this case, 'the involvement is not with the external dynamic of action but rather with the internal trauma of passion' (Walker 1982: 17). This second type can find embodiment in other genres including the women's film, comedy and the romance. And as their names imply, these particular types are intimately concerned with a gendered subject, although various male types and figures are also central to some of the concerns and ideological issues embodied in the broad category (Haskell 1973: 1–14; Affron 1982: 14–22; Basinger 1993: 1–45; Neale 2000: 179–88).

This is a highly pertinent and useful distinction in the present context. It helps in the demarcation of a particular type of melodrama and, in turn, also allows the researcher to see connections with the women's film. The designation facilitates consideration of some helpful remarks regarding narration in melodrama provided by Bordwell (1985: 70–3). This researcher characterizes the melodrama as a narrative concerned with emotional states and impact. Such narration has to do with a genre that is highly communicative concerning plot elements and mostly unrestrictive in range. Such an approach to film story telling maximizes the audience's desire to know what will happen next and, particularly, to notice how any specific character will react to what has occurred (1985: 72). Altogether, the melodrama (or the melodrama of passion) insists on a communicativeness that justifies shifts that reveal a range of emotional experiences. Bordwell notes a 'stylization' that is frequently detected in melodrama and which stems from a heightened narrative self-consciousness joined to a 'high degree of communicativeness, especially about emotional conditions and effects' (1985: 73).

Female Cinema

The final element of this introduction has to do with a brief survey of the term used as synonym or alternative to melodrama, namely the 'women's film'. Three kinds of accounts can be indicated here. The first is the approach that links screen image and industry and is interested in the woman both before and behind the camera (cf. Kaplan 1983; Butler 2002). Such accounts tend to concentrate on the women's film in particular decades such as the 1940s and are not especially helpful in relation to other periods closer to the present, a point conceded by Cook (2002).

Meanwhile, a second focus is provided by Basinger (1993) who, following an earlier lead by Haskell (1973), is ready to consider a far wider range of films other than family melodrama of the 1940s and 1950s as constituting the women's film. Basinger is especially interesting and useful. Not only is she alive to matters regarding narrative structure, imagery and ideology in Hollywood between 1930 and 1960 but she also writes in a highly accessible form, which is not always the case with various other writers interested in this genre. According to Basinger, the women's film includes not only the melodrama of passion and romance but also a wide range of other types in which the woman is prominent including adventure, comedy and crime. Similarly, Affron (1982) is also concerned with this genre of cinema. However, his particular focus concerns the affective qualities of such films and his purpose is to extend the range and vocabulary of emotional concepts through which the melodrama of passion can be analysed. Taking the term 'sentiment' as a key concept, Affron shows how the women's film has proceeded to tie the term to a range of situations, stories and characters, thereby considerably extending its range and resonance.

Altogether, using the label 'women's film' rather than 'melodrama', one is directed to part of the framing discourse of a particular kind of cinema that has immediate resonance in Australia. What might be broadly described as the women's film appears at least as early as *Jedda* (1955) and runs down to the recent present with films such as *Peaches* (2005) and *Little Fish* (2005). The women's film is, one might say, a major genre in the category of the melodrama of passion so that one issue that must be addressed is the inclusiveness or otherwise of such a type. As already implied, one of the most interesting accounts that leans in the former direction is that provided by Basinger (1993). Her particular focus is on this kind of film in Hollywood in the period 1930 to 1960. She defines the genre as follows:

> A women's film is one that places at the centre of its universe a female who is trying to deal with the emotional, social, and psychological problems that are specifically connected to the fact that she is a woman. These problems are made concrete by various plot developments, and since they are contradictory, they are represented in the story as a form of choice that the woman must make between options that are usually exclusive. (Basinger 1993: 505–6)

Because she is dealing with a period in which the Production Code was in operation in Hollywood such that the woman faced an impossible and irreconcilable choice of options, Basinger's account must be modified to suit a different time where such tragic alternatives do not necessarily operate. Be that as it may, the study has one major strength. This is that she treats the films as a generically coherent body of work and is aware of the need to trace a consistent pattern of form, style and discourse across the films of the period. To do so, Basinger examines women not only in what she calls 'the woman's world' (1993: 213–56) but also focusses on 'the woman in a man's world' (1993: 445–85). Put another way, the emphasis not only falls on those films centred on the home and family that have been recognised in the term 'the family melodrama' but also follows women into other settings and plots including those of crime and adventure. Her account constitutes an assertion that the women's film has to do not only with the melodrama of passion but also the melodrama of action.

The second writer, already mentioned, helpful in the matter of the women's film is Affron (1982). Without going as far as Basinger, he suggests that this second broad type of melodrama has to do with women characters in central roles in films that variously emphasize their vulnerability, powerlessness and passivity. Such films have to do with sentiment and feeling and frequently are tear-jerkers, not only in the reaction of audiences but also in the behaviour of characters. Above all, this kind of film involves broad emotional states on the part of the characters and often has a broad emotional impact on viewers. Again, as Bordwell notes (1985: 70–3), characters usually speak their minds so that nothing is held back. Instead, the generic impulse is to let it all hang out.

According to Affron, narrative structures deployed in this kind of cinema include a range of both happy and sad occasions with the plot often zigzagging between the two (1982: 11–51). Indeed, chance and coincidence not only guarantee surprise but also help to shift the action from one sphere to the other. Some of the former may consist of first meetings, dates, courtship, making love, anniversaries, celebrations and weddings, while the latter can encompass misalliances, initial or later repulsions, fatal misunderstandings, doomed love affairs, departures, betrayal, divorce, illness, death and funerals (Affron 1982: 30–45). Clearly, males are important cogs in such machinery but nevertheless women are central. And, indeed, the melodrama of passion can include films that concentrate on other relationships between a woman and another person, most especially those to do with offspring. In other words, as Neale points out, a series of different familial and related positions are available for women in this kind of film, which can include daughter, wife, mother, fiancée or would-be wife, 'other woman' or indeed the overlap of several of these (Neale 2000: 189–90).

Towards an Australian Tradition

It is time then to make more explicit connections between these observations and Australian cinema. In the remainder of this chapter, the focus is on four films that are reasonably representative of work in the genre. Obviously, there are many cycles and trajectories in feature film output since the Revival that belong to a large, multifarious tradition of the Australian women's film. Breen (1995: 127), for instance, has called attention to a 'feminist' cycle of narrative features that runs from at least *Journey Among Women* (1977) to *High Tide* (1987), while Collins has also written expansively on the general subject of women in the coming-of-age cycle in Australian cinema (1999b: 411–14). To emphasize the existence of other strains, four films have been chosen that can be seen as a more conservative, less liberationist group. The quartet to be discussed is drawn from the four decades that have followed the Revival. The films in question are *Tim* (1979), *Evil Angels* (1988), *Dance Me to My Song* (1996) and *Japanese Story* (2003). Despite the difference in the time of their appearance, these have a number of features in common. As Bordwell notes about the film melodrama, all feature a woman as central character and all occur in the present without flashback

193

and little reference to the past. More importantly, coincidence and chance play important structural roles in their narratives and surprise frequently comes upon characters as well as upon the viewer. Given the train of events, one can identify a series of 'dissociated' emotions that the films engender in the audience. Taking this as cue, the chapter has therefore arranged the analysis of each film around a particular feeling or sentiment.

Love

In the previous chapter concerning the teenpic, attention was drawn to a minor cycle of films having to do with the romantic and sexual liaison between an older woman and a younger man. In the case of *The Heartbreak Kid* (1993), the difference in age between the twenty-two-year-old teacher and her seventeen-year-old male student is underplayed as a means of suggesting that they are both youthful and equally ingenuous, on the threshold of an adult world. Although this particular tale is told as much from the woman's point of view as it is from that of the teenager, this is not usually the case. Hence, an early film of the Revival, *Tim* (1979), is interesting in the context of the subject of women's emotions, especially the various kinds of love that a woman can feel for another person. The film is worth extended consideration not only because of a marked age difference between the woman and the man – the woman is almost twice as old as the film's namesake – but also because the focus of attention falls primarily on the woman.

The plot is as follows. Mary Horton (Piper Laurie) is a middle-class, middle-aged single professional woman who hires Tim Melville (Mel Gibson), a twenty-four-year-old labourer as a gardener. Tim is slow in intelligence and can neither read nor write. He left school early to become a labourer and continues to live at home in an inner-city working-class Sydney suburb with his simple but loving father and mother. Mary is pleased at Tim's work and his friendliness and with his father's approval arranges to also take him to her beach weekender to undertake handyman work there. The friendship deepens but Dawnie, Tim's older sister, who has just become engaged to an affluent middle-class young man, is suspicious that Mary's interest in Tim may be physical. Tim himself is upset about Dawn leaving the family and Mary comforts him, positively responding to his plea never to leave him. Then, unexpectedly, Tim's mother dies and Mary helps Ron (Alwyn Kurts), Tim's father, through the funeral arrangements, not least by again taking Tim away with her. Both Ron and Mary now turn their thoughts to what will happen to Tim if and when Ron dies. Mary, who has been increasingly taking Tim under her care, including teaching him to read, decides to marry him to help settle the future. Dawn and her husband are noticeably absent at the wedding but Ron is on hand to toast the couple. Not long afterwards, Mary and Tim get word that Ron has collapsed and died. At the second funeral in the film, Mary attempts to commiserate with Dawn but she stalks off. Tim remonstrates with her to love Mary but the two couples leave separately.

As this summary suggests, *Tim* is about Mary as much as it is about Tim. And, equally, despite the outbursts and anger of Dawn, who gives voice to the suspicion that Mary is only interested in Tim in terms of a sexual relationship, in fact there is no prurient interest in the deepening bond between the two. Like the connection encapsulated in the film *All That Heaven Allows* (1955), directed by Douglas Sirk, which also features a middle-aged woman Cary Scott (Jane Wyman) and a mentally retarded younger man Ron Kirby (Rock Hudson), who works as her gardener, the film is as much about whether a physically retarded person has as much right to happiness as do other 'normal' people. In this respect, *Tim* also has interesting connections with a more neglected Hollywood romance, *Light in the Piazza* (1961). This domestic drama also has to do with matters of maternal and romantic love and concerns an American mother (Olivia de Havilland), who must decide whether to allow her beautiful but mentally retarded daughter (Yvette Mimieux) to marry a young, handsome Italian (George Hamilton III). In the event, romantic love prevails and the worries about retardation recede in the face of the physical beauty and charm of the couple. On the other hand, *Tim* is more successful in emphasizing the continued relevance of the matter about what Mary must do in relation to the young man. The film traces a relationship that begins as friendship, deepens into concern and feeling and finally, once the two are married, can become sexual. All of this occurs in a context of relative social isolation, especially for Mary, so that the relationship with Tim begins in part out of companionable friendship. This social void helps explain the extraordinarily choric and 'melodramatic' role assigned to Dawn, Tim's sister, who becomes the means of articulating the charge that the older woman's interest in Tim can only be sexual.

Mary is calm in the face of this accusation knowing that she has nothing to hide or be ashamed about. On the other hand, the film's narration is such that the progress and changing nature of her involvement with Tim can only find oblique expression in music and *mise en scène*. Their changing relationship is not explicitly articulated but must instead be inferred by the audience from looks, gesture and movement as well as from other elements, such as clothing. The only exception to this pattern is a single conversation between Mary and a professional associate, who is also a friend, about what to finally do about the relationship between her and Tim. (In fact, this fellow lawyer suggests that Mary marry Tim.)

Thus, the audience must reach its own conclusion about when friendship becomes love and the varieties of love that Mary feels for Tim, ranging from companionable through sisterly and maternal to romantic and sexual love.

Suffering

However, the social and psychological problems associated with friendship and love are only one kind of matter besetting a woman protagonist. Distress and anguish can have other sources. *Evil Angels* (1988) has already been mentioned in the chapter concerning the biopic but it is revisited because of the sustained representation of pain and agony that it offers.

In the melodrama of passion, suffering, pain and grief are by no means confined to women. So it is in this film where the ordeal of the loss of baby Azaria, the inquest and the trial affects both parents, Michael (Sam Neill) and Lindy Chamberlain (Meryl Streep). The fact that the former, a pastor in the Seventh Day Adventist church, is a gentle, spiritual even feminine man who becomes disoriented and confused during the trial underlines the point that protagonists are inevitably genderized in stereotypical ways in this kind of film. All the same, the main emphasis is that Lindy as mother and wife becomes especially vulnerable to the forces that assault them.

The events portrayed in the film would be striking enough in a work of fiction but in one based on an actual case are doubly remarkable because the events actually befell an Australian wife and husband, especially the former, in the early years of the 1980s. The actual story gained international attention and there is little need to recount it again. Suffice to say that in mid 1980 on a camping holiday at Ayers Rock, Lindy and Michael Chamberlain had a new-born baby, Azaria, stolen by a dingo that entered their tent. The body was not recovered and an inquest returned an open verdict. However, politicians and police in the Northern Territory re-opened an investigation and this led to the Chamberlains being charged with the baby's murder. The case was heard in Darwin and a guilty verdict was returned. Lindy was sentenced to life imprisonment with hard labour while Michael, a pastor, received a suspended sentence of eighteen months as an accessory to murder.

Evil Angels narrates these story events into a large number of segments focussing on the Chamberlains, especially on Lindy, and organised into three parts. The first begins with the disappearance and culminates in the inquest held in Alice Springs. Lindy and Michael are exonerated and an open verdict returned. They resume their lives in the community of their church only to find that the investigation has been re-opened. Shortly, the two are charged with murder in a Darwin courthouse. In the last part of the film, Lindy begins her prison term and finds that she is not allowed to keep a new baby with her. Meanwhile, a jacket that Azaria was wearing on the night of her disappearance is found, thereby confirming Lindy's innocence. The government releases her from jail but without either a pardon or an exoneration.

Undoubtedly, Lindy Chamberlain in *Evil Angels* is a protagonist whose pathway is one of suffering. Three forces oppress her and her husband, taking these innocents from the community of their church and their family along a path that eventually leads to prison. The first of Lindy's tormentors arrives in the shape of the state apparatus of police–forensic–judicial bodies–prison. As though to demonstrate the partiality of the state towards an apparently homicidal mother, she is sentenced to life imprisonment with hard labour while her husband is given a suspended sentence of eighteen months. Meanwhile, the media also assails the woman, manipulating both her statements and her silences over the course of eight years. In fact, Lindy learns the hard way that the reporters and journalists are not to be trusted and work only in their own interests. The other agent of torture is the public at large, in the shape of those gossiping, talking on the radio airwaves, interviewed on television, telling jokes, abusing Lindy in the street and even making bomb threats. All of this generates not only occasional anger, bewilderment and bemusement but also a stoic suffering and pain.

In fact, Lindy must walk a *via dolorosa* of anguish and torture that has a myriad of contributing elements. As a mother, she suffers shock and guilt to do with the disappearance of the new-born Azaria, the fact that she left her alone in the tent and may or may not have zipped up the front. Moreover, the prosecution in the trial pictures her as an evil parent, a monstrous mother rather than a merciful one, who would murder and decapitate her own child. Nor does her ordeal end there. Instead, the state shows a gross inequality in terms of the sentence imposed on her. She has an hour to hold her new-born baby before it is taken from her and given to her husband, who is looking after the children. And even then she can only see her children when Michael takes them near the prison walls where they wave to her.

In view of the concerns of this chapter with gender and film, it is worth ending this analysis by noting the fact that Lindy is caught in a bind so far as her behaviour in the trial is concerned. In a sense, it is Michael who publicly displays qualities that are thought to be feminine, the preserve of women. In the trial, he appears to become disoriented, confused and is visibly distressed by the judicial apparatus. In fact, later when sentence is passed, he is deemed

197

to be capable of acting as mother as well as father to the children so that his sentence is suspended. Lindy, on the other hand, appears to act in ways that are seen to be the opposite – cool, jokey, sarcastic, unflustered under cross-examination. Such behaviour is seen not to be appropriate so far as the media, the gallery or the many members of the public across Australia are concerned. These hard, even masculine qualities seem to be out of keeping with her gender and therefore, precisely because it is not stereotypical, to corroborate the prosecution's case that she is a monstrous mother, an evil angel. The suffering meted out to her by the state appears in part to be based on the perception that she does not conform to womanly type.

Romance

At first sight, it might seem somewhat unusual to treat *Dance Me to My Song* under the category of romance. After all, the central figure of Julia (Heather Ross) is a young woman who is inside a twisted body severely affected by cerebral palsy. As such, the film might seem to be social realist in the tradition of *Annie's Coming Out* (1984), with its emphasis on the need for society to recognize the severely disabled as people who have an equal right to live normal lives in the community rather than being shut away in institutions. In fact, *Dance Me to My Song* is another kind of film entirely, so despite the possibility of understanding it in terms of social realism, it is equally pertinent to recognize it as a women's film. Within that broad type, one can understand *Dance Me to My Song* as a magical tale of cruelty, romance and love. The opening segment helps set the parameters of the film, intercutting two young women wakening in different places in the city. Julia is severely disabled and relies on being able to buzz her carer to help her move off her bed and toilet her after the night. Meanwhile, Madelaine (Joey Kennedy) is her carer but self-absorbed and careless towards her charge. In fact, the narration shortly reveals her as cruel, a liar, vindictive, spying, larcenous and even jealous of Julia – a truly wicked kind of sister to the other woman.

   Dance Me to My Song has to do with the struggle of the two women. Madelaine inflicts more and more cruelties and outrages on Julia while the latter struggles to cope with the unfolding situation. The carer has shown herself especially prone to the possibilities of romance although several early encounters with men also prove to be disastrous and without affection. Prince Charming enters the film in the shape of Eddie (John Brumpton), a neighbour, who is progressively drawn to Julia despite various lies and blandishments from Madelaine. In the highly melodramatic climax of the film, Madelaine confronts Julia, angry and physically abusive because the latter has managed to have her fired. She is so outraged by the fact that the other woman has been able to assert some authority and autonomy that she is physically ready to kill her. However, some of Julia's friends visit and she is banished. The audience's last glimpse of the witch figure has her in long shot kicking her car which has broken down in busy traffic. The film ends with Julia reunited with Eddie.

Dance Me to My Song clearly belongs to the genre of the romance. However, it is also important to recognize it under the mantle of the woman's melodrama. The two women are distinguished along the most traditional of lines – Julia with blonde, fair hair and Madelaine with dark hair – and the plot moves in a straightforward fashion that allows concentration on the emotional states of the women. There is little or nothing in the way of background story so that the emphasis is directed to what will happen to the two and how Eddie may figure in the final arrangement. And, given Julia's physical handicap, the action is almost wholly set in the interiors of houses. In other words, *Dance Me to My Song* is very recognizably a women's film, ostensibly joined to the others under discussion here because it has to do with a woman's feelings and suffering, not so much because of the flow of circumstances but rather because of the wickedness and malevolence of another woman who is her enemy and rival.

Grief

The final example of the women's film has to do with another emotion even though elements of love, suffering and romance also come to the fore. Probably the most sustained imaging of grief in Australian cinema in recent years occurs in *Japanese Story* (2003). In particular, the film pictures the mutual sense of loss and sorrow of two women from different cultural backgrounds united by the death of a man that they both love. The film's narrative concerns Sandy Edwards (Toni Collette), a young, independent woman living close to the Pilbara region in Western Australia and a partner in a geological survey company that serves the mining industry. An executive from one of the mining industry's most important Japanese customers, Hiromitsu Tacibana (Gotaro Tsunashima) is visiting the area and Sandy is dragooned into acting as his guide. At first, relations between the two are highly formal. After visiting various mining operations, Hiro is hugely impressed by the space and size of the country and at his insistence they drive off into the 'dust and debris', off even gravel road. Their four-wheel-drive becomes bogged on a sandy track. Trying to free the wheels, Sandy and Hiro are forced to spend a night together in the open and finally manage to get the vehicle moving again. As they grow to know each other and their respective cultures a little more, relations thaw between them and they become lovers. A swim in a billabong to cool off from the heat of the day turns to tragedy when Hiro breaks his neck. He is dead when he floats to the surface. A distraught Sandy finally manages to get help. Hiro's widow, Yukiko (Yumiko Tanaka), arrives from Japan to take the body home for burial and she flies out leaving a very distressed Sandy in the airport lounge watching the last vestiges of her relationship disappear.

As a women's film, *Japanese Story* is methodical and painstaking in its build-up to the tragedy and its aftermath. The opening credits introduce the audience not only to a palette of non-figurative colours but especially to a measured six-beat musical piece, 'Chinsagu No Hana', played on a single-stringed instrument, which is simple and repetitive in structure. This is followed by two narrative segments that briefly introduce Hiro and Sandy before they meet. The film is cueing the audience to expect a relationship if not a romance and this, of course, proves to be the case. On the other hand, what surprises and even astonishes Sandy (and the audience) is the suddenness and completeness of the fatal accident. The adventure narrative that earlier could encompass a degree of gentle comedy and a developing cultural understanding and romance now must accommodate the grieving and trauma of the two women, Sandy and Yukiko. Although the latter's role in the film is brief, consisting of only five scenes, nevertheless her presence has been anticipated. When Sandy notices a picture of her and their children in Hiro's wallet she asks whether he loves her. And, of course, Yukiko enters the film after the figure of Hiro has departed, thereby suggesting both a continuity and a difference between the two narratives of romance and of grief.

However, the central protagonist in *Japanese Story* is Sandy, and her grief is especially acute and moving not least because she has no official status in relation to the deceased. Instead, there is first the agony of recovering the body, lifting it into the four-wheel vehicle and driving to where she can enlist the help of others. Cleaning and dressing the body, she is unaware that she is, in effect, engaged in a form of anointing, a bestowal of last rites. For once she does reach help, Sandy is dumbstruck to find that bureaucracy kicks in and that she is increasingly marginalized in arrangements concerning the body. The pace of the film slows deliberately and the duration of many shots of Sandy grow longer as a kind of objective correlative of the anguish and trauma that she is undergoing as she is more and more removed from events happening. Meanwhile, the musical number 'Chinsagu No Hana' returns insistently, suggesting the inexorable movement of events leading to the body departing.

However, Sandy does find a brief opportunity for inclusion when she meets Yukiko. The executive's widow sees some of the photos of the couple and realizes that Sandy brought her husband joy and opened his horizon. At the same time, he fully intended to return to her and his children. Yukiko gives Sandy a letter that Hiro had written to Sandy in anticipation of his return to Japan, so that she is able to draw some comfort from his words as the plane bearing the body and the widow departs. The slow, increasingly darkening tracking shot at the end of the film of Sandy watching the airport runway to the accompaniment of 'Chinsagu No Hana' is one of the most powerful embodiments of sorrow and trauma to be found in Australian women's cinema.

Yet, as suggested, it is important to realize that two women are affected by this grief and loss. Yukiko is given equal footing as Sandy, no matter how fleeting her appearance. The audience sees her mute grief and tears in the car after her arrival, has the point-of-view shot of her experience of the photographs and the evident happiness of her husband and Sandy therein, and is crying when she gives Sandy Hiro's letter as she leaves to board the plane. Altogether, these moments of contact suggest a mutual tact and sympathy between the women in their sorrow and anguish.

Last Words

Each of the four films examined in this chapter belongs to an Australian women's cinema. Although different in matters of form and style, all conform to the general type of the melodrama of passion. Each film is intimately concerned with a woman protagonist – Mary, Lindy, Julia and Sandy – and with the set of choices that they face as women. Mary must decide on Tim's domestic future; Lindy must arrange what is best for Michael and for her family; Julia has to make choices concerning both Madelaine and Eddie; and Sandy has to decide about what to do with Hiro's dead body and how she might relate to his widow. Although a combination of circumstances has brought each of these women to the point of emotional decisions, nevertheless the four are agents of free will within various domestic and familial settings. Composed in terms of 'zigzag' construction, each film develops in a straightforward manner which yet allows the operation of chance as a means of springing surprise on both characters and audience. In addition, 'big' emotional scenes appear in all four films, thereby confirming the operation of the women's film, the melodrama of passion.

Finally, it is also necessary to point out that the analysis of these films should be read in the context of inquiry into other films in previous chapters of the book. In Chapter 2, the operation of both *Shame* (1987) and *Rabbit Proof Fence* (2002) in the domain of the action-adventure film is examined. Several women-centred films, from *Picnic at Hanging Rock* (1975) to at least *The Piano* (1993), play their part in the local art film. Meanwhile, women also have central roles in romantic comedy, so this genre too is important to any full consideration of the women's film. The female investigator of crime received analysis in the chapter concerning the detective film. *Moulin Rouge* (2001) is an important Australian women's musical. And, finally, the cycle of socially concerned women's films, from *Journey Among Women* to at least *The Fringe Dwellers* (1987), figure in Chapter 11.

A more thorough investigation of the full field of the women's film in Australia would research each of these matters at greater length. Such an inquiry would also investigate this trajectory more historically. Nothing has been said about women in Australian cinema before 1970 but clearly such a generic investigation is overdue. Meanwhile, the coincidence of the women's movement and the Revival of the Australian feature film production industry also invites attention. It was a significant parallel development that saw second-wave feminism emerge in Australia at approximately the same time that the Australian government was establishing a state-supported film industry. Much work remains to be done.

15
Afterword

This book has sought to introduce the subject of Australian feature film from the standpoint of cinema genre.

In particular, it has been concerned to establish three matters regarding the subject. First, genre has been defined as a structural category differentiating it from other ways of approaching Australian cinema. While the book has not had anything to say about other approaches, such as those of *auteurism*, thematic considerations, institutional history, changing representations of such groups as Aborigines, women and the disabled, nevertheless by emphasizing genre above these other approaches, it has sought to champion a highly pertinent strategy for unravelling the narrative, stylistic and thematic complexities of local feature film.

In addition to this intervention, this book has also attempted to emphasize what seem to be the main genres of Australian cinema. While Australia shares in some of the same forms found in film industries elsewhere, it also differs – not least in terms of those categories that attract the imaginative energy not only of producers and writers but also of its audiences. Almost forty years ago, Alan Lovell (1968) suggested that British cinema comprised seven genres, consisting of comedy, documentary, horror, crime, historical drama, social realism and melodrama. In a similar desire for model-building, this book asserts the presence of thirteen different genres that account for the great bulk of Australian cinema output. Hence, although many overlaps and hybrids have been noted in passing, these pages have designated a series of distinct classes that are significant for Australian film makers and viewers alike.

In discussing these, *Film in Australia: An Introduction* has attempted to offer viable working definitions of each class of film, while recognizing at the same time that there is always a provisional dimension to such designations. This is no false modesty or understatement but arises instead from a recognition that new films contain the constant possibility of changing the sense of what is constituted by any particular genre as well as how such classes relate to each other. Further, as noted in Chapter 1, different genres frequently emphasize different elements whether these be matters of structure, style or theme so that, for example, a genre such as the crime film seems to have a stronger iconography and visual look than does another such as social realism. Neither, though, can one refer to historical tradition in Australian cinema, since genres such as those just named barely had a presence in the local industry before the 1970 Revival. Discussing this paradox of the time-bound nature of particular genres, Bordwell quotes the Russian Formalist Boris Tomashevsky:

> No firm logical classification of genres is possible. Their demarcation is always historical, that is to say, it is correct only for a specific moment of history; apart from this they are demarcated by many features at once, and the markers of one genre may be quite different in kind from the markers of another genre and logically they may not exclude one another, only being cultivated in different genres because of the natural connection of compositional devices. (Bordwell 1989: 147)

Over and above this double complication of the historical nature of genres and their frequent incommensurability is the problem of distinguishing genre from adjoining principles of organization, including cycle and format. In Chapter 1, this book was delimited to the investigation of narrative genres in Australian cinema. Among the different filmic types excluded were documentary and the avant-garde or experimental film. Yet these modes are referred to at particular points in the book in discussing both different boundaries and subtypes of particular genres. Various cycles and recurring formulas have also been noted, frequently without any attempt to pursue further the status of these categories. Hence, for example, an 'ocker' comedy cycle has been designated running from *The Naked Bunyip* (1970) to *Les Patterson Saves the World* (1987) without examining any earlier, pre-Revival precedents or later extensions of this output. Bordwell notes that Tomashevsky has hinted that 'the idea of genre is so historically changeable that no set of necessary and sufficient conditions can mark off genres from other kinds of categories' (Bordwell 1989: 147–8).

Despite this kind of contingency, these chapters have, all the same, tried to encourage understanding of Australian films in terms of genre principles and types. At the same time, this book is the first to admit that the types assembled here need further analysis and historical inquiry. The book has, for example, highlighted social realism as currently the most important film type operating in the local industry and culture. Yet so little is known about this genre in Australia. A more extended investigation of this class would mean, on one level, relating such films to each other, pinpointing their imagery and meanings, detailing their historical trajectory, and analysing the connection between their evolution and Australian social, legal, economic, and cultural development; and, on another level, to relate the whole of the genre of social realism to other genres or works which take advantage of the same archetypal narrative structures. In other words, instead of a single volume devoted to the subject of genre in Australian cinema, there is a pressing need for a series of studies of specific Australian film genres including comedy, adventure and social realism.

It also hardly needs saying that the films covered in this volume by no means exhaust the output of Australian narrative cinema. Nor was it intended that it would. Readers should be able to suggest other films that might have been discussed under particular headings. Although many films were viewed as part of the research, there were more that were not watched. The hope, therefore, is that additional titles furnish the opportunity to test the analytical strength and precision of this investigation as well as to further extend and refine the findings. Put another way, the expectation is that the reader will use this work in an active, critical manner, as a means of viewing new films and of reviewing older ones with an inclination to understand just how these employ sets of conventions particular to specific genres. Such an engagement will, it's hoped, be judicious and discriminatory, testing films but also the categories proposed in this book. For although films are constantly given generic labels in the film culture – this is a comedy, that is a sci-fi thriller and so on – this book furnishes the opportunity to think about this process in a more sustained, systematic, and – it's hoped – more thoughtful way.

In a fine metaphor for the film genre endeavour, Charles Derry likens the work of this kind of investigator to that of the map maker or cartographer (1988: 325–6). Such a figure attempts to map out various countries in terms of their boundaries, to estimate distances, calculate heights, notice physical features, pay attention to the location of cities and towns and otherwise provide a reliable chart of the regions being surveyed. Such efforts are, though, serviceable estimates rather than exact blueprints because the chart is always only a guide. In particular, it does not replace the actual sensation of touring in the region itself. And of course, places grow and others decline, borders are redrawn, old names disappear and others take their place, territories change hands and so on. Hence, *Film in Australia: An Introduction* represents an attempt to sketch out the uncharted lands of Australian narrative film genres. If it has drawn the frontiers a little too sharply or overlooked particular lands too strange, distant or unrecognizable, comfort is taken in the fact that it will assist other travellers in making richer and more thoughtful visits to this region.

Bibliography

Adams, P. 1979 'The dangerous pornography of death' *The Bulletin*, No. 100 1 May, 38–41

Affron, C. 1982 *Cinema and Sentiment*, Chicago: University of Chicago Press

Altman, R. 1987 *The American Film Musical*, Bloomington: Indiana University Press

Amis, K. 1976 'Starting points' in M. Rose (ed.), *Science fiction: a collection of critical essays*, Englewood Press: Prentice Hall

Anderson, C. 1988 'Biographical Film' in W. D. Gehring (ed.), *Handbook of American Film Genres*, Westport: Greenwood Press, 331–54

Anderson, C. and Lupo, J. 2002 'Hollywood Lives: The State of the Biopic at the Turn of the Century' in S. Neale (ed.), *Genre and Contemporary Hollywood*, London: British Film Institute, 91–104

Australian Film Commission 2004 <http\\www.afc.gov.au\filmsandawards\filmdbsearch.aspx?view=type&type.feature>

Bailey, S. and Hay, J. 2002 'Cinema and the Premises of Youth: "Teen Films" and their Sites in the 1980's and 1990's' in S. Neale (ed.), *Genre and Contemporary Hollywood*, London: British Film Institute, 186–204

Balio, T. 1990 *Hollywood in the Age of Television*, Boston: Unwin Hyman

Barlow, H. 1995 '*Dead Calm*' in S. Murray (ed.), *Australian Film 1978–1994: A Survey of Theatrical Features*, Melbourne: Oxford University Press, 272

Barr, C. 1977 *Ealing Studios*, London and Devon: Cameron, David and Charles Taylor

Basinger, J. 1993 *A Woman's View: How Hollywood Spoke to Women 1930–1960*, New York: Alfred A. Knopf

Bazin, A. 1971 'The Western or The American Film *Par Excellence*' in *What is Cinema?* Volume 2, Berkeley: University of California Press, 140–8

Bennet, T. and Carter, D. (eds) 2002 *Culture in Australia: An Introduction*, Melbourne: Cambridge University Press

Bergman, A. 1971 *We're in the Money: Depression America and Its Films*, New York: Harper and Row

Bernstein, J. 1997 *Pretty in Pink: The Golden Age of Teenage Movies*, New York: St. Martin's Griffin

Blackford, R., Ikin, V. and McMullen, S. 1999 *Strange constellations: a history of Australian science fiction*, Westport: Greenwood Press

Bordwell, D. 1979 'The Art Cinema as a Mode of Film Practice' *Film Criticism*, Vol. 4 No. 1, 56–64

1982 'Happily Ever After, Part Two' *The Velvet Light Trap*, No. 19, 27

1985 *Narration and the Fiction Film*, London: Methuen

1989 *Making Meaning: Inference and Rhetoric in the Interpretation of Cinema*, Harvard and London: Harvard University Press

Bordwell, D., Staiger, J. and Thompson, K. 1985 *The Classical Hollywood Cinema: Film Style and Mode of Production to 1960*, New York: Columbia University Press

Bordwell, D. and Thompson, K. 1979 1996 *Film Art: An Introduction*, New York: Knopf

Breen, M. 1995a '*Hard Knocks*' in S. Murray (ed.), *Australian Film 1978–1994: A Survey of Theatrical Features*, Melbourne: Oxford University Press, 60

— 1995b '*The Plains of Heaven*' in S. Murray (ed.), *Australian Film 1978–1994: A Survey of Theatrical Features*, Melbourne: Oxford University Press, 108

— 1995c '*Going Down*' in S. Murray (ed.), *Australian Film 1978–1994: A Survey of Theatrical Features*, Melbourne: Oxford University Press, 127

Brown, S. 1995a '*The Big Hurt*' in S. Murray (ed.), *Australian Film 1978–1994: A Survey of Theatrical Features*, Melbourne: Oxford University Press, 185

— 1995b '*Fair Game*' in S. Murray (ed.), *Australian Film 1978–1994: A Survey of Theatrical Features*, Melbourne: Oxford University Press, 194

Butler, A. 2002 *Women's Cinema: The Contested Screen*, London: Wallflower

Cameron, I. 1974 *Adventure in the Movies*, New York: Crescent Books

Caputo, R. 1995 '*Squizzy Taylor*' in S. Murray (ed.), *Australian Film 1978–1994: A Survey of Theatrical Features*, Melbourne: Oxford University Press, 111

— 1993 'Coming of Age: Notes towards a Reappraisal' *Cinema Papers*, No. 94 August, 1216

Cawelti, J. G. 1976 *Adventure, Mystery and Romance: Formula Stories as Art and Popular Culture*, Chicago: University of Chicago Press

Clancy, J. 1995 'The King of the Two Day Wonder' in S. Murray (ed.), *Australian Film 1978–1994: A Survey of Theatrical Features*, Melbourne: Oxford University Press, 36

Clover, C. J. 1992 *Men, Women and Chainsaws: Gender in the Modern Horror Film*, London: British Film Institute

Collins, F. 1999a 'Comedy' in B. McFarlane, G. Mayer and I. Bertrand (eds) 1999, *The Oxford Companion to Australian Film*, Melbourne: Oxford University Press, 74–6

— 1999b 'Rites of Passage' in B. McFarlane, G. Mayer and I. Bertrand (eds) 1999, *The Oxford Companion to Australian Film*, Melbourne: Oxford University Press, 411–14

Collins, J. M. 1988 'The Musical' in W. D. Gehring (ed.), *Handbook of American Film Genres*, Westport: Greenwood Press, 269–84

Conomos, J. 1995 '*The Heartbreak Kid*' in S. Murray (ed.), *Australian Film 1978–1994: A Survey of Theatrical Features*, Melbourne: Oxford University Press, 360

Considine, D. 1985 *The Cinema of Adolescence*, Jefferson, NC: McFarland

Cook, P. 2002 'No fixed address: The women's picture from *Outrage* to *Blue Steel*' in S. Neale (ed.), *Genre and Contemporary Hollywood*, London: British Film Institute, 231–45

Cowie, E. 1988 'The Popular Film as a Progressive Text – a Discussion of *Coma* Part 1 and Part 2' in C. Penley (ed.), *Feminism and Film Theory*, London: Routledge, 104–40

Crofts, S. 1993 *Identification, Gender And Genre In Film: The Case Of Shame*, Melbourne: Australian Film Institute

Cunningham, S. 1989 'The Decades of Survival 1930–1970' in A. Moran and T. O'Regan (eds), *The Australian Screen*, Melbourne: Penguin Books, 53–72

— 1991 *Featuring Australia: The Cinema of Charles Chauvel*, Sydney: Allen and Unwin

Custen, G. F. 1992 *Bio/Pics: How Hollywood Constructed Public History*, New Brunswick: Rutgers University Press

Davies, B. 1973 *The Thriller: The Suspense Film Since 1945*, London: Studio Vista

207

Davison, G. (ed.) 1991 *The Heritage Handbook*, Sydney: Allen and Unwin

2003 *The Use and Abuse of Australian History*, Sydney: Allen and Unwin

Dermody, S. and Jacka, E. 1987 *The Screening of Australia Volume 1: Anatomy of a Film Industry*, Sydney: Currency Press

1988 *The Screening of Australia Volume 2: Anatomy of a National Cinema*, Sydney: Currency Press

Derry, C. 1988 *The Suspense Thriller: Films in the Shadow of Alfred Hitchcock*, Jefferson, NC & London: McFarland & Co

Dixon, W. W. (ed.) 2000 *Film Genre 2000: New Critical Essays*, Albany: State University of New York

Dzenis A. 1995 'In Search of Anna' in S. Murray (ed.), *Australian Film 1978–1994: A Survey of Theatrical Features*, Melbourne: Oxford University Press, 32–3

Elsaesser, T. 1972 'Tales of Sound and Fury' *Monogram*, Vol. 4, 2–15

Fisher, J. 1977 *Funny Way to be a Hero*, London: Paladin

Foucault, M. 2001, *Madness and civilization: a history of insanity in the age of reason*, London: Routledge

Frye, N. 1957 *Anatomy of Criticism: Four Essays*, Princeton: Princeton University Press

Gardiner, G. 1995a '*Palm Beach*' in S. Murray (ed.), *Australian Film 1978–1994: A Survey of Theatrical Features*, Melbourne: Oxford University Press, 65

1995b '*Kitty And The Bagman*' in S. Murray (ed.), *Australian Film 1978–1994: A Survey of Theatrical Features*, Melbourne: Oxford University Press, 130

Gehring, W. D. 1986 *Screwball Comedy: A Genre of Madcap Romance*, Westport: Greenwood Press

(ed.) 1988 *Handbook of American Film Genres*, Westport: Greenwood Press

Gomery, D. 1992 *Shared Pleasures*, Madison: University of Wisconsin Press

Gow, G. 1968 *Suspense in the Movies*, New York: Castle

Grant, B. K. (ed.) 1977 *Film Genre: Theory and Criticism*, Metuchen, NJ, and London: Scarecrow Press

(ed.) 1986 *Film Genre Reader*, Austin: University of Texas Press

Hammond, L. 1974 *Thriller Movies: Classic Films of Suspense and Mystery*, London: Octopus

Harries, D. 2002 'Film parody and the resuscitation of genre' in S. Neale (ed.) *Genre and Contemporary Hollywood*, London: British Film Institute

Harris, P. 1995 '*Touch and Go*' in S. Murray (ed.), *Australian Film 1978–1994: A Survey of Theatrical Features*, Melbourne: Oxford University Press, 67

Harrison, T. 2005 *Australian Film & TV Companion*, 2nd Edition, Sydney: Citrus Press

Haskell, M. 1973 *From Reverence to Rape: The Treatment of Women in the Movies*, New York: Holt, Rinehart and Winston

Hodsdon, B. 1980 '*Palm Beach*' *Filmnews* January/February, 6

1985 'The Avant-garde Impulse and Australian Narrative: *Palm Beach* in Context' in A. Moran and T. O'Regan (eds), *An Australian Film Reader*, Sydney: Currency Press, 288–94

Holland, N. 1964 'The Puzzling Movies: An Analysis and a Guess at their Appeal' *Journal of Social Science*, No. 1 January, 71–96

Horton, A. S. 1991 *Comedy/Cinema/Theory*, Berkeley: University of California Press

Hunter, I. 1985 'Corsetway to Heaven: Looking Back at Hanging Rock' in A. Moran and T. O'Regan (eds), *An Australian Film Reader*, Sydney: Currency Press, 190–3

Jacka, E. 1991 *The ABC of Drama, 1975–1990*, Sydney: Australian Film, Television and Radio School

Jeffords, S. 1994 *Hard Bodies: Hollywood Masculinity in the Reagan Era*, New Brunswick: Rutgers University Press

Kaminsky, S. 1974 *American Film Genres: Approaches to a Critical Theory of Popular Film*, Dayton, Ohio: Pflaum

Kaplan, E. Ann 1983 *Women and Film: Both Sides of the Camera*, New York: Methuen

Karnick, K. B. and Jenkins, H. (eds) 1995 *Classical Hollywood Comedy*, New York and London: Routledge

Kawin, B. 1986, 'Children of the light' in B Grant (ed.), *Film Genre Reader*, Austin: University of Texas Press

Keane, S. 2004 *Disaster Movies: The Cinema of Catastrophe*, London: Wallflower

Kitses, J. 1969, *Horizons West*, Bloomington: Indiana University Press

Lawrence, P. 1995 '*The Year of Living Dangerously*' in S. Murray (ed.), *Australian Film 1978–1994: A Survey of Theatrical Features*, Melbourne: Oxford University Press, 117

Lay, S. 2002 *British Social Realism: From Documentary to Brit Grit*, London: Wallflower

Lev, P. 1993 *The Euro-American Cinema*, Austin: University of Texas Press

Lipkin, S. 1988 'Melodrama' in W. D. Gehring (ed.), *Handbook of American Film Genres*, Westport: Greenwood Press, 275–302

Lloyd, J. 2001 'The Politics Of Dislocation: Airport Types *The Castle*' in M. Shiel and T. Fitzmaurice (eds), *Cinema and the City: Film and Urban Society in a Global Context*, Oxford: Blackwell Publishing, 171–84

Lovell, A. 1968 *The British Cinema: The Unknown Cinema*, London: British Film Institute Education Department Seminar

Lucas, R. 1993 'Deadly Ambivalence, or The Family Romance in *Dead Calm*' *Literature/Film Quarterly*, Vol. 21 No. 2, 121–9

McFarlane, B. 1995 '*Gallipoli*' in S. Murray (ed.), *Australian Film 1978–1994: A Survey of Theatrical Features*, Melbourne: Oxford University Press, 74

2004 '*Dirty Deeds* and good clean fun' *Metro* No. 140 April, 48–52

McFarlane, B., Mayer, G. and Bertrand, I. (eds) 1999, *The Oxford Companion to Australian Film*, Melbourne: Oxford University Press

McGuinness, P. 1985 'Peter Weir's Hauntingly Beautiful Film Makes the World Sit Up' in A. Moran and T. O'Regan (eds), *An Australian Film Reader*, Sydney: Currency Press, 188–9

McKee, A. 2001 *Australian Television: A Genealogy of Great Moments*, Melbourne: Oxford University Press

Malard, C. S. 1988 'The Social Problem Film' in W. D. Gehring (ed.), *Handbook of American Film Genres*, Westport: Greenwood Press, 305–30

Maltby, R. 1983 *Harmless Entertainment: Hollywood and the Ideology of Consensus*, Metuchen: Scarecrow Press

1995 *Hollywood Cinema: An Introduction*, Oxford: Blackwell

Marchetti, G. 1989 'Action-Adventure as Ideology' in I. Angus and S. Jhally (eds), *Cultural Politics in Contemporary America*, New York: Routledge

Martin, A. 1995a '*Blood Money*' in S. Murray (ed.), *Australian Film 1978–1994: A Survey of Theatrical Features*, Melbourne: Oxford University Press, 52

1995b '*Mad Max: Beyond Thunderdome*' in S. Murray (ed.), *Australian Film 1978–1994: A Survey of Theatrical Features*, Melbourne: Oxford University Press, 78

1995c 'Hostage: The Christine Maresch Story' in S. Murray (ed.), Australian Film 1978–1994: A Survey of Theatrical Features, Melbourne: Oxford University Press, 129

1995d 'With Time To Kill' in S. Murray (ed.), Australian Film 1978–1994: A Survey of Theatrical Features, Melbourne: Oxford University Press, 236

1995e 'Jenny Kissed Me' in S. Murray (ed.), Australian Film 1978–1994: A Survey of Theatrical Features, Melbourne: Oxford University Press, 199

1995f 'The Delinquents' in S. Murray (ed.), Australian Film 1978–1994: A Survey of Theatrical Features, Melbourne: Oxford University Press, 274

2003, The Mad Max Movies, Sydney and Canberra: Currency Press and Screensound Australia

Mayer, G. 1993 'A Hard-Boiled World: Goodbye Paradise and The Empty Beach' Literature/Film Quarterly, Vol. 21 No. 2 April, 112–20

1999 'Genre' in B. McFarlane, G. Mayer and I. Bertrand (eds), The Oxford Companion to Australian Film, Melbourne: Oxford University Press, 177–80

Melehy, H. 2004, 'Bodies without organs: cyborg cinema of the 1980s' in G. Rickman (ed.), The Science Fiction Film Reader, New York: Limelight Editions

Mercer, J. and Shingler, M. 2004 Melodrama: Genre, Style, Sensibility, London and New York: Wallflower

Milner, A. 1994, 'On the Beach: Apocalyptic hedonism and the origins of postmodernism' in I. Craven (ed.), Australian Popular Culture, Melbourne: Cambridge University Press

Moran, A. 1985 Image and Industry: Australian Television Drama Production, Sydney: Currency Press

1991 Projecting Australia: Government Film Production since 1945, Sydney: Currency Press

1993 Moran's Guide to Australian Television Series, Sydney: Australian Film, Television and Radio School

Moran, A. and O'Regan, T. 1985 (eds) An Australian Film Reader, Sydney: Currency Press

Moran, A. and Vieth, E. 2005 Historical Dictionary of Australian and New Zealand Cinema, Langham, Md: Scarecrow Press

Murray, S. 1975 'Picnic at Hanging Rock' Cinema Papers, November-December, 264–5

(ed.) 1995a Australian Film 1978–1994: A Survey of Theatrical Features, Melbourne: Oxford University Press

1995b 'Hurricane Smith' in S. Murray (ed.), Australian Film 1978–1994: A Survey of Theatrical Features, Melbourne: Oxford University Press, 319

1995c 'Running From The Guns' in S. Murray (ed.), Australian Film 1978–1994: A Survey of Theatrical Features, Melbourne: Oxford University Press, 228

1995d 'Grievous Bodily Harm' in S. Murray (ed.), Australian Film 1978–1994: A Survey of Theatrical Features, Melbourne: Oxford University Press, 251

Murray, S. and Beilby, P. (eds) 1980 The New Australian Cinema, Melbourne: Nelson

Neale, S. 1980 Genre, London: British Film Institute

2000 Genre and Hollywood, London and New York: Routledge

(ed.) 2002 Genre and Contemporary Hollywood, London: British Film Institute

Neale, S. and Krutnik, F. 1990 Popular Film and Television Comedy, London: Routledge

Nerlich, M. 1987 Ideology of Adventure: Studies in Modern Consciousness 1100–1750, 2 volumes, Minneapolis: University of Minnesota Press

Nichols, B. 1981 Ideology and the Image, Bloomington: Indiana University Press

O'Pray, M. 2003 Avant-Garde Film: Form, Themes and Passions, London: Wallflower

O'Regan, T. 1985 '*The Man From Snowy River* and Australian Popular Culture' in A. Moran and T. O'Regan (eds), *An Australian Film Reader*, Sydney: Currency Press, 242–51

Palmer, J. 1978 *Thrillers: Genesis and Structure of a Popular Genre*, London: Edward Arnold

1987 *The Logic of the Absurd*, London: British Film Institute

1995 *Taking Humour Seriously*, London: Routledge

Pike, A. and Cooper, R. 1980 *Australian film 1900–1977: a guide to feature film production*, Melbourne: Oxford University Press

Pirie, D. (ed.) 1981 *Anatomy of the Movies*, New York: Macmillan Publishing Company

Plunkett, F. 2002 'The detective, the poet and the femme fatale: Mourning and Hermeneutics in *The Monkey's Mask*' *Metro Magazine*, No. 131/2 March, 66–72

Purdon, N. 1980 '*Palm Beach*' *Cinema Papers*, December 1979/January 1980, 660

Quinn, K. 1995 '*Deadly*' in S. Murray (ed.), *Australian Cinema 1978–1994: A Survey of Theatrical Features*, Melbourne: Oxford University Press, 336

Rickman, G. 2004 'Introduction', in G. Rickman (ed.), *The Science Fiction Film Reader*, New York: Limelight Editions

Roffman, P. and Purdy, J. 1981 *The Hollywood Social Problem Film: Madness, Despair and Politics from the Depression to the Fifties*, Bloomington: Indiana University Press

Rogers, M., Epstein, M. and Reeves, J. 2002 '*The Sopranos* as HBO Brand Equity: The Art of Commerce in the Age of Digital Reproduction' in D. Lavery (ed.), *This Thing of Ours: Investigating* The Sopranos, New York: Columbia University Press; London: Wallflower Press, 42–57

Rohdie, S. 1985 '*Gallipoli*, Peter Weir and an Australian Art Cinema' in A. Moran and T. O'Regan (eds), *An Australian Film Reader*, Sydney: Currency Press, 194–7

Roth, M. 1981 'Some Warner Musicals and the Spirit of the New Deal' in R. Altman (ed.), *Genre: The Musical*, London: Routledge Kegan Paul/British Film Institute, 41–56

Routt, W. D. 1985 'On the Expressionism of Colonialism in Early Australian Cinema – Charles Chauvel and Naive Cinema' in A. Moran and T. O'Regan (eds), *An Australian Film Reader*, Sydney: Currency Press, 55–71

Rowe, K. 1995 *The Unruly Woman: Gender and the Genres of Laughter*, Austin: University of Texas Press

Ryan, T. 1980 'The Historical Film' in S. Murray and P. Beilby (eds), *The New Australian Cinema*, Melbourne: Nelson, 113–37

Saenz, M. 1997 'Programming' in H. Newcomb (ed.), *The Museum of Broadcasting Communication Encyclopedia of Television*, Chicago and London: Fitzroy Dearborn Publishing, 1301–8

Schary, T. 2002 *Generation Multiplex: The Image of Youth in Contemporary American Culture*, Austin: University of Texas Press

Seidman, S. 1981 *Comedian Comedy: A Tradition in the Hollywood Film*, Ann Arbor: UMI Research Press.

Shirley, G. and Adams, B. 1983 *Australian Cinema: The First 80 Years*, Sydney: Angus and Robertson and Currency Press

Siska, W. C. 1988 'The Art Film' in W. D. Gehring (ed.), *Handbook of American Film Genres*, Westport: Greenwood Press, 331–54

Smith, S. 2004 *The Musical: Race, Gender and Performance*, London: Wallflower

Sobchack, T. 1988 'The Adventure Film' in W. D. Gehring (ed.), *Handbook of American Film Genres*, Westport: Greenwood Press, 9–21

Sobchack, V. 1987 *Screening Space: the American science fiction film*, New York: Ungar

Solomon, S. 1976 *Beyond Formula: American Film Genres*, New York: Harcourt Brace Jovanovich

Stratton, D. 1990 *The Avocado Plantation: Australian Film in the 1980's*, Sydney: Macmillan

Tasker, Y. 1993 *Spectacular Bodies: Gender, Genre and the Action Cinema*, London and New York: Routledge

Telotte, J. P. 2002 'The New Hollywood Musical: From *Saturday Night Fever* to *Footloose*' in S. Neale (ed.), *Genre and Contemporary Hollywood*, London: British Film Institute, 48–61

Thompson, K. 1988 '"No, Lestrade, in this case nothing was left to chance"' in K. Thompson, *Breaking the Glass Armor: Neoformalist Film Analysis*, Princeton, NJ: Princeton University Press, 49–86

Todorov, T. 1975 *The Fantastic: A Structural Approach to a Literary Genre*, Ithaca: Cornell University Press

1977 'The Typology of Detective Fiction' in *The Poetics of Prose*, Ithaca: Cornell University Press, 42–65

Truffaut, F. 1967 *Hitchcock*, London: Secker and Warburg

Tudor, A. 1974 *Image and Influence*, London: Allen and Unwin

2002, 'From paranoia to postmodernism? The horror movie in late modern society' in S. Neale (ed.), *Genre and Contemporary Hollywood*, London: British Film Institute

Turner, G. 1989 'Transgressive TV: From *In Melbourne Tonight* to *Perfect Match*' in J. Tulloch and G. Turner (eds), *Australian Television: Programs, Pleasures and Politics*, Sydney: Allen and Unwin, 25–38

1993 'The Genres are American: Australian Film, and the Problem of Genre' *Literature/Film Quarterly*, Vol. 21 No. 2, 102–11

Turner, G. and Cunningham, S. (eds) 2000, *The Australian TV Book*, Sydney: Allen and Unwin

Verevis, C. 2004 Remaking Film. Unpublished paper delivered at the 12th Biannual Conference of the Australian and New Zealand Film and History Association, Canberra

Verhoeven D. (ed.) 1999 *Twin peeks: Australian and New Zealand feature films*, Melbourne: Damned Publishing

Vieth, E. 2001, *Screening science: context, texts and science in fifties science fiction films*, Maryland: Scarecrow Press

Walker, M. 1982 'Melodrama and the American Cinema' *Movie*, 29/30, 2–38

Warshow, R. 1962 *The Immediate Experience: Movies, Comics and Other Aspects of Popular Culture*, New York: Doubleday

Watson, J. 1984 'Urgent Images' *Art and Text*, No. 14 Winter, 8

Willis, D. (ed.) 1985, *Variety's complete science fiction reviews*, New York: Garland Publishing

Index